Footprints on the Mountains

High praise for *Footprints on the Mountains*

Dennis (Dr. Renshaw) has combined a helpful and careful commentary of hiking the AT with powerful insights that will help anyone who reads this book begin to understand the lure of the Appalachian Trail. I was saddened to reach the end of the book, as I was so enjoying his stories and descriptions of the Trail. I felt as if I was going to summit Katahdin with him.
—*Dr. Don Thrasher, pastor*

We are preparing to thru-hike the Appalachian Trail in 2020. We found this account extremely insightful on how the Trail affects you both physically and mentally. What makes this book so special, though, is the spiritual journey on which the writer takes you.
—*Sarah and Jonathan Baker, future Appalachian Trail hikers*

Footprints on the Mountains

Hiking the Appalachian Trail from Georgia to Maine

Dr. Dennis Renshaw

Copyright 2019 Dr. Dennis Renshaw

All rights reserved. No part of this book may be reproduced or utilized in any form or by any means, electronic or mechanical, including photocopy, recording, or by an information storage and retrieval system, without permission in writing from the publisher.

Library of Congress Cataloging-in-Publication Data

ISBN: 9780996345897

Printed and bound in the United States of America by Ingram Lightning Source

First edition

Cover and professional photography: Dennis Renshaw, Jr.

Other photography: The author and friends

Editing, layout, and design: Jacque Hillman and Katie Gould

Cover and map design: Wanda Stanfill

Scripture verses are taken from the New Revised Standard Version of the Bible.

The HillHelen Group LLC
127 Fairmont Ave.
Jackson, TN 38301
hillhelengroup@gmail.com

To my lovely wife, Judy Carol Renshaw.
I could not have completed the Appalachian Trail nor written this book without the help and encouragement of my lovely wife, Judy Carol Renshaw. She is the greatest joy in my life and I love her dearly. We have been married over 36 years, during which time we have raised a family of four children, and now have seven grandchildren. She continues to be the center of our family and my greatest advocate. She exemplifies the wonderful characteristics of a godly woman more perfectly than anyone I know and she always points me and others toward our Lord and Savior, Jesus Christ. I thank God every day that He sent her my way and that she is my closest friend and companion.
Thank you, Judy, for who you are and for being my wife.

Acknowledgments

Thanks:

To Jacque Hillman, who edited this book and—along with her team of Jesse Hillman, Wanda Stanfill, Amy McDaniel, and Katie Gould—advised and helped me through a maze of getting this book to the publisher. Their hard work, superb knowledge, constant encouragement, and integrity were evident in all they did.

To my son, Dennis Renshaw, Jr., for getting me off and on the Trail in New York and for sharing his wonderful talent of photography with me and you, the reader, in the fabulous pictures he took of me and the Trail. But mostly, for being the type of person and son he is.

To all the invisible people who shared their Trail Magic with me. I can only name a few of the things they did for me, including caring for the Trail itself and keeping bushes and trees cut when they grew or fell across the Trail; building and maintaining shelters; leaving food, drinks, and water along the Trail; holding sporadic cookouts for all hikers who came by; and picking me up along the road to carry me into and from towns when I zeroed. Especially, a great big thanks to Fat Man Walking for his hospitality shuttling me and others over the course of several weeks.

To Scott (Freebyrd) Garner for our time together on the Trail and his encouragement as we hiked together those last few hundred miles and summited Mount Katahdin in Maine. Also, to his precious wife, Phyllis, who, along with Scott, drove half the night to get me to the Boston airport on my way home the night I had summited with Freebyrd.

To our four children, Camille Renshaw, Kristi Pettigrew, Heather Renshaw Vucetin, and Dennis Renshaw, Jr., for their encouragement, help, and convincing Judy I would be safe hiking the Trail.

To my lovely, wonderful wife, Judy, for allowing me to be gone for weeks at a time while I hiked. I could not have made the journey if she had not encouraged me, helped me plan, sent supply packages to me, kept our home and yard while I was gone, helped edit this book, and, above all, prayed for me constantly. I know she worried about me every day but, in spite of that, she was always willing to change all she was doing to enable me to hike. And when I got home, she nursed me back to health. God blessed me with an incredible and beautiful partner.

Table of Contents

Chapter 1. What You Don't Know Can Hurt You	1
Chapter 2. Egos Come and Egos Go	11
Chapter 3. So Many Questions	21
Chapter 4. Everything Starts with the First Step	33
Chapter 5. Helped by Trail Angels	47
Chapter 6. Staying Warm and Dry Is Not an Option	55
Chapter 7. It's a Family Affair	65
Chapter 8. Hiking Rain or Shine	75
Chapter 9. Missteps Can Ruin Your Whole Day	89
Chapter 10. Leaving Tennessee Behind	97
Intermission 1. Decision Time—to Go or Not to Go	107
Chapter 11. Saying Goodbye Is Hard	111
Chapter 12. Meeting Place of South and North	139
Chapter 13. Crossing the Halfway Point	145
Chapter 14. Almost Finished, or So I Thought	159
Intermission 2. Time to Pause for Family	167
Chapter 15. Plans Can Change in a Flash	173
Intermission 3. Falling Isn't a Failure Unless You Don't Get Up	189
Chapter 16. Someone Looks Out for Me	193
Chapter 17. Climbing through New Hampshire	211
Intermission 4. Timeout before the Big Push	227
Chapter 18. Challenging Mount Washington	231
Chapter 19. The Final Steps	241
Chapter 20. Epilogue	263
Devotional	267
About the Author	269

Dennis pauses in full gear near Newfound Gap, Tennessee.

> "Now shall I walk or shall I ride?
> 'Ride,' Pleasure said.
> 'Walk,' Joy replied."
> —*W.H. Davies, a Welsh poet who spent much of his life as a hobo*

CHAPTER ONE

What You Don't Know Can Hurt You

We sometimes start something when we have no concept of what we are starting! So it was when, in March 2012, I called our oldest daughter, Camille, and said, "We've both been too busy to spend much time together, so let's get together and go hiking. Do you know of somewhere we can hike together for about three or four days on the Appalachian Trail?"

I had no idea what God was setting into motion and the way it would change our lives, my wife Judy's and mine. At that point, I thought it was all my idea and God had little to do with it. Looking back, I can't say whether this was my idea or God's, but what I can say is, "God certainly used it for my benefit and, I hope, for the benefit of others."

It all started the year Camille went to college at the University of Tennessee in Knoxville. That was way back in 1989! We live in Jackson, Tennessee, which is nearly at the other end of the state from Knoxville, and some 300 miles by car. Like most college kids, Camille had come home often during her freshman year but more sporadically each year thereafter. After graduation, she moved around a bit with jobs in Nashville, Tennessee; Florida; and finally Brooklyn, New York. Between her job and my job, we rarely seemed to have time for one another. It wasn't due to animosity or any other issues between us; we were just too busy. In addition to that, I had gone through a midlife career change. For 25 years, I had been a sales engineer selling industrial equipment in West Tennessee and West Kentucky until God called me into the ordained ministry as a pastor.

I will explain more about that midlife change later, but for now I will simply say I spent four years getting the master of divinity and then three more years obtaining the doctor of ministries. During those seven years, I also continued to work full time serving churches in West Tennessee, so there was little time for family, friends, or daughters living in New York City, no matter how sweet they are.

While in school in Knoxville, Camille had hiked a bit in the Smokies on the AT and loved it. She had also been instrumental in introducing our second-oldest daughter, Kristi, to hiking, which would lead to some good advice and encouragement from her when I decided to hike the entire Trail. Camille has continued to section-hike whenever she has time. She hikes sections of the AT as opposed to thru-hiking the Trail entirely in one year. When I thought of doing something with her that we both would enjoy, it was a no-brainer to suggest hiking. Camille jumped at the chance both to hike and spend time with her dad, and she immediately knew of a section we could hike together. It was "flat," had shelters about every 10 miles, and ended at the only place on the AT where a train will stop and take you into New York City. There is nothing flat on the Trail, but I didn't know that yet! I can't think of a better place for an AT hiker to begin, but it wasn't going to be a "piece of cake," although I didn't know that yet, either!

Now the tough stuff started: TRAINING! In high school and college, I had been a distance runner. I even had a four-year scholarship running at Lambuth College in Jackson, Tennessee, and did well. I was captain of the track and the cross-country teams for all four years, and I still hold some distance records there, but that was more than 45 years ago. Since that time, I had not run at all and seldom did anything that resembled working out. All of that is to say that I was out of shape. I called Camille, and she suggested I start running, preferably up and down stairs.

That didn't sound good to me, so I called my old running buddy from college, Jimmy Carmichael, who has spent his working years as a high school coach. We literally had run thousands of miles together, so I trusted his ideas and suggestions. He, too, suggested running and added weight lifting. That definitely sounded like work, so I developed my own unaggressive workout schedule. It consisted of walking at a comfortable (slow) speed up and down a small hill near our home. It was a mile each way. That worked fairly well until I decided it was time to add some weights. After all, I'd be carrying a fully loaded 35- to 40-pound pack hiking the AT!

With some hesitation, I got two 5-pound hand weights to carry while I was walking. That sounded simple enough, and surely I could do that. At least, it was simple for the first quarter of a mile when I hid them in the grass next to the road to be retrieved on my way back down the hill. I found it much more difficult to get into shape than when I was 19 years old and in college. Now I was 64, had a middle-age waistline bulge, and was a little flabby. I had to take working out a bit more seriously. I just didn't know how seriously yet.

In addition to getting into shape, I began to think about gear. I knew nothing about boots, packs, cookstoves, or tents, and I knew even less about what kind of food I should eat while hiking. The realizations that all my equipment had to be carried on my back and that hiking on the AT consumes between 4,000 and 8,000 calories a day had not fully registered. I had been a Boy Scout as a kid and a troop Scoutmaster as a young adult. But in Scouting, our leaders carried most gear to the campsite via an automobile and eating consisted of s'mores, which were marshmallows and chocolate melted between two graham crackers. Fortunately, I always had Camille, the Internet, and a place where I spent a lot of time, Recreational Equipment, Inc. (REI) in Nashville.

I found out quickly that my old tennis shoes and cotton socks would not work on the Trail. Camille and REI introduced me to the debates about wearing boots versus running shoes for the Trail; using a sleeping pad under my bedroll versus no pad to save the weight; and carrying a $90 cookstove with the latest technology, such as a Jetboil, versus a lightweight stove burning white gas for $10 that goes out in a light breeze. Should I carry an extra pair of "heavy" underwear? How many pairs of socks should I carry so I would always have at least one dry pair? In case you are wondering, I found about three days is the max for one pair of underwear between washings, most times! Forgive me, Mom! And socks stay dry inside a hot, sweaty hiking boot only for about three hours, max!

All of this is to say that getting prepared to hike something as daunting as the AT should be taken seriously and with the help and advice of as many people as possible. Do seek out those who have hiked the AT and did not just read books or search the Internet. Each hiker will make different decisions as to what equipment to purchase and how to train. I was still in that naive state of mind believing that an extra five pounds in my pack didn't matter, and hiking the AT was the same as walking a few blocks around my home. But I would learn the hard way!

I continued to train, walking two, then three miles, and slowly increasing until I was up to 10 miles, simultaneously adding a pack and a few more pounds each week. I was getting stronger and cockier every day. I could do this!

I arrived in New York on Wednesday, September 19, 2012, unaware of how much I had to learn and how much I needed to increase my strength and endurance. Fortunately, my education continued that evening in Camille's apartment, where she took apart my pack and all that was in it, item by item. Every new hiker should have an experienced hiker do this before they hike. Camille, I found out, is what is known as an ultralight hiker, meaning she is willing to forgo some niceties and comfort in order to carry fewer pounds in her pack. She even cuts two inches off the handle of her toothbrush to conserve weight!

I have found that I like a light pack but am not willing to forgo too many "comfort" items. I can go without a sleeping pad or carry fewer clothes and risk being uncomfortably cool for a short hike of a day or two when I know what the weather and terrain are like, although I never risk being too cold if safety is a factor. For long-distance hiking, I prefer to sleep well, be comfortable, and cover as many contingencies as I can. I have seen some hikers go to the extreme for comfort by carrying items such as a lawn chair, a 10-inch iron skillet, and a full cooking grill. I have also seen those same hikers lying beside the Trail totally exhausted and determined to leave the Trail and never come back at the next road!

Camille was kind enough to help me remove some of my extra clothes, my larger and heavier writing items, duplicates of supplies she already had such as maps and a cookstove, and my extra food, although she didn't find everything, including the two pounds of chocolate candy that she still teases me about. I still remind her she didn't mind eating it as we hiked!

The next morning, I took my first steps on the Trail near Canopus Lake and New York State Route 301. Looking back, I am amused at myself. Over the next three days, we hiked 24.5 miles to Pawling, New York, averaging 8.2 miles per day, and each of those days, I was tired and ready for a restful night. Three years later, I hiked through the same area in a little over one day and was surprised that it was not at all as I had remembered. I remembered it having some steep climbs and difficult terrain, but when compared to the rest of the Trail, it is one of the easier places to hike. Note I said "easier" and not "easy." I have found there really is almost no part of the Trail that is easy unless you are talking about a very short section of the Trail.

Camille had chosen a good place for me to learn about the Trail and develop some of the skills I would need to hike and camp on the Trail. I had no idea that in the coming three years, I would hike the entire 2,186 miles from Georgia to Maine and spend more than 100 nights along the Trail, most of that by myself. But before I could do that, I had a lot to learn, much studying about equipment to discern what I needed, and many miles to hike to get into shape.

That first day, Camille and I hiked seven miles to the Ralph's Peak Hikers (RPH) Club shelter on a good trail and in good weather. There we found one of the nicest, most comfortable shelters on the Trail. It's a painted block building with a front door, windows, and an opening on the other end leading out to a covered patio complete with a table and benches. Inside we saw a writing desk and four sets of bunk beds where eight people can sleep, and outside is a well with an old-time hand pump for water. My first night on the Trail was almost like being at home. Three years later, I would stay in the same shelter and order pizza from a local restaurant delivered for supper! How ironic and misleading is that for the first night on the Trail?

I remember a "southbounder," a hiker traveling from north to south, or from Maine to Georgia, arriving about dusk and how impressed I was to learn he had hiked 20 miles that day. A year later, I would join that group who thought nothing of hiking 20 or 25 miles a day for several days in a row, but at that moment I was just happy and proud to have hiked seven miles and still be alive to tell about it.

The next day, we hiked nine miles to the Morgan Stewart shelter. The first night out, I had

Shelter: Near the Trail are hundreds of small buildings normally spaced 2 to 10 miles apart where hikers can spend the night. They are usually three-sided with the fourth open to the woods. Floors are usually raised 2 feet above the surrounding terrain and may be wood, concrete, or dirt. Campers come on a first-come-first-served basis and sleep side by side. Many shelters have picnic tables, bear cables, and privies (outdoor bathrooms similar to an outhouse) located nearby.

experienced one of the nicer shelters, so it was appropriate that the next night I would stay at one of the older and more rustic shelters, built in 1986. It sleeps six people lying side by side in about a 10-by-16-foot space.

I distinctly remember two things about Morgan Stewart. The first is that the ceiling slopes away from the front of the shelter and in mid-ceiling is a log running the length of the building whose purpose is to support the ceiling. I was wearing a hat that obscured my vision above my head, which was not helpful, because each time I crawled back to the rear of the shelter, I couldn't see the log above me before cracking my head on it. After I had done this for about the third time, Camille called my attention to what someone had written on the log. It said, "Hit head here." I wasn't the first to have found that log, and for once I was glad to have a hard head!

The second thing I remember is that it was there I learned about the importance of hanging your food. One unfortunate fact about shelters is that animals have found that we humans often leave food out and it's easy pickings for them. Mice thrive in shelters as a result. Camille helped me hang my pack from a string suspended from the ceiling. About halfway up the string was an aluminum soft drink can with the string running through it. Mice can run up and down a string or rope, but they can't navigate around or over the can, thus it prevents the mouse from getting to your pack. That does NOT prevent them from crawling over your bedroll with you in it during the night, though. For that reason and others, I would later learn that I prefer to sleep in my tent rather than in a shelter.

The following morning, we woke up early and hiked with what little speed we could muster because we had a train to catch. Eight miles ahead was the Appalachian Trail railroad station, a wooden platform about 16 feet by 24 feet where the Metro-North train stops on Saturday and Sunday, and for about $25, you can ride the train into Grand Central Station in New York City. It's designed as a service for hikers who come up out of the city for a day hike, and it takes you back to yesteryear as you stand there and literally wave the train down. We got to the station with plenty of time to spare, waved the train down, and paid the conductor after we got on the train. We deliberately sat a bit back in the car, away from other commuters, since we had just spent the last three days on a hot, dirty trail. We had taken "birdbaths," but that doesn't account for everything. We were tired and dirty, and we certainly didn't want to offend anyone.

At one of the stops, four young ladies, dressed to kill and obviously going into New York to party, boarded and sat down across from us. I haven't mentioned that Camille's large Labrador retriever had hiked with us. I had given him the Trail name Scout, because he had spent all his time running up the Trail several hundred yards and then back to see if we were still coming. He was "scouting" the Trail. Scout was lying on the floor between us, oblivious to everything going on around us. He was tired and had slept for most of the hour's ride to Grand Central Station. Camille and I had already decided to stay put and allow others to depart first so we wouldn't offend anyone with our not-so-clean bodies. To put it bluntly, we smelled, folks!

But Scout didn't know we were staying put and was anxious to jump up and do some more "scouting," so as the train slowed to a stop, one of the young ladies sitting across from us stood up, and as she turned around to retrieve her belongings from her seat, Scout also stood up and "checked her out." That is, he cold-nosed her! For those of you who are not from the South or did not grow up on a farm, he stuck his nose directly up her dress and placed his cold nose directly on her butt to get a good smell of her, as animals are apt to do. Fortunately, the girls thought it was hilarious, and I had the good sense to say nothing and let Camille do all the explaining. I am just pleased they thought it was funny, too, and they didn't think it was my dog!

We took the subway from Grand Central Station to Brooklyn and ate some of the best food I've ever had. I say that as if all the food I've eaten after dehydrated food on the Trail isn't the best I've ever eaten! This was the first of many meals I would eat after hiking on the Trail and being self-conscious about how I looked and smelled while others around me ate. Later that evening, I concluded my latest adventure by taking a cab across town to the home of our son Denny Jr., daughter-in-law Leigh, and their daughter Vivian. Judy had flown in from Tennessee and was waiting at their home so, being the husband that I am, I gave Judy the first kiss and, being the grandfather that I am, I gave two-year-old granddaughter Vivian Kate the most attention!

My main purpose for this initial hike was to spend time with Camille, and that goal was fulfilled in its entirety. I truly enjoyed our time together, and we still have hiking as a common subject to share along with many other things. She is a beautiful person inside and out, and I so cherish our time together, whether on the Trail or anywhere and anytime we can be together. I feel closer to her after spending those three days hiking with her, and I know that time was a blessing from God. Little did I know that three years later we would hike together in North Carolina when I passed through on my way from Georgia to Maine. We did something similar in the summer of 2017, hiking 70 miles on the AT, starting at Springer Mountain and going to Dicks Creek Gap.

I learned a lot in New York while hiking with Camille, but I had many decisions to make before hiking almost 2,200 miles. My choices about food and equipment included:

1. Pack: REI has qualified salespeople who helped me in many of my decisions. The only piece of equipment that I started and finished with was the type of pack I carried. I did have to replace it after some 500 miles of training and 1,350 miles of the AT because it finally wore out.

2. Bedroll(s): I wasn't sure how much hiking I would do, so I started with a $29 bedroll from Dick's Sporting Goods. It was rated for 50-degree weather but was too heavy for long-distance hiking. Later I replaced it with an ultra-lightweight rated for 50 degrees for warm weather and another bedroll rated for 15 degrees for cold weather. I swapped them out as the seasons changed by having Judy mail me the bedroll I needed and returning the one I was replacing.

3. Food: I started with packages of dehydrated food for each meal, which required two cups of boiling water and waiting about 15 minutes before eating. That works well but does get old eating the same basic foods all the time. It also means stopping and cooking at noon and takes about 50 minutes for lunch, which is a bit too long. I gravitated toward more store-bought food the longer I hiked, meaning pita bread, packaged tuna salads, raisins, nuts, etc.

4. Boots: I have yet to be comfortable with the size and type of boot I have. Most people's feet swell after hiking several hundred miles and may never go back to their original size. I went through about four or five sizes and types of boots. Initially, I got huge blisters on my feet and couldn't find a good size. Michael Hughes at Cumberland Transit in Nashville was recommended to me as someone who can fit boots well. I drove 120 miles each way to see him, and he does know his stuff! He suggested two different boots, either of which he thought would work for me, but he also said he thought the boots I had were fine. I just needed to tie them in a different way. Unfortunately for Michael, I didn't buy anything from him, but I am very grateful. I've been tying my boots his way now for three years, and it works much better.

When I got home that day, Judy summed it up this way: "Let's see now. You drove 240 miles and spent most of an entire day, all just to learn how to tie your shoes!" It must be our wives' job to always keep us guys humble! But I would never have Judy any other way.

The purposes of shoelaces are, first, to keep the boot snug on one's foot, and second, to keep one's toes from being shoved into the front or toe of the boot, especially when going downhill. Michael suggested that I tie the laces on the lower part of the boot as loosely as possible while keeping the boot just snug around the foot. The key becomes how to tie the laces beginning at the bend where the foot turns up and becomes the leg or shin.

    I would tie the lace in a loose knot at the bend so the lower part was snug, but make the upper part a bit tighter so that my foot couldn't slide forward in the boot. This left a space of about one-half inch in the toe so my toes wouldn't slide forward and bruise my toenails. Unfortunately, I had to learn this after losing all my toenails at least four times!

Daughter Camille and her dog, Trail-named Scout, rest at a shelter in New York.

Dennis in rain gear is prepared for all types of weather.

CHAPTER TWO

Egos Come and Egos Go

I went to New York thinking it was more or less a onetime hike, but it wasn't long before I found myself longing for the freedom and excitement of the Trail. The bug had bitten, but I didn't yet know how hard and how much of my time and energy it would consume over the next three years.

I sought out Camille again, and she suggested I solo-hike a section she was familiar with from her college days when she attended the University of Tennessee at Knoxville, 60 miles away. It was 33 miles from Clingmans Dome to Fontana Dam, and since this was my first section in the mountains, she thought going in that direction, from north to south, would be easier as the net fall in elevation is a little over 4,700 feet, or nearly a mile straight down. That was certainly good advice, as I wasn't in shape yet for the kind of climb I would have had in the other direction. To be sure, it's not all downhill, as the Trail goes up and down continuously.

I was to learn in the coming months, however, that going down a mountain is often more damaging to one's legs than going up. A step downhill, someone has figured, is six times more stressful on the knees and feet than going uphill. I also learned that when (not if) I fell, I would fall farther—literally—while going downhill than if I had been going up the hill. Something makes us want to run a few steps trying to catch up with our downhill momentum, but the only thing that really does is speed us up, so that when we do finally take that plunge, we launch ourselves into space going faster and higher for a much harder landing. I never did learn to fall quickly rather than fighting it and ending up with worse cuts and bruises.

Planning the hike was a back-to-the-basics course for me. First, where would I leave my car and how would I get back to it? Should I leave it at the point where I started hiking and then find a ride back to my car somehow, or leave it at Fontana Dam so it would be there when I came off the Trail? And who would transport me?

The Internet, I found, has all kinds of information about the Trail, and there are two books on every hiker's must-buy list. *Appalachian Trail Thru-Hikers' Companion*, published by the Appalachian Long Distance Hikers Association, and *The A.T. Guide*, written by David "Awol" Miller, have most of the information needed to hike the AT and are the first places to look for any information about the Trail. Between those three sources, I found several people who will drop hikers off or pick them up almost anywhere a road crosses the AT. I contacted The Hike Inn, located six miles from Fontana Dam and operated by Jeff and Nancy Hoch. They quickly agreed that one of them would pick me up at six in the morning on Monday, October 15, 2012, and take me to Clingmans Dome.

Second, the *Thru-Hikers' Companion* helped me estimate that three days of hiking 11 miles a day would get me the 33 miles required and, after I looked at a map, showed me two shelters where I planned to stay.

Third, I duplicated equipment and food from my original hike in New York but added more clothing for the cooler weather.

Fourth, a quick phone call to the Smoky Mountains Visitor Center got me the required reservations for the shelters. I was ready! I had no idea really what to expect or how I would do, but I was R-E-A-D-Y, or as ready as I could be.

Noon on Sunday, October 14, finally came. I was a pastor serving the Decaturville, Tennessee, First United Methodist Church at that time. As soon as the last person left the sanctuary, I hurried next door to the parsonage, changed clothes, added ice to my cooler, kissed Judy goodbye, and headed for Fontana Dam on the Tennessee-North Carolina line. It's a six-hour, 320-mile drive.

The first part is interstate, so I set the cruise and sat back, but the last hour is through the Tail of the Dragon, a winding, dangerous road that follows the Chilhowee River. The scenery is beautiful but, with hairpin curves set one after another, I dared not take my eyes off the road. Besides, I had a destination: the Smoky Mountains and three wonderful days of hiking.

I arrived at Fontana Dam shortly after dark, but I was prepared. I drove across the dam to a picnic site beside Fontana Lake, parked the car, and got out my trusty lightweight stove and a dehydrated pouch of noodles and chicken that weighed only 5.5 ounces but had 480 calories. This was still exciting, eating ready-made "gourmet" food that needed only two cups of boiling water and 10 minutes to hydrate. Dessert was a Mars bar and a Coke. It also was easy to clean up: just fold the empty food pouch up with the Mars bar wrapper, place it in the garbage, and lick the spoon clean. Supper was delicious, although not quite like Mother used to make. After supper, I set out making my bed for the night. I had planned to sleep outside under the stars, but as I threw the last bit of trash away, it dawned on me that I was sitting next to a bear-proof garbage bin made of extra-thick steel, childproof (maybe that's bear-proof) handles for opening, and attached to a concrete pad using large, heat-resistant, earthquake-proof bolts. Kind of made me think there might be a bear around!

That night, I laid the seat down in the back of my van, blew up my air mattress, rolled out my sleeping bag, and slept in the car. I would learn to sleep with the bears another night. As I dozed off, somewhere in the back of my mind I remembered bears smell approximately 60 times better than humans and have been known to break car windows in order to get to the food inside. I slept a bit fitfully that night, thinking of hiking the next few days, going over my equipment in my mind, and worrying a bear might be nearby. I was glad when morning came and it was finally time to get going.

Nancy Hoch picked me up promptly at six o'clock. I piled my hiking poles, large-brimmed hat, and an overloaded backpack into her car trunk. I wore new, military green hiking pants, a red shirt, polished hiking boots, and a silver whistle around my neck. A one-pound can of bear spray hung from my belt. I was sure she couldn't tell I was a novice hiker. I was ready.

The ride to Clingmans Dome took an hour and a half, climbing steadily up the mountain for 66 miles. We drove through Bryson City and Cherokee, North Carolina, and then continued past Newfound Gap. The road past Newfound Gap is a winding, two-lane, paved road with beautiful mountain-vista lookouts appearing about every quarter mile leading to Clingmans Dome, which is the highest point on the AT at 6,643 feet.

The trees had dropped their leaves, so the views were spectacular. My excitement grew with each passing curve, and suddenly there we were, the only car stopped in the parking lot that early morning. I was in a hurry to get started, so after paying Nancy for the ride, I lifted my pack and awkwardly pulled the straps tight. This would become second nature to me after a few months, but right then I experimented to determine which strap to tighten and which to loosen as I hiked.

At that moment, all I wanted to do was get on the Trail and hike. I was focused; I was ready; I was about to become a solo AT hiker! The sidewalk from the parking lot leads up about 300 feet in elevation over half a mile of paved sidewalk to a 45-foot-tall circular observation tower. The Trail comes out briefly beside the tower and then disappears back into the thick undergrowth. All that stood between me and the AT was this "short" walk up to the observation tower. I was winded halfway up, but I wasn't going to let this uphill walk keep me from 33 miles on the Trail.

By the time I reached the tower, I was totally out of breath and more than happy to drop my pack on the ground while I made the mandatory trip up the tower to capture the view. At least it became mandatory when I was passed by an elderly lady who seemed to have no trouble walking. I was an AT hiker now and wasn't going to be outdone by her or anyone else, even if they weren't carrying a pack. And so began three days of an ego trip that said I could do this. Then reality set in, confirming what all AT hikers agree on: Hiking the Trail is one of the toughest things they have ever done.

Somehow, I made it to the top of the observation tower and was rewarded with a spectacular 360-degree panoramic view of the Smoky Mountains. Basically, I was standing on the line that separates Tennessee and North Carolina. From there is a view of mountain range after mountain range separated by deep valleys, all covered by magnificent trees, with a few streams and rivers winding endlessly through it all. To the west, so small one could hardly make it out, was a view of Fontana Lake and the dam where in three days I would arrive as a slightly experienced AT hiker. Or, at least, I would have begun to realize I had a lot to learn. Those three days would be memorable. I would gain confidence that I could hike these mountains and survive. I would learn a bit about the equipment and skills needed to hike and camp. But far more important was that on the Trail I would be made very aware of the care and presence of our living God. This awareness is something I will carry with me the rest of my life.

The Psalmist put it this way in Psalm 32:8: "I will instruct you and teach you in the way you should go; I will counsel you and watch over you."

At about eight thirty in the morning, I set out on the Trail. It drops off sharply from the paved sidewalk to trampled dirt and rock, and winds along the mountain crest where one's right foot may be in Tennessee while the left is in North Carolina. On either side are wonderful views of the mountains and valley. It's treacherous due to the rocks, tree roots, sharp up-and-downs, and the steepness of the mountain sloping away from the Trail on both sides, as well as the fact that I was carrying a pack weighing 43 pounds.

I found it difficult to see the view unless I stopped for a moment. Instead of watching scenery, I was watching my feet. Each step had to be carefully placed, and failure to do so often resulted in a nasty fall. In fact, I would fall an average of three to five times a day. Most falls were minor and with no harm done, but occasionally they skinned a hand or knee. I was fortunate that I fell very little during that section.

By noon, I was ready for a break and food. I stopped at Silers Bald Shelter, where I had both a water source and a log cut flat on one side for a table. Water was a spring about 75 yards from the shelter, but it takes a process to get water and purify it. I soon developed a routine: Immediately upon stopping, I would get water in the bag used for filtering, attach the filter to the bag, and squeeze the bag to force the water through the filter and into my water bottle or cooking stove. It takes about 20 minutes to filter enough water to cook and refill my water bottle.

Each evening, I would fill my two-liter water bag inside my pack so it was ready for the next day. Water was of paramount importance, and I asked everyone I met on the trail, "What does the water look like behind you?" And, of course, they wished to know how the water supply was behind me. Based on that information, I would know how much water to carry. One gallon of water weighs eight pounds, so carrying an extra quart of water is carrying two pounds. That doesn't sound like much until you've carried the extra weight for 10 or 20 miles, in addition to all your other supplies.

The Silers Bald Shelter got the name Siler from a farmer by that name in the area. A bald is a clear-cut or treeless area on the side or top of a mountain. Oftentimes, the bald has become overgrown with trees and bushes and no longer resembles a bald, but the name sticks.

By late afternoon, I arrived at Derrick Knob Shelter. It was designed to sleep 12, but AT courtesy means there is always room for one more if additional hikers show up late, especially if the weather is bad. That night I shared the shelter with only two other hikers. They had already made a fire in the fireplace, which most shelters don't have, so I had both a place to warm myself and a place to hang my socks to dry from the day's perspiration.

Two things made an impression on me that evening. First, two bears came up about dusk and began to eat termites from an old log near the shelter. They were fun to watch until the two men I was sharing the shelter with decided they wanted the bears to leave. They began to shout and throw rocks and sticks at the bears to scare them away. No harm there, as the bears went right on intently eating the termites, which they found by occasionally pulling the log apart with their sharp claws and strong legs. That was enough to tell me these were powerful animals and should be respected. They are wild animals and, when provoked, can protect themselves in remarkable and consequential ways. Black bears can climb trees faster than we can walk and can run up to 30 miles per hour. They are not to be played with. I also figured that they could not differentiate between the two men who were trying to disturb their dinner and me, who did not want to become any part of their dinner!

When the bears remained oblivious to us, my two new associates suddenly, and in unison, ran quickly to within about 15 yards of the bears before the animals bolted and ran off into the woods. I was astonished by what the hikers had done, and I suspect they had no idea of the danger they had put all of us in. I was so surprised I didn't know what to say or how to react. This could have been a devastating situation, and I didn't need to be convinced to hang my food as high up in the air as I could using the metal bear cables provided.

The second thing I remember was that to my surprise, I was not hungry at all and had to force my supper down that evening. I found this to be true of almost every meal for the first five days or so each time I began hiking a new section. This became a serious situation for me because I lost about a pound of weight each day I hiked unless I found a way to make myself eat. It was a continual problem that I never completely overcame. Most hikers require 5,000 to 8,000 calories a day. It's difficult to consume that much a day, especially if you aren't hungry. I would lose more than 20 pounds on each long section hike of more than 800 miles and about 5 pounds a week on my shorter hikes. I'm a small-framed guy of 5 feet 8 inches and started out at 170 pounds, so I didn't have any extra weight to lose.

The next day was beautiful with sunshine and temperatures around 60 degrees. The mountains had lost their foliage, so the trees were evergreens or brown. What was lost in color was gained by being able to see beyond a few yards. Clearly evident is the great loss of the Fraser firs and the red spruce due to a non-native insect, balsam woolly adelgid, as many of the formerly beautiful, tall, proud trees are now dead and rotting ghosts. The 12-mile hike was a relatively easy one but, as always, I was glad to get to the shelter that evening. Mollies Ridge Shelter is made of stone and has a fireplace, but no one seemed interested in finding firewood that evening. Its name comes from an old legend that a Cherokee maiden froze to death while looking for a lost hunter, and the legend says her ghost still resides on the mountain. Fortunately, I don't believe in ghosts, so sleep came easily that evening. But I was still glad I had a warm bedroll as the wind came up, or my fate could have been similar to that of the Indian maiden.

The next morning, the wind was still blowing at an estimated 20 to 25 miles per hour. I most likely would not remember that if not for the fact that I was unable to boil water for my oatmeal and hot chocolate using my cheap, lightweight stove. I moved to the rear of the shelter to get out of the wind, but still the wind blew the heat away before it warmed the water. After several tries, one of the other men staying in the shelter kindly pulled out his Jetboil stove and heated all the water I needed in less than two minutes.

I found that's the way the Trail works. Everyone helps take care of the others, and most people will share whatever they have even to the point of not having enough for themselves if

Bear cables: Some shelters provide a metal cable that is hung between two trees so a pack or food bag can be suspended in the air. The food is attached to a hook on the cable and hoisted up about 16 to 20 feet. Bears can't climb the cable, and the cable is positioned far enough away from the surrounding trees to prevent a bear from climbing the tree and snagging the food. Thus, bears don't get your food, and they don't learn to come around the shelters looking for food.

it helps someone else. After thanking him for cooking my "breakfast," I carefully pulled out my notebook and made a note to buy a Jetboil stove before my next hike. Most hikers are willing to talk about what equipment works for them. For the most part, that's the way I learned what equipment or food worked and what did not.

The following day's hike down to Fontana Dam was an easy one. The Trail is clearly marked and well worn. About noon, I spotted a black bear some 200 yards in front of me. He appeared to be a young male. I tried to get pictures, but he succeeded in staying just out of range. Mostly, I was just concerned about getting too close and friendly, and he soon disappeared into the forest. Other than the bears, I didn't see much wildlife on that hike.

I reached Fontana Dam about three o'clock and found my car as I had left it. There is a public shower at the dam with hot water, so after a shower and clean clothes, I was ready for the six-hour drive to West Tennessee. I was tired but exuberant that I had successfully taken my first solo hike and had no major cuts or bruises, and my equipment and food had gotten me through except for my stove. However, I knew that if I was to hike more of the AT, I would need to be in better shape and buy equipment more specific to the weather and the harsh wear and tear of the Trail. I was learning but had a lot more to learn.

A typical winter Trail offers a clearer view and easier hiking but less protection from the wind.

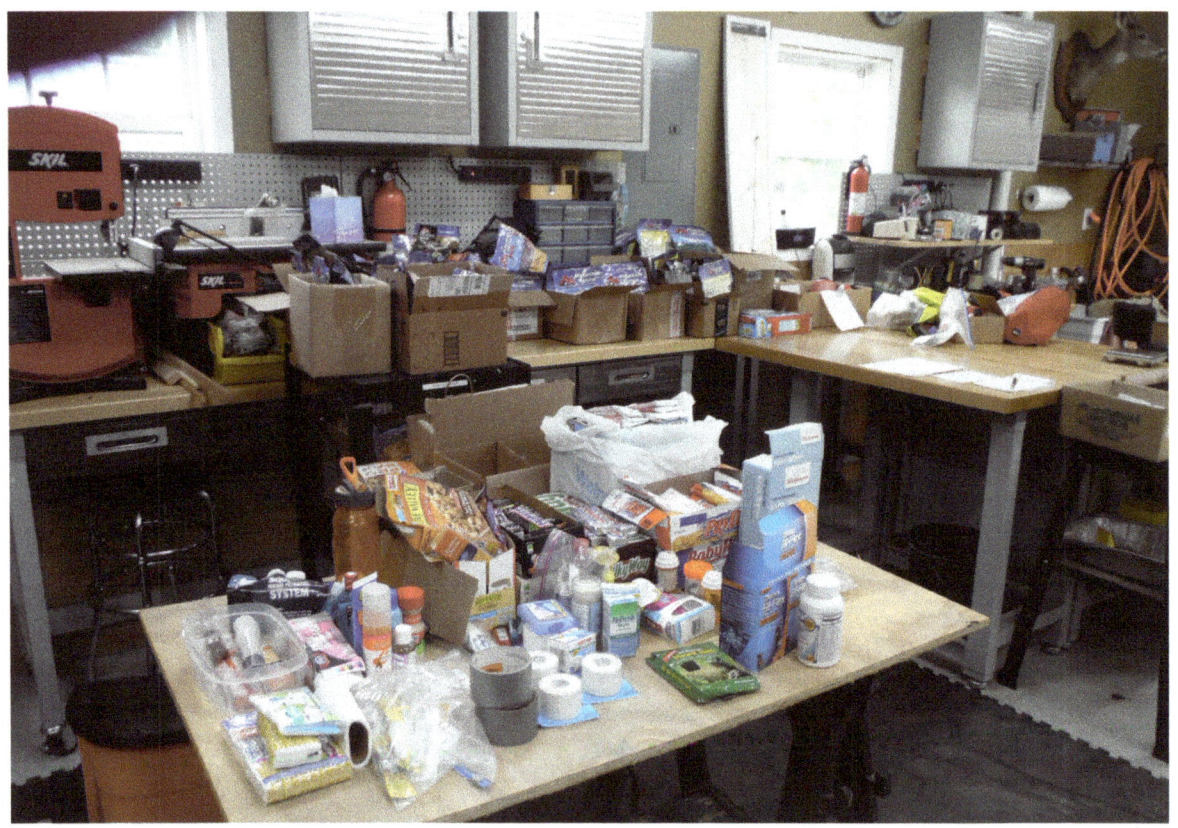
The Renshaws' stock room has Trail supplies that Judy kept filled for Dennis and ready to ship.

CHAPTER THREE

So Many Questions

My hike in the Smoky Mountains had given me a feeling of self-confidence and invincibility. I had now hiked 24 miles in New York and 33 miles in the Smokies, and I began to think I could do anything on the Trail. Surely it couldn't be rougher or more difficult than what I had already experienced. Clingmans Dome, after all, is the highest place on the Trail and I had hiked it!

The Trail leading down from there was long, or so I thought then, but I had conquered it as if I was made for it. If I could hike that, I could surely hike anything the Trail could throw at me! When I talked with people who had never hiked, they were amazed at what I had done. I was beginning to call myself a semi-experienced hiker. I had a lot to learn! And perhaps I had forgotten Matthew 23:12: "For whoever exalts himself will be humbled, and whoever humbles himself will be exalted."

With the confidence of Christopher Columbus, I began planning and training for a 2,186-mile thru-hike from Georgia to Maine in the spring. Of course, there were some "minor" hurdles ahead. I had not told my lovely bride, Judy, I might leave her alone for five or six months. I was still employed as a full-time pastor, and I had not planned to retire yet. I wasn't in shape for such a long hike. I didn't have all my equipment in place and didn't know exactly how to choose the right gear. I had much to learn about nutrition. I also needed to figure out the logistics of getting myself and all my equipment and food to the right place and at the right time on the Trail.

Who would do all the yard work, such as mowing the lawn, while I was gone? The seasons would transition from winter to spring to fall while I was hiking and thus necessitate changes in equipment and clothes as the temperatures and climate changed. What would I do when equipment broke or I was hurt on the Trail? What if it started to rain and continued for days at a time? Or worse, some of the mountains get snow every month of the year! And what about all the wild animals on the Trail? Bears, snakes, and moose all can be very dangerous. I had so many questions, so much to learn, and so little time. I had found on the Internet that most hikers started between March 1 and the end of April. That only gave me 3.5 to 5.5 months before I'd be leaving Springer Mountain, and I needed to answer all those questions and hundreds more, as well as make arrangements. Time was wasting.

Getting permission

I had so many questions and so much to learn that I began to spend every free hour planning or doing something for the hike. The first, and most difficult, task was to convince Judy that I'd be safe on the Trail. She wasn't any happier about us being apart for an extended time than I was. But my safety was her primary concern. She began to ask as many questions and accumulate as much information about the Trail as she could. To my advantage was the fact that all three of our daughters have hiked some of the AT and offered encouragement and good advice. They told Judy that "at my age," 65, this would be good for me to get in shape, and it would be especially good for my heart and cardio, thus prolonging my life. That's encouraging! Judy came around slowly, and became my number one encourager and helper. I never could have hiked the whole Trail without her help.

My entire family helped in one way or another. Camille, our oldest daughter, who then lived in Brooklyn, was a great help in giving advice about the Trail and equipment. Kristi, our second-oldest daughter, who lives almost next door to us, convinced her mother it would be good for me to hike and then helped pack and send supplies to me while I was on the Trail. Heather, our third-oldest child, who lives in San Francisco, was a great encourager, gave me information she found on the Internet, and not only wanted me to hike the AT but also the Pacific Crest Trail running from Mexico to Canada with her. Our son, Denny, who lives in Brooklyn, helped each time I went through New York to get on or off the Trail. He also picked me up in Kent, Connecticut, when I hurt my foot and put me back on the Trail after it healed.

One of many things Judy did while I was gone was mow the lawn. First, you should understand, she has an allergy, so mowing is not something she really should be doing. Second, she had never driven a zero-turn mower. That's a professional-type mower that has a 60-inch-wide cut and can turn 360 degrees, rotating around either the right or left rear tire. It's fast and the controls are "tight" like a sports car, and it takes some getting used to. I gave her some lessons before I left on my hike. Judy grew up on a farm and drove most all the farming equipment you can imagine while helping her dad. She's a good driver, but did I say that it takes some getting used to?

Our joke during the first summer of hiking became Judy telling me over the phone: "I have some good news and some bad news!" I quickly learned the good news was she had mowed the lawn. The bad news would be things like, "Remember the lights lining the sidewalk? Well, there's one less now!" Or "Remember that little shrub by the back corner of the house? Well, we need a new one." Or "My brother David replaced the mailbox for us! It was the roll bar's fault!" The mower has a safety roll bar behind the driver's seat that protrudes above the driver's head and is not in the driver's line of sight. Judy did run over a few things in the yard, but she kept the lawn cut and the bushes trimmed, and that's a lot considering our yard covers about 1.5 acres. Just before I left for the second year's hiking, I bought a new zero-turn mower. Our daughter Kristi assured me her mother would like this one better or, as she put it, "Mom will love it. It's faster!"

Judy is a real hero for all that she did to keep me on the Trail and take care of the home chores and duties. She accomplished all this in addition to her stressful job as senior vice president of business and community services at the Jackson, Tennessee, Chamber of Commerce, where she served for 40 years. And she did everything while being a grandmother, which comes first before anything else in life except her strong faith in God. She is truly an angel in my mind.

Training

Training for the hike was an intentional and difficult process. As stated earlier, I had trouble walking two miles and carrying two five-pound weights when I started to consider hiking in New

York with Camille. But when I returned, I trained in earnest all through the winter, for four to six days a week. For two or three days a week, I trained at a local fitness center called The LIFT, which is an 84,000-square-foot facility that is a department of West Tennessee Healthcare.

The LIFT is a complete training center, including a walking track, numerous weight machines, and three pools. It covers two floors, which was important, as I used the steps for training. Most days I trained carrying a pack weighing up to 43 pounds and wearing my hiking boots, even while training indoors at The LIFT. I put an emphasis on my midsection and legs as these, I assumed, would be the body parts that would do the most work while hiking. Also, since the AT is never flat, I walked up and down flights of stairs to simulate climbing the mountains. Often during one workout, I would climb as many as 50 flights of stairs, plus walking 10 miles or more on the track while carrying my backpack.

At least twice a week, I drove to Mousetail Landing State Park to hike real trails and train on the hills there. This also got me into the habit of watching for rattlesnakes and other vermin, which fortunately I saw little of, although other hikers and the park rangers constantly warned me about them. I often hiked up to 19 miles a day, but in no way would I compare that to hiking the AT with its strenuous ups and downs of several thousand feet at a time.

This regimen worked well because I was a pastor. I usually would get up around three in the morning and hike for an hour or more using my headlamp. Starting that early, I could be back in the parish by noon and still fulfill my duties there. This also became a special time of communing with God in the quiet of the dawn and rising sun. What a blessing that became for me, and on the Trail I kept the habit of rising early and hiking before daylight. It also was a wonderful time because the deer, turkeys, and other animals would be moving and easily seen during those early hours. I often saw as many as 20 deer and 25 turkeys each day, and I began to notice their patterns of movement and know where they would be each morning. It became a holy time with God and all of God's natural beauty. God is good.

Food

What one eats and how to get food on the Trail is of major importance. There were two general ideas: The first is to buy all your food along the Trail from local grocery stores and quick markets. The problem is that there is no way to know with certainty where these stores will be and how close to the Trail they are. Most groceries do not carry many dehydrated foods like what is needed on the Trail, and carrying canned goods is out of the question because the liquid in them makes them heavy. The people who do it this way commonly eat rice and macaroni products, combined with tuna fish in pouches, but some go to elaborate ends to season and combine these foods with vegetables and spices. Additionally, foods high in calories such as peanut butter, chocolate, honey, and dried fruits and nuts are liberally used for snacks and desserts. A few hikers find room in their packs for items such as titanium skillets and coffeepots, becoming somewhat like a chef and cooking some rather exotic meals over their little gas stoves.

One such "chef" was a hiker from Austria who carried a complete coffee-making set including four little metal cups, metal teaspoons, and a coffeepot, which he used to perk coffee using his propane cookstove. He made coffee from scratch four or five times a day, sharing it with anyone lucky enough to be close by and accept his gracious hospitality. He hiked with me for about a week but got off the Trail in Manchester Center, Vermont, to return to Austria. He was a manager in a manufacturing plant and got a month's vacation once a year, and he spent that month traveling to the United States and section-hiking the Trail. I have wonderful memories of waking to the smell of coffee perking nearby. He only perked enough for four little cups, so it was a race to get out of your bedroll and be one of the first three people in line behind him for coffee. His English was not the best, and my German is worse, but he was such a gentleman.

The last night before we parted ways, we ate dinner at Ye Olde Tavern in Manchester Center, where I ate pot roast while explaining the limited history I knew of that area. The restaurant is located in an old New England home built more than 200 years ago, which was helpful, as I only had to point around the room at all the artifacts. Our differences in language and background were nullified by the fact that we had just shared a week of hiking together and had helped one another climb over some tough terrain. Need I say, we concluded a nice dinner with a cup of coffee? We began to hike together after we happened to tent close to each other and his coffee lured me over to meet him. Yes, his appropriate Trail name is Coffeeman. The morning after that meal, we stood on the porch of Sutton's Place, where we had stayed two nights, and said our goodbyes. A friend of his was picking him up and driving him to New York for a flight to Austria that evening. One Trail lesson is you meet good people with whom you would be good friends except you will never see them again, at least in this life.

Some hikers, like Coffeeman, hike to eat. And, as you can guess, some hikers eat so they can hike. One who ate so he could hike was a young man, about 25 years old, whom I met just north of Newfound Gap in the Smokies. I will call him Mr. Macaroni. He had a garbage bag filled with macaroni from which he ate three meals a day without adding anything other than water. He simply added water to the macaroni in a pot and boiled them until they were soft enough to eat. That evening, everyone was cooking their supper at the same time when a discussion started between this young man and three medically trained people who were staying there for the night. The young man began to tell the medical group about a wound he'd had for several weeks that would not heal, and he asked for their advice.

In the course of that conversation, one person who had noticed the plain macaroni he was eating asked him about his diet. Mr. Macaroni replied that macaroni was all he had eaten for several weeks. All three medical guys began to lecture him on the importance of a balanced diet and said that could very well be the reason his wound would not heal. It became rather comical when Mr. Macaroni insisted three times he ate a well-balanced diet; after all, he was taking a one-a-day vitamin! I don't think Mr. Macaroni ever did understand, and I didn't see him up the Trail after that, so I don't know if he made it to Maine as he had planned.

The second method of cooking, which is the one I used for the first 1,800 miles of my hike, is to buy dehydrated food already prepared in ziplock packages. These require adding about two cups of boiling water, and then you wait about 10 minutes to have a full meal. They come in many varieties including several types of breakfast and some desserts. There are perhaps as many as 30 or 40 flavors of meals, including several menu items featuring entrees from Mexico, Italy, and the Orient. The main difficulty of preparing these meals was that it required filtering water; getting the stove out of your pack; boiling the water, which was not a big problem because the water boiled in about 1.5 minutes; and then waiting about 20 minutes for the meal to cool. Altogether, it took close to an hour to prepare and eat a meal. This was a long time to stop for lunch at noon, and I often was too tired in the evening to wait an hour before I crawled into my bedroll. All-day snacks included candy bars, peanut butter packages, dried fruits, and nuts.

I often crossed a road that had a minute market or restaurant within a mile of the crossing. I seldom missed those opportunities to get off the Trail and hike to the store or restaurant for "real

This is the Southern Terminus Sign at Springer Mountain, Georgia.

food." It was vitally important to supplement one's diet with foods such as greasy hamburgers, pizza, and milk. Restaurants with a buffet were rare treats, but wonderful places to gorge myself. I found, though, many restaurants had modified their menus and increased the price of a salad bar or buffet by $2 to $5 or more for hikers. I can't say I blame them; I sometimes felt the restaurant was losing money even at the higher price since we hikers definitely eat more than average folks. I often ordered the equivalent of two or even three meals and could almost always eat it all in one sitting. It was no wonder, because no matter how much I ate on the Trail, I was usually 2,000 to 3,000 calories a day behind on my calorie count.

Supplies

In the months leading up to my hikes, I stocked my own little "supply room" on one side of my shop. On top of boxes, tables, and the floor, I collected most everything I would need on the Trail. While hiking, I could call Judy about once a week and give her a list of the supplies I would need on the next leg of my hike. She would pack those supplies in a box and mail or ship them to the hotel or post office in the next major town I would come close to in the coming week. These supplies would be waiting, with a few exceptions that I will tell about later, when I got there. This way, I had exactly what I wanted in the quantity I needed and at a reasonable cost, having ordered them on the Internet in most cases.

In my "supply room" were all kinds of supplies and backup equipment, including more than 200 packages of dehydrated meals; boxes of candy and peanut butter packages; bottles of 100 percent DEET mosquito repellent; toothpaste; toilet paper; clothing of all kinds, especially socks; spare hiking poles; a summer bedroll, to be exchanged for my winter bedroll when it got cold in New Hampshire in the fall; cleaning wipes for my glasses; soap; batteries; vitamins; athletic tape; medical supplies; small plastic garbage bags; spare boots; and much more. These were items I would either use on a regular basis or possibly need as equipment wore out or broke. I broke so many hiking poles that whenever Judy shipped me a complete pole, I would ship the remaining good sections of the broken pole home, so Judy could ship me one of those sections back when I broke a similar section of my pole again.

Most items can be purchased on the Trail, but often either the correct type of equipment was not available, such as high-quality but ultralight hiking poles, or the available quantity was too high. Who wants to either buy four batteries when only three are needed and throw one away, or carry 24 batteries, less the three you needed at the time, because that is the cheapest way to buy them? Logistics can be a major problem, so taking care of details was important.

It's amazing how much packaging we use in America. That's great for advertising on the store shelf or for proper identification, but all that paper and plastic weighs quite a bit, and the total for all that is used in a week can weigh several pounds. Judy would tear off as much of the packaging as she could before shipping, and I would put my trash in a plastic bag to be dumped in the first garbage container I could find along the Trail. Much of my trash had the scent of food on it, so it became a liability when the smell attracted mice or other wild animals. Attention to detail is not only good sense but also essential to one's safety and well-being in the mountains.

Retirement

I did not retire until the first week of June 2013, and since I wanted to begin hiking in late February or early March, this became a bit of a problem. I had turned 65 the previous year, so according to the rules of my denomination, I could retire any time after that and receive full benefits. But because most moves by a pastor to a different church occur around the third week of June in our tradition, I presented those who would appoint a pastor to follow me with a dilemma. They couldn't deny my request for retirement, but they didn't have a "spare" pastor to send in my place any old time I decided to retire.

I knew that but decided to try the system anyway. I sent a letter announcing my retirement to the bishop, and shortly thereafter I received a letter affirming my request. The bishop really didn't have a choice since I was eligible for retirement, but that didn't make someone just appear to take my place. Therefore, I wasn't surprised when I got a call from my district superintendent, the Reverend Dr. Richard Clark, gently urging me to reconsider and wait until June to retire when there would be several pastors available for appointment to my church. Richard was one of my former pastors whom I grew to like and love, and we became good friends through the years. He was personally responsible for finding a pastor for my church. As only a good friend can do in a situation like this, I assured Richard that this was "his problem and that is why he was being paid the big bucks!" He suggested I reconsider my "early" retirement and pray about it. So it went for several weeks. He was unable to find a pastor and continued to urge me to reconsider, and I continued to remind him he made the "big" bucks.

About a month later on a Sunday afternoon, Richard and his lovely wife, Susan, showed up at our home, having "just been passing by." Now, he lives in Jackson, and the church parsonage is in Decaturville, which is about 45 miles away tucked in a corner of the Tennessee River where you rarely go to get to somewhere else unless you are going fishing. I had never known Richard to go fishing unless it was fishing for a little white ball on the golf course—mine, of course. They had made a trip specifically to ask me to reconsider the timing of my retirement. After some idle chitchat, Richard again began to tell me he had been unable to find a replacement for me, to which I reminded him again "that's why he made the big bucks." We're good friends, but I could tell my humor was beginning to rub him the wrong way.

Now, Richard was my boss. I reported to him, so when asking the nice way didn't seem to be working, he used the "reprimand" method. He reminded me I had missed a district meeting of all the pastors, which I was supposed to have attended.

The truth was I had forgotten about it, but pastors always have an "out." With a slight grin, I told him, "I 'think' I had a funeral that day and couldn't make it."

Not to be outdone, Richard reminded me, "Well, there was the Saturday makeup meeting you could have been at then."

I replied with a bigger grin, "When was that? I 'think' I had a funeral that day, too."

Richard's face got noticeably a little red. He had a church that needed a pastor, and he had no other options. He needed me to postpone my retirement and my hike, and I wasn't helping him a bit. Not only that, but I was making light of it and cracking jokes. He had had enough!

Susan had been sitting quietly by his side on the couch and, I think, enjoying listening to two old friends banter back and forth. Susan and I have been great friends going back at least 25 years, when she was our pastor's wife in Beech Bluff, Tennessee. We were constantly pranking each other. One Christmas morning, I hung switches and ashes on their front door with her name on them from "Santa Claus." She gave it back just as strongly. It took me 10 years to get her to admit she was the one who put a toilet seat with a sign in the chair I always sat in to teach Sunday school that read, "Dennis. This is the only throne you will ever sit on."

When she spoke up that day and said, "Dennis, just go ahead . . . tell Richard to fire you," I wasn't surprised at the humor. Richard wasn't the least bit amused, though, as he told Susan to "just be quiet." Susan and I still laugh about that almost every time we all get together.

In the end, I couldn't leave the church I so loved there in Decaturville without a pastor for two and a half months, and those wonderful people were willing to also take care of me. We worked it out so that I would hike every other week but be in the pulpit every Sunday, and I requested to be paid only half my salary since they were graciously letting me begin my hike. And I wouldn't retire until the normal third week in June, which made my good friend Richard happy.

It had taken a lot of time and energy to plan and execute all my preparations, but I was READY! Judy was still concerned about my safety, but she was completely supportive. It was now time to hoist my pack, pick up my hiking poles, and begin a journey of 2,186 miles from Georgia to Maine. God willing.

Isaiah 30:21: Whether you turn to the right or to the left, your ears will hear a voice behind you, saying, 'This is the way, walk it.'

On the Trail, hikers can enjoy the beauty but deal with difficulty at the same time.

CHAPTER FOUR

Everything Starts with the First Step

 Sunday morning had seemed like it would never come. It was the last week of February 2013. The weather was cold, and the forecast for the coming week called for continued cold but dry conditions. It sounded doable. I was ready to start hiking the next morning. Now, I just needed to get through this busy Sunday morning, and I'd be on my way to the Georgia mountains.

 The last week had been spent laying out equipment and supplies before putting them all in my pack and carefully weighing them using our bathroom scales. I had lists upon lists of what to take and the weight of each item. My first "weigh-in" for my pack was around 48 pounds, which was far too much. What should I do? I had to get my pack down at least below 40 pounds. But how? Should I take one pair of heavy pants and do without long johns, insulated underwear, or take a lightweight pair of pants and two pairs of long johns? How many pairs of socks would I really need? Could I wear the same pair of underwear for four days? And what would happen if I tore a hole in some of my clothes or my equipment broke? The thought of being miles away from help and having several days before I could get off the Trail haunted me. I would be alone, and the weather reports in the mountains couldn't be counted on. People have frozen to death after getting lost in unpredicted snowstorms.

I had so many questions and options to consider before I left, and with each one came issues of weight. It's said an ounce of weight in the morning feels like a pound that night, so what did I need to have and what could be left at home? My final tally for the week was 35 pounds including my tent, food for five days, and a liter of water. Much better than I originally had thought I could do. And I was still taking an extra day's rations just in case I had trouble or hiked more slowly than I had hoped. I was packed. I was in shape. I had my maps, and I had a plan. But I never dreamed how much I still had to learn.

I rose early, going through my normal Sunday morning routine of showering and dressing before spending an hour at my desk in prayer and reviewing my sermon. I always feel a bit nervous about standing before a hundred or more people to preach the Gospel. Was it relevant? Was it the Gospel as I had heard God speaking to me in the previous few days of preparation? Would it speak to the hearts and minds of those in attendance? Then, as I seemed to do every Sunday, I hurriedly printed the notes I would use before running out the door to church.

Judy and I own our home outside of Jackson, Tennessee, on the family farm. We've lived there for more than 30 years and have remodeled several times, and now we have the house and property just about the way we want it. It's home and it's comfortable, so when I was asked to pastor the First United Methodist Church in Decaturville, about 45 miles away, I had a dilemma. It's hard to pastor a church and not spend a lot of time in the community getting to know people and being present with them when they need a pastor. The church in Decaturville also recognized this and offered their nice parsonage, which is next door to the church, as our home during our tenure as their clergy couple. But Judy was the senior vice president at the Jackson Area Chamber of Commerce, where she was strongly encouraged to live inside the Madison County limits, and she wasn't quite ready to end her 38-year career there.

When the congregation heard this, they were the most gracious and loving church anyone has ever pastored. Together we agreed that I would live in the parsonage three or four days a week and spend the rest of the time with Judy in our home in Jackson. Judy and I were ecstatic with this arrangement, and it worked well for the year and a half I remained there. We had equipped the parsonage with everything we needed to live there. We had furnished the parsonage, stored extra clothes there for each of us, kept food in the refrigerator, and had all we needed to stay any time under most circumstances. I have to add here that those wonderful people in Decaturville were so gracious and loving to us both during our tenure there. Truly God is in that place.

We had spent that particular Saturday night in Jackson, so I left for church Sunday morning driving my car and Judy was coming about an hour later. I had my car packed with all my clothing and gear, and the GPS was programmed for Hiawassee, Georgia. I even had snacks and an ice chest with soft drinks ready for the long drive that afternoon.

My sermon that morning was titled "God is in the wilderness, too." I had no idea how prophetic that would be as I hiked in the wilderness called the Appalachian Trail and experienced anew the wonderful and powerful presence of God. I went on the Trail, as we so often do throughout life, thinking I was prepared and that I was ready for anything life could throw at me. Then we find we are unprepared and inadequate to face life unless God is there and ready to help us. And He is always there way ahead of us, fully prepared to pick us up and carry us when we fall or fail. It's almost like God knows we will fail on our own but, as I discovered again, He is more prepared to help us than we are to ask Him for help. His footprints where He carried me are all over the Appalachian Trail. God is so good.

I was ready to jump out of the pulpit and straight into my car to leave for Hiawassee, but the church had planned that Sunday to honor the Cub Scouts. They even provided them with a delicious, enticing, potluck dinner, and I was invited. It wasn't easy, but I forced myself to go easy on the food. I believe I only went back twice for the main course and three times for dessert! I had a 340-mile, 5.5-hour drive ahead and it had been an early morning for me, and I was missing my usual Sunday afternoon nap. I stayed awake with lots of caffeine, a loud radio stuck on the jazz station, and the anticipation of hiking the next morning. The drive was long as the somewhat flat West Tennessee countryside turned into the rolling hills of Middle Tennessee before Interstate 40 climbs up the Cumberland Mountains into East Tennessee.

I arrived in Hiawassee, Georgia, about eight o'clock eastern time and found the Holiday Inn Express to be comfortable and reliable. In fact, for the rest of the Trail, I would attempt to stay at that chain of hotels whenever possible. I ate a supper of waffles and bacon at the local Huddle House restaurant. I would learn quickly to add milk to every meal for the extra fat content and calories, but that evening I drank perhaps the last Diet Coke I would drink for several months, as the 260 calories in a regular Coke or Pepsi is important to a hiker. Before going to bed, I set three alarm clocks for fear I'd be late the next morning. There wasn't much use in doing that, as I was so excited I didn't sleep very well that night.

The next morning I took a "last shower," wondering why I was taking one. In a few hours, I'd be soaking wet from perspiration, undoing all the cleaning and grooming of the morning, but somehow we're programmed to be clean. I'd soon get over that, and I often think I took showers on the Trail more for the benefit of others than myself. Many things we think are necessities in life are not necessary at all and can get in the way of what really matters. That's true whether it's growing too busy for relationships, the way we view material goods, or anything else that gets in the way of communing with God.

'North' and 'south': Those directions on the AT do not mean a compass direction, but rather 'north' is to be headed toward Mount Katahdin in Maine, and 'south' is to be headed toward Springer. The Trail wanders in every direction, so a compass never helps one to know whether one is going toward Springer or toward Katahdin.

Sally Smith picked me up promptly at seven thirty for a 90-minute drive to the forestry road near Springer Mountain. While looking on the Internet for someone to shuttle me to the AT, I had found Sally and Joyce Monroe. I called on them several times and found them to be reliable, and I add, good-naturedly, they are not early risers because about seven thirty was the earliest I could get them to pick me up. I enjoyed my conversation with Sally as she drove me over some of the roughest roads on the AT. She had retired and moved to Hiawassee from Florida, as I recall, and supplements her income by shuttling hikers. She charged me $90 for this trip.

Sally dropped me in the parking lot on the unpaved Forest Service Road 42, which is nine-tenths of a mile "north" of Springer, so to start the Trail I had to hike "south" to Springer and then retrace my steps back the way I had come. It was cold and windy that morning, especially because the leaves were still off the trees. I hiked just 300 yards before I made my first stop, realizing that I had forgotten to retrieve my toboggan, as we call it in the South but stocking or ski hat to others, from my pack and I had to take off the pack to get it. Four days later, when I got into the car to go back to the hotel for the night, I realized I had not taken my toboggan off even to sleep or wash my face. It was just too cold!

I summited my first mountain, Springer Mountain, about 25 minutes later. That was the first of hundreds of summits over the months of hiking to come. Actually, the climb to the summit from the parking lot is not much of a change in elevation at 432 feet over almost a mile. But for my first "climb," I was proud to be at the start of a long journey. To commemorate the event, I took my first selfie on the Trail with the bronze plaque marking the start of the Trail behind me. While I was soaking in the moment, two young men from Oregon and Massachusetts appeared, having climbed Katahdin from the other direction. That Trail up the mountain is definitely more daunting, as it is a steep climb of 8.8 miles from Amicalola Falls State Park. They participated in another first for me: They were kind enough to take a picture of me using my camera, and I reciprocated. I remember signing the quest book as "Dennis Renshaw, Preacher." I had decided to give myself a Trail name until someone gave me a better one.

At 9:20 a.m. on February 24, I took the first step of many heading north toward Maine, wondering if I'd really make it, even though I had registered as a thru-hiker. I encountered no real trouble all day, but it was exhausting. I felt slightly sick at my stomach from the excitement of finally hiking. I ate only one meal besides breakfast and almost no snacks that day, which was a problem for me on the Trail. A combination of being too tired to eat, not always liking the food, and getting into too much of a hurry to stop and cook a meal led me to lose more weight than I should have during my hike. Also, I did not drink enough fluids.

Trail name: Most hikers do not use their real name but prefer a nickname called their Trail name. This can be a serious name or one given in jest. The name often tells something about the person, their interests, or their life.

The Trail that day had no significant climbs and was wide and smooth for the most part. It's a good way to start the AT, but I didn't know that, nor did most of the hikers I met on the Trail. I met one lady sitting squarely in the middle of the Trail, crying. She was wearing heavy, cotton-insulated overalls that definitely were not made for hiking; she was obviously out of shape and overweight; and she was trying to carry a pack that looked as if it weighed 60 or 70 pounds. She was exhausted and ready to give up. Another hiker had already

The tent needed drying out after multiple days of rain.

stopped with her to make sure she was okay, so after I tried to encourage her and saw I wasn't any help, I hiked onward. A year later, Sally Smith was shuttling me again, and I told her about the lady I had met. I didn't know her name and assumed she had given up. Sally, however, remembered giving her a ride several months later, and she was of the opinion that this lady, whose name we couldn't recall, had gone on and made it to Katahdin. It goes to show that hikers do not fit any one mold, and some who appear to be the least likely to hike the whole Trail, or even part of it, do indeed succeed.

By about five that afternoon, the wind had come up and a slight mist had begun to fall, and soon it turned to sleet. I had in mind that I had to hike to a designated campsite to spend the night. Later I learned I could camp most anywhere I found myself, but that evening, I thought I had to go on. I was cold and tired, and all I could think of was a warm bedroll inside my tent. By the time I finally stopped at Woody Gap, I was exhausted and cold, and the wind was howling. I had hiked until about eight o'clock, one hour after dark, and covered some 23 miles that day. It had been a tough, cold, and exhausting day, but it was a success. I was 23 miles closer to Maine!

My tent, which I had partially assembled in the garage at home, would not cooperate in the wind. The wind was blowing about 30 miles per hour by then, and I couldn't put up the tent while wearing gloves, so my fingers quickly grew numb. When I finally got my tent up, I threw my pack inside and ignored the idea that bears could be interested in any food left within reach. I was just relieved I was finally in my bedroll. That night, the wind blew so hard that I thought there was a train nearby and even heard a sound resembling a train's whistle. After a couple of hours, I realized no train was that long, nor could any train be up that high in these mountains. I was hearing the wind in the trees and around the mountain. Maybe it was nature's way of singing me a lullaby before I went to sleep.

The wind continued to blow hard during the night, and several times I felt the tent tilting badly and even wondered whether it would blow over. I didn't realize until the next morning in the daylight that I had not assembled my tent right, and thus it tilted and the wind blew into it. Fortunately, I had a good bedroll, or else I could have suffered frostbite. I had learned two more lessons that evening. First, make camp when the weather turns bad before it gets to the danger stage. Second, know your equipment. Setting up a tent in the garage is quite different than doing it on a mountain with the wind and sleet blowing.

Each day, I saw fewer and fewer hikers. I estimated I saw 25 hikers on the first day, with all but one going north, and most said they were thru-hikers. It was interesting that I saw about 15 hikers the second day, 8 or 10 the third day, and no hikers the final day except the pair in the shelter with me that morning! Of course, one reason I didn't see as many hikers is that we were getting spread out on the Trail. But the other reason is that many hikers quit in the first few days. Like I did, they found that although we had trained hard for the hike, we had not encountered anything as difficult as the steep, long hills of North Georgia. Of course, we had not yet seen the White Mountains of New Hampshire and Maine, either!

Thru-hiker: A thru-hiker is a person who hikes the entire AT in one 12-month period, either from Georgia to Maine or from Maine to Georgia. It doesn't matter how many times the hiker comes off the Trail, and the entire distance does not need to be hiked all in one direction. Any combination of hiking north or south is okay.

I woke up the next morning to a cold wind and temperatures slightly below freezing. I had left my hiking boots outside the main part of my tent under a flap. Since I had not anchored my tent properly, my boots were soaked inside and out. This was not good, as wet boots are not only uncomfortable but can easily lead to blisters forming on your feet.

It was too cold and wet for me to cook breakfast comfortably, so I hurriedly packed my gear, but my wet tent was a different matter. The tent was partially frozen, so it was difficult to fold, and I had no way to dry it, so I carried a badly folded tent that would stay wet for a couple of days. I never did learn how to put up a tent or take it down in the rain without getting the inside of it wet, nor did I ever find a way to deal with a wet tent except to stop during the day and lay it out to dry. This assumed that the rain would stop and the sun would come out later during the day. A few times, I went several days before my tent fully dried out.

I hiked for about an hour and a half before stopping for breakfast. By then, I had warmed up and my boots, although still wet, felt normal again. I threw my pack down in the middle of the Trail and boiled enough water for two cups of hot chocolate and two packages of instant oatmeal. It wasn't the way I had envisioned my first night and breakfast on the Trail, but I had gotten my first taste of how weather and terrain can dictate a new plan for the night.

The climb up Blood Mountain is uphill for 1,500 feet in elevation over about five miles. It's the first of many steady uphill hikes before a drop of nearly the same amount in just 2.5 miles. I arrived at the bottom of the descent at Neel Gap to a greatly appreciated full-service outfitter called Walasi-Yi Interpretive Center. The Trail literally goes through an archway that is part of the building. Inside is most anything a hiker could need. They will weigh your pack, make suggestions, sell you what you don't have, and mail what you don't need to your home. Also available are all kinds of equipment and clothing, hot showers for a $3.50 fee, hot and cold drinks, and food. A bunk room and a tenting area are nearby. I bought a hamburger and Coke and sat in a chair near the fireplace while a local pet dog sat patiently in front of me, begging for a bite. Unfortunately for him, I was hungry and ate every crumb of the burger.

I left at about two thirty. I noticed many hikers were taking advantage of the convenience of hot food and a warm bed for the night, but I pushed on. I had only gone about 200 yards when I saw a sign that caused me to have second thoughts about staying the night. The sign warned in detail about a bear that had come out of hibernation early and would be scrounging for whatever food she could find. She had two cubs, which made her more dangerous. The sign cautioned all hikers to take particular care not to surprise the bear or leave out food; particularly, do not keep food, including candy bars or other snacks, in a tent. The sign advised hikers to hang all food and packs from a tree at least 16 feet up in the air and 6 feet away from the trunk of the tree. Needless to say, I hung my food from the highest limb I could throw a rope over that night.

I tented that evening at Hogpen Gap, arriving about seven thirty. I had hiked about 17.5 miles that day and was well pleased. However, I was exhausted and again shorted myself on a meal that evening, having eaten a late lunch. This was not a good thing to do, especially as this was the second day in a row, but I had no encounters with any bears or other animals that day, and that was good.

The next morning, I rose to some light snow and cold temperatures. Again, I was so cold that the thought of pausing long enough to heat water and eat breakfast was uninviting. Instead, I packed my equipment, rolled up my wet tent, and began hiking as quickly as I could without breakfast or any liquids to drink. A heavy fog had rolled in overnight, creating limited visibility of less than 100 yards. It's a bit eerie to look out and only see what is immediately around you, and to follow a path that disappears into the mist. The fog lifted about noon, but for most of that afternoon, I hiked between layers of clouds that still gave low visibility and the impression of being lost in the sky with no references either in the sky or down in the valley as to which direction I was hiking. Fortunately, the Trail was well marked . . . and I was going north, as best I could tell, by shelters and creeks I passed.

I thought I should have been famished at noon, but I had to force my food down when I stopped. I could eat only about two-thirds of a package of chicken and noodles, and I was well aware that wasn't enough. But try as I could to eat, I just wasn't hungry.

As I had done the first day, I hiked until about an hour after dark, using my headlamp, before arriving at the Tray Mountain shelter. I found two young men already asleep at the shelter, so I quietly got out my bedroll, hung my pack on the nearby bear cables, and found sleep came easily. However, I rose to go to the bathroom at about three in the morning, only to find that I had severe vertigo! I was stumbling as much as four feet in every direction, making it difficult to get back to the shelter. The next morning, I discovered I had lost my hat the night before, but luckily I found it on the ground by the bear cables, covered with a light layer of new snow.

I have had vertigo several times and found it to be debilitating. Most times I can barely stand up, and it often lasts for three or four days. During that time, I am forced to stay in bed and not move my head any more than is absolutely necessary. I carry meclizine, which is a medication for vertigo, with me on most trips, but it always leaves me feeling drugged and sleepy. That night, I was afraid to take the meclizine for fear it would put me to sleep or make it impossible to have the motor skills needed even to walk, let alone hike down a mountain carrying a pack. This, I knew, could be a dangerous situation, and I must use extreme caution and good common sense. Hoping for the best, I lay down and slept until around five forty-five

Gap: A low area between or along mountains. Over time, these gaps became natural passageways for animals and other wildlife, Native Americans, and the early settlers. Today, most roadways go through these gaps rather than over the surrounding higher terrain. Since the AT often follows the mountain ridges, the hiker goes down into a gap, where often there is a water supply, and then back up the mountain, still following the ridge. These gaps may have names such as Hogpen Gap and Neel Gap.

in the morning, when the two young men got up and quietly left for the Trail. I think they were the same two whom I had met on Springer Mountain, and we had shared taking pictures, but I could not be sure, as I remained in my bedroll hoping I would feel better.

After they left, I got up and found I was in the same shape I had been before, so I took half of a dose of meclizine and lay back down in my sleeping bag. By eight in the morning, I knew I had to try to hike. I felt better and found that with my two hiking poles, and holding my head still, I could keep my balance and walk slowly. It had snowed during the night about a quarter inch, making the world as beautiful as any winter scene on a Christmas card. Right then, I didn't notice except to be aware that the snow could make things a bit slicker.

The rest of the day is a blur. I remember staggering a great deal. I must have looked drunk to anyone who might have seen me. I don't remember seeing anyone, but I recall knowing what a perilous position I was in. I couldn't walk straight and felt extremely tired. At one point, I felt like I couldn't go on. I was climbing up to Kelly Knob, ascending almost 900 feet, and wasn't sure I could make it. Even after going up that mountain, I still had to go down and then back up Powell Mountain before descending more than 1,200 feet into Dicks Creek Gap.

At some point along that climb, I told God I couldn't make it up the mountain. Nor did I think I had the energy or stamina to continue fighting my vertigo. In my prayer, I told God how each step was difficult and dangerous, and that I was hiking over some treacherous rocks and mountains, with steep climbs and descents. I couldn't do this on my own, so He would have to help me. My prayer was simply that Jesus would take me through this wilderness and land me safely at Dicks Creek Gap. I don't remember any more than that until I reached the descent into Dicks Creek Gap. I truly do not know if it was a loss of memory or a miracle that took me over those mountains. What I do know with certainty is I reached the parking lot of Dicks Creek Gap, some 11 miles from the Tray Mountain shelter, about four that afternoon. I was exhausted and cold but convinced God had been with me and carried me over the mountain safely.

I feel certain that if I had looked back that day, there would have been only one set of footprints in the snow, and perhaps a bit deeper than normal, where someone had carried me down the mountain. There are several times when I have no doubt that God carried me either physically or in spirit, but always safely, and it could only have been He who saved me that day.

Using my cell phone from the parking lot at Dicks Creek Gap, I called Joyce Monroe, a shuttle partner with Sally Smith, who picked me up 30 minutes later and for $15 delivered me to the Holiday Inn Express & Suites in Hiawassee, where I had left my car and I would spend the night. I was tired, hungry, cold, and dizzy, but I had hiked my first 70 miles of 2,186 miles on the AT. Now only 2,116 miles to Katahdin, and I still felt I could make it somehow!

That night, after checking in at the motel, I took a long, hot soak in the jetted tub and slept until midnight. Then I got up, dressed, and went back to the same Huddle House where I'd eaten four days earlier. I found eating to be difficult, but I forced myself to consume as much as I could. It felt good to be back in a place where there were luxuries such as hot water, real food, a mattress to sleep on, and clean clothes. I woke at seven o'clock the following morning, still a bit woozy from the vertigo but able to drive the 350 miles home. What a blessing it was to finally get home that Friday afternoon! I knew Judy would worry, so I had not told her of the vertigo, from which it took a full week to recover.

Proverbs 16:9: In his heart a man plans his course, but the Lord determines his steps.

I had planned to go hiking again the next week, but a combination of poor weather in North Georgia and my recovery from the first trip convinced me to wait an additional week. I had lost seven, yes, seven pounds during those four days of hiking.

But, most important, I had learned that we indeed have a God who never leaves us and who desires the very best for us. We believe in Him; we ask for help from Him; we follow Him as best we can; and we share Him with others. And through it all, God loves us unconditionally. That's what Jesus came to show us. Amen.

Dennis squeezes through the boulders.

A plaque honors those who hiked the Trail.

CHAPTER FIVE

Helped by Trail Angels

Weather is perhaps the most dangerous and most unpredictable factor of any hike. The forecast can be quite good for surrounding cities, but the effects of increased elevations and the wind blowing through valleys and over mountaintops can create sudden changes within a few miles. If you are unfortunate enough to be in that area, you can experience sudden drops in temperature, almost instant changes in wind velocity, and unforeseen rain and snowstorms that can become quite violent.

Because of predicted bad weather in East Tennessee, I delayed returning to the AT for an additional week. The time wasn't wasted, as I experimented with my pack while attempting to lighten my load. One of my ideas was to leave my tent at home and thus reduce my pack's weight by 2.5 pounds. This would make it necessary to spend my nights on the Trail in a shelter, and I learned later from a soon-to-be Trail Angel that depending on finding a shelter can be a dangerous thing to do.

I left Decaturville after church on Sunday as soon as I finished leading worship and changed clothes, and I drove to the Holiday Inn Express & Suites in Hiawassee. Early the next morning, I drove 52 miles to the Nantahala Outdoor Center (NOC) in Bryson City, North Carolina, where I left my car. I intended to hike back to my car from Dicks Creek Gap, which is 67 miles by trail.

"Nantahala" is a Cherokee word meaning "land of the noonday sun," because the sun doesn't shine in the valley between the mountains until noon. Several weeks later, when I hiked down the steep mountain on one side into Nantahala and then up the even-steeper mountain on the other side, I appreciated the true meaning of "land of the noonday sun." The sky can be perfectly clear and brilliant, but it really is noon before sunshine reaches the valley below.

As scheduled, Sally Monroe picked me up at eight in the morning and drove me back through Hiawassee to Dicks Creek Gap, where she dropped me off. I was on my way again, joining all the other thru-hikers. We all said we were thru-hikers even if we weren't. I felt again like I was in the "big boys and big girls" club! It's amazing how our egos and minds can make us feel bigger, less vulnerable, and more important than we really are. So it is on the Trail. We are brash enough to think that on our own and using our own powers, we can hike from Springer, Georgia, to Katahdin, Maine. I learned the hard way like all the others that we are not alone in this world. God is with us, and God also sends angels to help us along the trail of life.

However, we don't always recognize those we meet as angels. I met a southbounder who was a rough-looking man, gruff in his manners, in need of a haircut, with clothes that had seen a lot of the Trail, a medium-gray beard, tall, and obviously attuned to hiking. I asked him about the Trail behind him, water sources, and how crowded the shelters were. On the other hand, he asked me about my equipment and specifically whether I was carrying a tent or emergency tarp to use to make a tent if I became stranded on the Trail. Trying to travel light, I wasn't carrying either a tent or a tarp. In a gruff and stern manner, he reprimanded me for not being prepared in case I should become stranded.

He lectured me unmercifully: "Protection from the elements is paramount. Rain, sleet, snow, and high winds can occur very fast in the mountains, and weather reports are useless as mountains have their own weather patterns. People get stranded or hurt daily, and rescue teams have to come out to get people off the mountains, all the while leaving their own jobs and families and risking their own health to get some fool off the mountain who didn't have proper protection or supplies." He went on for several minutes and succeeded in both offending me right then and saving me in later weeks and months when I did experience unusual, fast-moving weather patterns that required me to hunker down in a tent that was hastily thrown down in the middle of rain and sleet. He would also be a Trail Angel to me within the next 48 hours.

I spent the rest of the day climbing. From Dicks Creek Gap up 1,000 feet to Buzzard Knob, then down a bit before climbing up another 1,600 feet to Standing Indian Shelter, I hiked a little over 16 miles that day. Considering I got a late start and the Trail had some rather long, steep climbs, I was feeling good about myself. The shelter that night was a bit crowded as more hikers took to the Trail when the weather warmed a bit and got closer to spring. The conversation around any shelter is always about the weather, the Trail, and what animals each hiker had seen that day. That night was no different, although no one had seen many animals. As I would soon learn, hikers don't see many animals; we are too busy looking at our feet and where we are going, and the animals shy away from human smells and all the noise we make.

During the day, I had passed what was always a milestone—a state line. Officially, I had hiked Georgia and now was in North Carolina. I had one state down and 13 more states to go before reaching that magical goal called Katahdin in Maine. Like the other hikers that day, I took a selfie standing beside the sign announcing I was in North Carolina. I would eventually have a selfie beside every state-line sign, like thousands of other hikers who record those milestones.

I had seen other signs that day that were a bit more concerning. They read, "CAUTION: This is a bear sanctuary." I also had seen in the *Appalachian Trail Thru-Hikers' Companion* a note in italics that read, "Recent bear sightings; use bear-proofing techniques." I would have preferred a sign reading, "Bears: This is a human sanctuary. Stay away!" But look as I might, I never saw that one. The truth is that nature belongs to all of God's creatures; it's just more obvious to whoever is not at the top of the food chain that day!

I like to wake up at four thirty and get on the Trail early enough to see the animals moving before other hikers scare them away. I was out early that morning, but unfortunately, no animals seemed to be roaming near me. The first 1.5 miles were a climb of just over 1,000 feet up Standing Indian Mountain, with an elevation of 5,498 feet. The view going up was not particularly good, as it is shrouded in trees, and a long climb is not the way I usually liked to warm up in the morning.

What I remember most about the day started while I was climbing Albert Mountain to a fire tower on top. The last three-tenths of a mile was a steep climb where it was often necessary to use my hands to help. Not only was it exhausting, but my right knee began to ache. By the time I reached the fire tower, it was more than an ache and was hurting to the point I was having trouble walking. Four hikers had passed me on the steep climb and were on top of the fire tower encouraging me to join them for the great view. One of the young men was complimenting everyone, including himself, about the fact that we had hiked the first 100 miles of the AT. Only one-third of all hikers, he said, ever made it as far as this 100-mile point, and we should be proud of ourselves. He was jumping up and down on top of the tower, shouting that we were better than two out of every three hikers who started on the AT, but all I could think about was that I was hurting and wondering if I could continue.

The next six miles to Rock Gap Shelter are a blur. I was walking stiff-legged with my right leg and attempting to put as much weight as I could on my left. The pain in my knee was killing me, but I finally reached the shelter around six that evening. The last 200 yards were downhill through some brush, and normal-size step-downs felt like deep canyons. When I got to the shelter, four people immediately came to meet me. I wish I knew their names, but perhaps they will read this one day and know they were angels to me. They helped me get my pack off; they got water from the spring nearby; they helped me cook my supper and get into my bedroll; and, to keep the bears out of my food, they hung my pack on a rope they had thrown over a branch.

I didn't get much sleep that night because I couldn't get comfortable with my knee. I didn't know how I was going to get off the mountain, but I was sure this trip was over, so I was glad when dawn finally came. The crew of four went to work again to get all my equipment together. They checked the maps and found a service road went within 300 yards of the shelter. One of them carried my pack while another gentleman helped me walk. I was still hurting badly, and I didn't know what I had done to my leg. I didn't remember hitting or twisting it. It had just begun to hurt for no apparent reason.

When we got to the road, there was a small parking area, and an SUV was stopped there with the engine running and a man and woman sitting in the back. When they saw me, they opened the door and invited me to sit in the warm vehicle while I waited for help. They had spent the night in the SUV and were waiting on another man to meet them. They were walking the Trail, and the man was ferrying their car up the Trail four miles where it would be waiting when they got there. The man they were waiting for turned out to be the same stern, gruff hiker whom I had met two days before and who had lectured me about carrying a tent in case I got hurt. I'm sure he remembered our conversation, but he was too kind to rub it in. Right then I needed a ride down the mountain, and he was kind enough to take me to Winding Stair Gap, where a van picked up hikers and took them into Franklin, North Carolina, to a motel and restaurant. This was the motel's way of getting hikers from the Trail to spend the night with them in town and take a zero day if they wished. The van showed up about an hour later for a 30-minute trip into town, and I gladly but gingerly climbed aboard.

No one that morning accepted a gratuity or asked for a fee to help me off the Trail. I was told, "No one ever accepts anything for helping someone hurt off the mountain." I was slowly learning that almost all hikers help each other out, and that while one moment we may receive help from an angel, the next we may be an angel to someone else. Without that care and love, no hiker would ever complete the Trail, and perhaps that's a lesson that can be applied to life. In fact, Jesus taught us a lot about love as told to us through His disciples in the Bible.

John 13:34-35: A new command I give you: Love one another. As I have loved you, so you must love another. All men (and women) will know that you are my disciples if you love one another.

There in Franklin, even though I wasn't staying overnight, the motel clerk made phone calls for me until she located a gentleman named Bob to shuttle me to my car in Nantahala. Bob turned out to be a retired policeman, approximately 80–85 years old, who needed to make some money even more than I needed a ride. He had an old, junky sedan, and threw papers and other items from the front seat to the back so I could get in. Before we left the parking lot, he asked if I minded giving him the $60 he was charging me for the ride right then, so he could buy some gas and get $10 added to his pay-as-you-go cell phone before we left town.

Of course, I didn't mind. Gas is a good thing to have when driving in the mountains. And when we stopped for the update to his phone, Bob asked me to go inside and pay for it. Even with my leg withering in pain, I could walk better than he could. I just hoped he could drive all right. Then he asked if it would bother me to take a shortcut he knew, which turned out to be a gravel service road that ran right beside a riverbed through the mountains. There were places where streams coming to the river had eroded the road, so it was necessary to slowly maneuver around the cuts. We were a pair, and the road was at best passable. But the gas held out; the car didn't break down; we both made it to Nantahala, where my car was parked; and we didn't have to use his cell phone to call for help even once! I can only pray he made it home safely.

I can count 10 people who directly made it possible for me to get off the mountain and safely to my car, and another person helped me at a rest area where I had stopped on the side of the interstate to use the restroom and had a soft drink can to throw away. When I got out, using one of my hiking poles as a cane and holding the can in my other hand, a stranger on the sidewalk saw me, politely took the can, and threw it into a garbage can some 20 feet away so I would not have to walk over to it. That's at least 11 people who helped me. Most people, by nature, have something in them that resembles the grace of God, and most people have a desire to reflect that to others. God is good. And all the time, God is good!

Zero day: A zero day is a day off the Trail during which hikers rest. Most hikers prefer to zero in a nearby town and usually rent a motel room and find the local restaurants. Washing clothes, replenishing supplies, and enjoying local activities are ways to relax, rest, and get ready for the next week of hiking.

I am reminded of an old story about a young Roman soldier named Martin, dating back to approximately 300 years after the birth of Christ. It was a time when Rome ruled the world and the Romans' word was gospel, or so they thought. In fact, the Roman emperor often saw himself as divine, and his word could mean life or death to those around him. But it was the Roman soldiers who kept the peace, or the Roman Pax, which really meant, "Leave Rome alone or risk your life!" They were rough and tough, often without any discipline or belief other than what was best for Rome. They were trained killers and had no compunction about killing anyone who opposed Rome or didn't think as they thought. They most often cared about themselves and Rome, but little else.

But Martin had become convicted that Jesus was the Son of God, and he was described as a seeker of the faith. One day, he met an unclothed man begging for alms in the freezing cold, so he stopped, cut his own coat in half, and gave it to the shivering stranger. That night, Martin had a dream in which he saw the heavenly court with Jesus robed in a torn cloak.

One of the angels asked, "Master, why do you wear that battered cloak?"

Jesus replied, "My servant Martin gave it to me."

That very night, young Martin went to be baptized.

Surely the Trail Angels who helped me were all Christ's little ones.

Five days after I got off the mountain, I was able to see Dr. David Johnson, who is a fine, Christian, orthopedic surgeon in Jackson. I first met him on a Walk to Emmaus, where he was the lay director and I was one of the spiritual directors. Since then, I have called him a friend and brother in Christ. He diagnosed me as having an irritated iliotibial (IT) band. The IT band is a tendon that runs from the knee to the hip. It can become irritated by overuse or not stretching it properly before exercise. I continued to have some problems with the IT but now know how to stretch it, and Aleve is great for treating the pain. I should have bought stock in Aleve long ago, as it is now a standard on my supply list when hiking.

As part of the treatment Dr. Johnson prescribed, I underwent several weeks of physical therapy. In the midst of the last therapy session as I lay on my back doing exercises, the therapist suddenly looked at me, stopped what she was doing, and said, "You're getting up off this table and going back hiking, aren't you?" I think the hiking pants and wool socks gave me away!

And she was right. I had my car packed and sitting in the parking lot, ready to head to the mountains for more hiking. If you are going to hike the entire Appalachian Trail, you have to decide beyond a doubt that finishing is a top priority. As I write this, I finished the AT from Georgia to Maine two months ago, and I'm in my second week of physical therapy on both knees for different causes, on both my shoulders, and for a sprained ankle that doesn't want to heal. If you hike the AT, you will get nicks, cuts, sore muscles, blisters, lost toenails, infections, and maybe a lot more. I had all the above and, yes, more of the more!

> **1 John 4:7-8, 11:**
> Dear friends, let us love one another, for love comes from God. Everyone who loves has been born of God and knows God. Whoever does not love does not know God, because God is love. . . . Dear friends, since God so loved us we also ought to love one another.

ABOVE: Checking your path meant looking down a lot at the Trail.

RIGHT: The path leads up mountains and down into the valleys.

CHAPTER SIX

Staying Warm and Dry Is Not an Option

The first Monday in April 2013, I got off the table from physical therapy on my knee and drove to Kodak, Tennessee, which is 24 miles from Gatlinburg, on Interstate 40 and Tennessee Route 66. I chose to spend the night there in order to be as close to Gatlinburg as possible, but not in the tourist areas of Pigeon Forge or Gatlinburg, where motel prices are higher.

I planned to park my car in Gatlinburg, hitch a ride to Newfound Gap, and hike southbound to Fontana Dam, where Judy would pick me up in three days. Then we would drive two hours to Pigeon Forge, where we would spend the night. The next morning, we planned to pick up my car in Gatlinburg before driving to Hot Springs, North Carolina, where we would spend a night. The following morning, we would pick up two of our daughters, Camille and Heather, in Asheville, North Carolina, and take them back to Hot Springs. Judy would drive home Sunday morning while the girls and I hiked for a few days. Most of the plan worked.

Early Tuesday morning, I grabbed two sausage biscuits from a local Burger King and ate them on the way to the NOC in Gatlinburg, where I parked. As a courtesy to AT hikers, NOC will shuttle thru-hikers up and down from Newfound Gap at no charge. A fine courtesy and, I suspect, a fine addition to their daily sales of hiking equipment and supplies. Judy and I would add to those sales four days later. Either way, I greatly appreciated the ride. I sat with five other hikers between packs and hiking poles on the floor in the back of the van. The seats had been removed to create room for more hikers, making for a rough ride on an unpadded floor, but 40 minutes of discomfort sure beats hiking up the mountain for some 18 miles. At the mountaintop, the other five hikers went north while I went south. I had planned the southbound hike so that Judy could pick me up on the way to Gatlinburg and we would not have to backtrack as much to retrieve my car.

The preceding days had been rough on the Trail. The entire Smokies had gotten a foot of snow on the Trail that stranded scores of hikers in shelters for three days. Most hikers did all right, but a few had problems. At least one had to be helicoptered out, and many ran out of food. I arrived on the second day hikers could begin moving again on the AT, although the snow was still treacherous. It was especially bad between Newfound Gap and Clingmans Dome, where the snow had been packed by the hikers coming through and then refroze overnight, making travel even worse. I arrived to a Trail of ice, so I hiked on the fringes and even off the Trail as much as possible, but the density of the trees and brush, and the steep inclines just off the Trail, forced me to hike on the Trail most of the time. Consequently, I think I fell at least 30 times during the first half of the day, and I was lucky that I wasn't hurt.

I met one northbounder who, when I got close, looked really bad. His face appeared strained, and he was moving slowly and with difficulty. Even to the most untrained eye, it was obvious something was wrong. I asked him if he was okay, to which he answered with a soft "Yes."

I said, "No, I hate to say this, but you look like something is wrong. Are you really okay?"

He replied, "I've been stranded on the Trail along with 30 others in Mollies Ridge Shelter. I ran out of food like most people did, and I haven't eaten in about two days. How far is it to Clingmans Dome? Can I get some food there?"

Mollies Ridge normally sleeps a maximum of 12 people. I replied, "It's about two miles, but take some of my food." I gave him two candy bars and tried to give him more, but he wouldn't take it. I also offered to hike back with him to Clingmans Dome, but he insisted he was all right.

I reluctantly went on, but I also knew there were other hikers in the area who would assist him if he needed any more help. Hikers help each other. That's just the rule of the Trail. I was helped many more times than I was able to help others, but I found for most of us, including myself, it is far easier to give than to receive.

Perhaps that is also true of forgiveness. Is that one reason when we hear those wonderful words in our Communion meditation, "In the name of Jesus Christ, you are forgiven," that we find it difficult to accept that forgiveness? We can give forgiveness, but it is difficult for us to accept that same forgiveness even though we know it comes from our Triune God.

I had hiked this Trail section the year before when I was deciding if hiking was for me and if I could see myself hiking the entire Trail. This time the hike was easier. I was in better shape, and I knew more about what to expect. I wanted to hike those 40 miles in two days, but the spacing between the shelters did not work for me, nor would it do any good to get to Fontana Dam a day early, as Judy wouldn't be there for three days.

On the third day, as I was hiking down to Fontana Dam, the weather started to change and a light mist of rain started. I was only about three hours from the dam, so I didn't worry about it. As the mist got a little stronger, I thought about putting on my rain pants, but that would mean stopping, taking off my pack, and removing my boots before I could pull on the pants. Then I'd have to put my boots back on before I could re-shoulder my pack. Besides, the rain might stop any minute. This went on for some time, and then I began to notice that the raindrops were freezing on the tree branches. The rain was not letting up, and it was getting colder, but I didn't feel cold. I was hiking, and my increased circulation was keeping me warm, or so I thought.

Isaiah 30:18: Yet the Lord longs to be gracious to you; He rises to show you compassion. For the Lord is a God of justice. Blessed are all who wait for Him.

Job 11:6: . . . Know this: God has even forgotten some of your sin.

Hosea 2:23: I will show my love to the one I called 'Not my loved one.' I will say to those called 'Not my people,' 'You are my people'; and they will say, 'You are my God.'

When I finally got to Fontana Dam, my pants were soaked through, and the rain had run down my shirt and jacket, getting me at least damp in most other parts of my body. I stopped under the canopy at the dam and immediately began to feel chilled. Judy wasn't due for at least another hour, I figured, but what I didn't know was that she had left Jackson about an hour late.

I had not had cell phone service, so there was no way for me to know she would be running late.

I was learning a valuable lesson. A chill on the mountain can quickly turn into hypothermia. The Mayo Clinic website defines this as: ". . . A medical emergency that occurs when your body loses heat faster than it can produce heat, causing a dangerously low body temperature. Normal body temperature is around 98.6 F (37 C). Hypothermia (hi-poe-THUR-me-uh) occurs as your body temperature passes below 95 F (35 C). When your body temperature drops, your heart, nervous system, and other organs can't work normally. Left untreated, hypothermia can eventually lead to complete failure of your heart and respiratory system and to death. Hypothermia is most often caused by exposure to cold weather or immersion in a cold body of water. Primary treatments for hypothermia are methods to warm the body back to a normal temperature."

This was a life-altering experience that caused me to take seriously all weather changes and always to err on the side of safety. I purchased another pair of rain pants that zipped all the way from the cuff to the waist so I didn't need to remove my boots to put on or take off my rain pants.

After I stopped, the chill continued to increase and I started to shiver with cold, so I went into the men's restroom, where I found an electric hand dryer. Ingenuity always helps. I took the plastic waste can from under the sink and turned it over, making a chair for myself, and set it under the hand dryer. Then, sitting on the waste can, I could get the dryer to blow warm air down my neck, and every 30 seconds, I'd take my elbow and hit the start button on the hand dryer, and so it went. I did that for almost two hours while waiting on Judy.

Picture it! I'm shivering, wet through and through, still in the clothes I'd been wearing for four days, dirty, hair uncombed, needing a shave, and sitting on a waste can in a public restroom, just as it's getting dark outside. What would you have thought if you had walked in on a picture like that? Well, a young man did come in! He looked around, a bit bewildered, and slowly exited the bathroom. Then about every 10 to 15 minutes, he would return, step in about five feet, give me some more odd looks, and back out of the restroom. I had no idea who he was, and I began to feel uncomfortable with him coming into the bathroom, looking at me for a minute, and then leaving. Each time, I tried to explain what I was doing, but he never told me who he was or what he wanted. He would just look and leave without a word. I'm not sure which of us was more uncomfortable with the other, but I was glad when I finally heard a car honking outside.

As it turned out, Judy had been in the area for about an hour and a half, but she went to the bottom of the dam, rather than the top where I was. Neither of our cell phones had service, so she was driving around trying to figure out where I could be. She finally drove up in front of the restroom and honked her car horn in the hopes that I might be within hearing range. I heard her and came out, much to the relief of us both. The guy who kept coming into the restroom was a security guard who was not in uniform, wearing a badge, or showing identification. I figured out who he was when he helped me put my equipment into the car. I'm not sure which of us was more relieved to discover the other was normal, or at least he was. I was a hiker, and there is nothing normal about us at times, at least to those who have never hiked the Trail.

By then, it was eight o'clock and dark. We had motel reservations in Pigeon Forge, but we couldn't get there from where we were. We had to take North Carolina Route 28 to US Route 129, which is affectionately known as the Tail of the Dragon because of its many curves. Many of the curves are marked 10 miles per hour, and you do have to slow down to 10 miles per hour or you won't make the curve. There are many accidents on that stretch, and motorcyclists and many sports car enthusiasts enjoy racing on that road. It seems like there is at least one accident each weekend, and some involve fatalities. When we reached that stretch, it was after dark, so the racers had gone home, but that did not make the road much safer.

Judy drove, so I didn't pay much attention to the road. I tried to get warm and had a great deal of difficulty doing it. I turned on the seat warmer and turned the temperature up to around 80 degrees. The heat nearly ran poor Judy out of the car, but I wasn't warming up very fast. I hadn't realized until then how cold I was and how close I had come to some serious physical problems. Looking back, upon arriving at Fontana Dam, I should have changed out of my wet clothes, put on whatever I could that was warm and dry, and gotten into my bedroll to get warm. But at that point, I was still learning some tough lessons. I had read as many of the "how-to" books as I could find, but until you experience many of those situations, it's difficult to do what they tell you to do. I didn't fully warm up until I got a hot shower several hours later in the motel.

From the Tail of the Dragon, we took the Foothills Parkway, which is a shortcut over the mountains. That evening, it was "short" but not so fast, as a heavy fog had rolled in and it was perhaps the thickest fog I have ever witnessed. We could see the white centerline of the road most of the time, but with visibility often less than 10 feet, when we crossed an intersection

Slick snow and ice make for a hazardous day.

where the white line didn't go completely across, we were strictly driving blind. Fortunately, there was no other traffic. We crawled along at about 10 miles per hour for more than an hour before finally dropping to a lower elevation and getting out of most of the fog. It was a tremendous relief to finally arrive in Sevierville and especially good to find a Five Guys Burgers and Fries. After being on the Trail for several days, a good ole hamburger can't be beat.

One downside of long-distance hiking is the aroma that hikers give off to those around them. Most hikers can be "appreciated" only if they remain at least six feet away from you while in the open air and in the next room if inside. That night we stayed at the Sevierville Holiday Inn Express, and I can't express how good it was to get a hot shower after not having a bath for four days and experiencing hypothermia. Judy also appreciated my bath and was quick to pick up my dirty hiking clothes and seal them in a plastic bag. I don't know where she found a can of Lysol, but she sprayed the room with it more than once before carefully washing her hands. She must really love me to have traveled with me for a couple of hours cooped up together in a car.

Judy and I had breakfast at the Cracker Barrel in Sevierville the next day. I ate two breakfasts. First, I had the biggest breakfast I could find on the menu, including a big slab of country ham, three eggs, biscuits, and gravy. Then I ordered a side order of pancakes, and I ate almost all of it! Hikers do get hungry!

We still had to retrieve my car from the NOC in Gatlinburg and drive to Hot Springs, North Carolina, but when we got to my car in Gatlinburg, I discovered I had inadvertently left the driver's side window down. I don't know why it was down to begin with, but there it was, wide open for the fifth day. I had left several pieces of hiking equipment, as well as my food supplies for the coming week, but no one had bothered anything, and apparently it had not rained there. I was very lucky. Or once again, had God been on the mountain in the freezing mist above Fontana Dam, in the fog the night before, and kept my car safe and dry? God is so good. I was learning that there would be many times when things happened and I would be surprised that I was safe from harm. His footprints are on the mountains!

Judy followed me in her car from Gatlinburg to Hot Springs. It's a 1.5-hour drive over winding roads through the mountains where we saw a sign saying we were just five miles from Hot Springs. Suddenly, we were directed to take a long detour around a bridge that was being rebuilt, and it took us some 30 to 45 minutes out of the way. The locals told us later that we could have gotten through easily by ignoring the bypass signs and going on the main road. On the return trip, we went by the main highway, and the locals were right. Local knowledge can be priceless.

Hot Springs is an old resort town nestled between the French Broad River and Spring Creek, with a population of between 600 and 700 people. Its history dates back to the Native Americans who discovered its mineral waters of 100-plus degrees. Later, European immigrants settled the area, and by 1778, people were visiting from other states for the water's reported healing powers. A major road, the Buncombe Turnpike, was built in 1828, and a railroad was constructed in 1882, making the area more accessible. Several large hotels were built to support tourism in bygone years, but most of them burned and were not rebuilt. Today, the mineral springs and hot baths are still there, but tourism has diminished. In 1917, during World War I, the United States government leased several hotels and kept German and Italian prisoners of war there. A number remained after the war and became residents of the community. Today, the AT comes into town on one end of the main street, goes across the French Broad River bridge at the other end, and turns and goes back up into the mountains. The street is appropriately named Bridge Street.

Deuteronomy 7:9: Know therefore that the Lord your God is God; He is the faithful God, keeping His covenant of love to a thousand generations of those who love Him and keep His commands.

Each town the Trail goes through has a list of unusually great people whose life stories have seldom been told outside of a few miles but who made important contributions to the community and the world. Two such people were Rev. Luke Dorland and his wife, Juliette, who came to Hot Springs in 1886 to retire and rest from 36 years pastoring in the Presbyterian Church. He was 71 years old, but God wasn't finished with him or his wife yet.

The townspeople soon discovered the Dorlands' gift for teaching and convinced them to start a school for the community's children. They started in their own living room with 25 children and soon grew to more than 60 students, and by 1890, they were serving more than 100 children. In 1893, the Presbyterian Mission Board took over the school and built a five-story building for boys' and girls' dormitories and more classrooms, and it became The Dorland-Bell School in 1918. Today it is known as Warren-Wilson College.

The Reverend and Mrs. Dorland set out to retire, but God had other plans and called them again in their declining years to serve Him and His smallest children around Hot Springs. I can only imagine what they might have said! Perhaps things like this: "We're too old." "I'm tired and need to rest." "We don't know how." Or perhaps, "We would rather sit back and let others do it. We've done our share."

Many of those I met on the Trail were people like that. At first, they appeared to have too many medical problems, were too old or too frail, or seemed to lack ambition, but they would finish hiking the Trail to wherever they set out to go. Many others were Trail Angels helping others. But what we do know about them all is that they did say: "Yes, here I am, God, use me," and "With your help, I can do it."

We stayed two nights in Hot Springs at the Mountain Magnolia Inn, which is a beautifully restored Victorian home, now turned into a hotel and restaurant. The first night was about settling in and getting some rest. The day had been an easy one, but we both were weary: Judy was tired from all the driving the day before after a full week in the office, and I was still trying to recover from hiking for three days. The second day there, we drove into Asheville, North Carolina, and picked up two of our daughters, Heather Vucetin and Camille Renshaw, at the airport before returning to Hot Springs. They came on separate flights, so we spent a good bit of time waiting on planes, but it was good to relax and not be hiking up a mountain.

The food at the inn was delicious and, important for a hiker, there was lots of it. As usual, I was also interested in finding the washer and dryer so I could clean my stinky clothes. Judy and the other hotel guests appreciated it, too. I'm sure the hotel owners were not entirely happy when I spread my bedroll, tent, and some other items from my pack on the beautifully manicured lawn to dry in the afternoon sun, but it had to be done somewhere. Lots of people who stay there also hike, so I'm sure I was not the first to do it. I hated to make a clothesline out of their lawn, but my equipment was still wet from hiking to Fontana Dam. It's amazing that clothes and equipment can get wet inside a pack, but they never dry until laid out in the sun to dry.

Other facilities around town catered to hikers, such as one motel and an inn; the Bluff Mountain Outfitters; and the Smoky Mountain Diner, where I ate twice. Located where hikers enter the town is a camping area complete with showers and a place to wash clothes. We enjoyed the small, quaint town located in a majestic valley with the French Broad River surrounded by the grand mountains, and it was a good break for me.

ABOVE: The beauty from the mountaintops was an incentive to climb out of the valleys.

RIGHT: Daughters Heather and Camille stopped for a photo op on the Trail.

CHAPTER SEVEN

It's a Family Affair

 On Sunday, April 7, Camille, Heather, and I hired a shuttle to take us to Sam's Gap. The driver arrived about eight in the morning in a little car that was much too small for herself, three hikers, and all our gear, but we made it into the car with each of us holding something in our lap. We were so tightly squeezed that we joked about what was going to happen when we arrived and opened the doors. The driver was trying to make ends meet by shuttling hikers. She was "between jobs," but worked part time at two other jobs when she wasn't shuttling hikers. She had hit a hard time in her life but was doing all she could to overcome it, and we were glad to help financially by hiring her and tried to be particularly generous with our tip.

 Judy left right behind us but went in the other direction heading home. It would take her about six hours to drive to Jackson, where we would meet again when I got home in four days. As always, leaving one another even for a short time was difficult. We've been married for more than 30 years and have developed a particularly strong relationship. This is the second marriage for us both and, perhaps because of that, we know how precious a true marriage is. We've worked hard to keep our relationship fresh and strong, and being separated during these weeks and months was hard, perhaps the most difficult part of my entire hike. Judy made a family of the two of us, her daughter Kristi, my two daughters Camille and Heather, and my son Denny. As I write this, I have difficulty saying "her" daughter and "my" children. Judy is largely responsible for making us into one family where neither of us differentiates between children, but rather it's always our children. I am eternally grateful to God and to Judy for our wonderful, loving family.

The girls and I hiked 33.5 miles southbound back into Hot Springs over the next three days. I had been on the Trail for nearly 200 miles and was developing my "Trail legs," but I still felt quite a bit of pain in my right knee from the bruised IT. Aleve was my new best friend! The doctor had told me I could take two tablets twice a day, as that was the prescribed dose, but I was adding another tablet sometime during the early afternoon as the morning dose began to wear off. Stopping every mile or so, I stretched my legs to help keep them from tightening. Still, several times during those three days, I found myself lying on the ground in deep pain, waiting on the Aleve to kick in. Despite the knee problems, though, I thoroughly enjoyed having the girls with me.

1 John 4:7-8: Dear friends, let us love one another, for love comes from God. Everyone who loves has been born of God and knows God. Whoever does not love does not know God, because God is love.

Our driver dropped us off at an overpass over Interstate 26 about nine in the morning. The sun was shining and a light breeze greeted us, making it an ideal day to hike. Even the temperature stayed in the 60s most of the day. We hiked 11.2 miles, not as far as I would have liked to cover in a day's time, but that was about the girls' limit. We had two climbs that day—the first about 600 feet and the second about 800 feet—before dropping some 1,500 feet to where we spent the night. The climbs were tough on the girls, and the downhill was particularly painful for my leg, but the joy of having company, especially my girls, made the day pleasant.

That night, we made camp near Flint Mountain Shelter, 20 yards off the Trail. Other hikers had already arrived, so we had to use our feet and a small branch as a broom to sweep leaves and limbs out of the way so we could pitch our tents. The campsite wasn't much, but it was relatively flat, and water was available down the hill about 300 yards away. The stream was small and not very deep, so we had to scoop up the water and pour it into the filter bladder, which adds a little time and energy in getting enough water for the evening and the next day.

Flint Mountain Shelter was about 100 yards away and could sleep eight people. Someone had hung a paper sign that said several hikers were sick with a stomach virus and advised us to keep our distance, which we readily did, but even with the sign, the shelter was full. About 10 other hikers camped in tents nearby. Everyone was courteous and quiet, a tribute to the goodness of humanity, although there were a few times on the Trail when common courtesy was not at its best.

The 2012 version of the *Thru-Hikers' Companion* describes an attention-getting experience of a hiker with a wild animal at this shelter. It is the "site of one of the more unusual animal encounters in Trail history. In 1994, a sleeping thru-hiker was bitten on the hand by a fox in the middle of the night, despite the presence of other hikers and two dogs."

This was not an encouraging thought to go to sleep by. But all was well that night, and the forest sounds lulled me to sleep. In particular, I enjoyed the owls hooting; they let the world know all was well. I slept well but suspect the girls were still adjusting to sleeping on the hard ground and the occasional twig snapping during the night.

The next morning, we each made our own breakfasts. I ate my standard two packets of maple and brown sugar oatmeal with two packets of hot chocolate. That required boiling four cups of water in my stove and pouring it into a cup. Washing the cup and spoon was more of a lick-and-a-rinse than a wash. I figured no one else was going to eat after me, and I would use them again before much mold could set in, so why bother? It must have worked, as in nearly 2,200 miles and multiple meals, I never got sick.

Camille is an ultralight backpacker, but that didn't stop her from producing amenities such as goodies for dessert the night before and a coffeepot for coffee in the morning. She goes to extremes to cut out any extra weight in her pack. For instance, she has cut the handle of her toothbrush off midway to reduce its weight, and she carries a sleeping pad that stops just below her waist, again to save a few ounces. On the other hand, I hike for days at a time and

Trail legs: Term used to describe a hiker who has developed a good bit of stamina and can hike longer distances, and go up and down mountains with some ease.

The peacefulness of the Trail is reflected in this moment by the water.

am willing to carry a little extra weight in order to be comfortable. How much to carry is always a give and take, because every extra ounce feels like a pound by the end of the day.

After breakfast and breaking camp, we made our way past the sign warning of the stomach virus in the nearby shelter and turned south, following the white blazes. It was another beautiful day with temperatures in the low 70s and a gentle breeze. The sun was shining, but the forest canopy blocks the sun's rays so effectively that I never wore sunscreen and never burned. I did always wear my wide-brimmed hat, both to block whatever sun did make its way through to the ground and to help protect my eyes from the small branches waiting for some unsuspecting hiker who had become momentarily entranced by the beauty of the mountains.

We spent the day hiking the ridge of Flint Mountain at an elevation of about 4,500 feet. We began with a climb of two miles and a little over 1,300 feet before what, for the AT, is a flat nine miles of hiking through the forest with only slight elevation changes of 50 to 200 feet. Despite the good trail, my knee bothered me, particularly when I was going downhill, so I would hike ahead of the girls going up and they would catch up to me going down. Spring had come to the lower elevations, but the trees and flowers were just starting to bud at our elevation. As a result, we could see a good distance, but the view was mostly of the forest hibernating. Unfortunately, enough hikers had already passed through the area that spring to scare most animals away, so we didn't see any wildlife except the occasional squirrel. It amazes me how the animals know just how close to get to humans without being seen. I only wish we could have seen a few of the multitude of God's little creatures that observed us from the recesses of the woods.

We made camp that evening in the middle of an old forestry road about 40 yards from the main Trail. A little stream came down out of the mountains and made a small pool 20 yards from where we pitched our tents, and a previous camper had pulled some old logs into a circle and made a fire pit in the middle. It was perfect. We had readily available water for cooking and drinking, and we were able to rinse off in the stream, removing the day's sweat and dirt, before preparing and eating dinner.

Camille had made a fire, and we sat on the logs around it after eating dinner and before finding our tents and bedrolls for the night. It was nice to have a campfire and enjoy the small talk on those three nights we were together, as they were the only campfires I sat around during my entire hiking experience. I did visit other hikers' fires occasionally while on the Trail, but only for short periods, because sleep was much more important than small talk. Camille and Heather again slept in Camille's two-person tent, which we had pitched next to my tent. I don't know how the girls slept, but I slept like a log. Perhaps I rested better because I had two other sets of ears to listen for any wildlife that might come snooping around.

In the morning, after eating breakfast and filtering drinking water from the stream for the day's hike, we hoisted our packs and began our hike toward Spring Mountain Shelter. Before long, I noticed the girls seemed to have a joke between them, and several times I saw them with half-concealed laughs. Now, as a father of three daughters and a son, I learned long ago there are secrets that children, especially daughters, don't readily share with their dad. It must be written somewhere in the instructions to daughters that they should keep their dad as uninformed as possible and make fun of him when he doesn't understand what's going on. This was one of those mornings where the girls followed instructions, and I was the last to know the joke!

Across the back of my pack, I had stretched a string with binder clips so I could hang my wet socks and shirts to dry as I hike. The night before, Heather had washed her black lace panties in the spring, but they had not dried overnight so, unbeknownst to me—you guessed it—that morning she had hung them on the back of my pack to finish drying. We stopped to rest about two hours into the hike, and as I slung my pack down to the ground, my eyes caught sight of those black silk panties. The girls were cracking up! They had already placed a picture of my pack with the panties on Facebook! Between laughs, they said that several times young men had passed me on the Trail and courteously greeted me with a "Good morning, sir," before noticing "my" black lace panties. Then they, as the girls put it, "made a wide path around me." Dads, beware of hiking with grown daughters, especially if they carry a camera!

I got a little revenge the next day, though. Heather, unfortunately, had come down with a stomach virus that kept her running for the woods the previous day. It was tough on her and took a lot of the fun out of her hike. I hate that. But after she began to get over her stomach problems, I came up with a new Trail name for her. When she was in high school, she was an excellent runner in both track and cross-country. Even up until her late 30s, she continued to run in marathons. I put that together with the fact that she had been doing a lot of running into the woods and gave her the name Runner. I told her she was welcome to explain her name to others either by saying she had been a runner in school, or by telling them the "real reason," which she and I would always know was in retaliation for her black lace panties being hung on my pack. Payback is always fun.

That night, after hiking a little over 10 miles, we camped near the old Spring Mountain Shelter, which sleeps only five hikers. Most hikers, including us, prefer to tent rather than sleep in the shelters, especially when they are old and appear to be infested with insects and rodents. The water was a small spring about 100 yards from where we had chosen to camp.

By now, the three of us had settled into a routine, so each of us got lost in our own world until our attention was drawn to Camille's shouts and laughter. She and a nearby camper were attempting to throw a small rope over a branch so we could hang our food pouches for the night, but they were not being very successful, to say the least.

The idea is to find a branch that is at least 16 feet from the ground and is small enough that a bear will not attempt to crawl on it but strong enough to hold our food pouches. The pouches also need to hang at least 6 feet from the tree trunk, or else an enterprising bear will snag them with a long, outstretched front paw while climbing the tree. It also helps if there are no obstructing branches that will catch and tangle a rope when it is slung up over the branch. I found this exercise to be difficult throughout my entire hike, and I never mastered the art of throwing one end of the rope over the limb and having it fall close enough to the ground that I could pull it down. As a consequence, I kept my food pouch in my tent most nights unless I was in an area especially known to have bears.

Acts 16:31: Paul replied, 'Believe in the Lord Jesus, and you will be saved—you and your household.'

Acts 2:39: The promise is for you and your children and for all who are far off—for all whom the Lord our God will call.

Camille and her new friend also found this task to be difficult. They first tried tying a stone to one end of the rope, which made it easier to throw, but the rock didn't want to stay on the rope. After several tries, they finally tied a bottle full of water to the rope and managed to get the rope across its proper place on the limb with both ends of the rope near the ground. Now the only problem was that we had one rope and about eight food pouches to hang on the same limb. I decided I'd let them figure it out, and I kept my food and pack in my tent.

Our original plan had been to spend four nights on the Trail and hike into Hot Springs on the fifth day. We had hiked a few more miles each day than the girls had anticipated, so around the campfire that night, we discussed whether we would prefer to go ahead and hike 11 miles into Hot Springs or to have two short days. We all agreed we'd been out long enough, so we hiked into Hot Springs on the fourth day, arriving in time for a late lunch.

The hike into Hot Springs is beautiful, especially during the last two miles. It's a steep descent that overlooks the French Broad River and a bridge leading into the town on the other side. The day was gorgeous with temperatures in the upper 60s and low 70s. Except for a steep climb of about 700 feet early in the morning, the hike that day had been primarily downhill. All morning, I anticipated a "real" meal at the Smoky Mountain Diner. We had eaten there before, and I wanted the same meal: a huge cheeseburger with bacon and all the trimmings, sweet potato fries, and all the iced tea I could drink, followed up with a big slice of lemon pie. And it was good—especially after eating dehydrated food for several days!

After a leisurely lunch, we walked a few blocks to the Mountain Magnolia Inn, where we had left my car. It was only about an hour's drive into Asheville, where I dropped the girls at the home of Richard and Melinda Douglass. They are the parents of our son's lovely wife, Leigh, and were kind enough to leave a key for the girls to go in, rest, and shower before catching a taxi to the airport. I had a wonderful time with the girls and will never forget it. I only wish they could have hiked more with me, but their careers and family would not allow it.

It had been a mixed-up few days. I drove from the physical therapist's table in Jackson, Tennessee, to Kodak, Tennessee; spent the night there; drove to Gatlinburg and got a ride to Clingmans Dome; hiked four days to Fontana Dam, where Judy met me; drove to Sevierville, Tennessee, and spent the night; drove to Gatlinburg, picked up my car, and drove to Hot Springs, North Carolina, where we stayed at the Mountain Magnolia Inn; drove to Asheville, North Carolina, and picked up the girls at the airport before driving back to Hot Springs; hired a driver to take us to Sam's Gap; hiked back into Hot Springs in four days; took the girls to Asheville; and now I was on my way home.

I was exhausted but glad I had stayed healthy on the Trail, and even happier that I drove the

550-mile, eight-hour trip from Asheville to Jackson safely and without going to sleep behind the wheel.

A lot of planning and coordination had gone into this part of the hike, but the AT requires that everywhere one goes. There are always the unknowns of how long it will take to reach the next supply drop; whether the supplies will arrive on time; how the weather will cooperate; whether the Trail can be hiked as marked, or if there are bypasses or swollen rivers to conquer; what the towns, restaurants, and motels will be like; how your body will hold up; and, equally important, how your mental strength and spirit will fare.

The Trail is not easy, but the support of family does make it easier.

This bridge is typical of those built by volunteer Trail clubs.

CHAPTER EIGHT

Hiking Rain or Shine

My ride to Abingdon, Virginia, on the afternoon of Sunday, April 21, was not unlike the other rides from Decaturville to the AT. I left church immediately after the worship service and drove all afternoon, finding the Holiday Inn Express & Suites late that evening. During the drive, I anticipated a supper of a huge cheese and ham omelet, pancakes, and hash browns, but the closest all-night restaurant I was familiar with was 20 miles back down Interstate 40. I debated whether to drive that far when I could get a quick hamburger right next door to the motel, but my hankering (a good Southern word for "a strong desire") overrode my reluctance to make another drive. I focused on enjoying my last meal before a week of dehydrated food. My supper was delicious and more than I could eat, but it was well worth the drive.

I had arranged to meet a man from Mt. Rogers Outfitters in Damascus, Virginia, at seven o'clock, so the night was short, but morning dawned bright and beautiful with the promise of good weather all week, a hiker's dream! Getting on the Trail always takes a bit of dreaming, planning, and then hoping the person scheduled to meet you early one morning hasn't forgotten, overslept, or had car trouble. But my ride met me exactly on time and pointed out a safe place to leave my car, across the street from Mt. Rogers Outfitters and right on the Trail. I couldn't ask for a better place to leave my car, especially knowing it would be waiting when I came through a week later, hot, sweaty, and tired.

In a little more than an hour, I was on the Trail again, excited and anticipating what would be around the next bend and what wonders God would provide for me to feast my eyes and mind upon. Every hike must begin with a climb, and this one rose and fell until I had ascended some 1,700 feet over about 7.5 miles to Bald Mountain before dropping down for a night's rest near No Business Knob Shelter.

During the day, I crossed Big Bald, where there still exist stories of lost love; a man's life lived somewhat aimlessly on the mountain; and a murder where the killer was never charged. The story is that a man known as Hog Greer lived on the mountain from 1802 to 1834, claiming the mountain as his personal property. Spurned by his lover, he became a cantankerous loner who lived in a cave. Local folks gave him his name on account of his personal appearance and hygiene. He lived up to his reputation of having a short temper by allegedly killing a man during an argument over property, but he was acquitted on grounds of insanity. Eventually, a local blacksmith shot him in the back and killed him, but the blacksmith was never charged in the murder. I often wondered, as I hiked over mountains and through valleys and towns, what stories I would never know about those who lived in those mountains long ago.

The next day proved to be grueling with a drop of nearly 3,000 feet before climbing 4,000 feet to a small area where I set up my tent near a piped spring. A piped spring is where a small amount of water surfaces, forming a spring so small that the water can only be obtained because a Trail Angel put a one-inch pipe into the ground so that the water runs out through the pipe rather than on the ground. There are numerous places like this where the water may come out as slowly as a few drops per minute or as a steady stream, although usually the velocity of the piped water is directly related to the amount of recent rainfall. That can become a major problem because a hiker never knows whether there will be sufficient water to fill bottles and hydrate food. For that reason, everyone asks, "How's the water up the Trail?"

The next morning, I came upon Uncle Johnny's Nolichucky Hostel and Outfitter, where I spent about an hour resting and drinking two quart-size chocolate milks. I wanted a third but was afraid I wouldn't be able to climb the ridge facing me across the Chestoa Bridge. I also found a gift left there for all the hikers. A drugstore had provided a box of hand sanitizers for anyone to pick up and carry with them. Various stomach ailments were being passed up and down the Trail, carried primarily by unwashed hands, so I took four small bottles and used all of them within the week. Trail Angels aren't always just individuals, but sometimes are the businesses along the way. Thanks to some caring druggists.

That night, I camped near Clyde Smith Shelter in my new tent, a half-moon design that uses a hiking pole for the center support and forms a half-circle that leaves an inch or so of space between the ground and the tent itself. I had never used one of these tents and had much to learn. First, I should have brought a plastic ground cloth to go under my sleeping bag. When it rained that night, the water ran in under the tent and got the bottom of my bedroll and my sleeping pad wet. Second, the seams were not waterproofed, so the rain came in through the tent itself in what seemed like buckets. The water dripped continuously from multiple spots so, just in case the water had not soaked up from the ground, this guaranteed that the top part would get wet as well!

By morning, everything I had was soaked. To make matters worse, the water that seeped into my belongings added what seemed like five pounds to my pack. That wasn't good, as two steep climbs lay ahead of me. The first was a climb of about 600 feet, followed by a drop of 1,000 feet and then a climb of 2,200 feet up Roan Mountain. The climb would have been tough without the added weight from the rainwater, but with that burden, the hike became extraordinarily difficult. The mountaintop flattens out through a meadow where the Trail becomes one of a multitude of little trails, so I was confused as to whether I was staying on the Trail.

At the top is a large parking lot and bathhouse. The parking lot was empty and the bathhouse was locked, but the concrete and asphalt, combined with a brilliantly sunny day, made the ideal place to lay all my gear out to dry. After turning items a couple of times to speed the process, everything was dry in about an hour and ready for the next rainstorm.

The half-moon tent had saved me about one pound in my pack but was not what I needed for my tenting experience. I had decided sometime during the night that my old tent performed well and was worth the added weight of just one pound. It had a floor, a mosquito net, and a cover that could be used in rain or cold weather but could be removed, leaving only the mosquito net for hot nights where a breeze felt good. Additionally, it had a flap on the front where I could leave my wet boots to dry at night. Most important right then was that it always kept me dry! I was lucky that the previous night had not been extremely cold or I could have faced hypothermia. That was another time when I learned a hard lesson but did not have to pay serious or life-threatening consequences.

I was rewarded two miles farther with spectacular views in every direction on Round Bald. Several section hikers had parked on a nearby road and were walking up, taking full advantage of the warm spring morning and panoramic views. Roan Mountain and the adjacent areas are some of the highest on the Trail and the most easily reachable for the general public. A month later, the parking lot below and the adjacent roads would be a mass of people doing what I was doing, hiking and taking in the scenery.

That evening, I camped about 300 yards from the Overmountain Shelter, which is an old, converted barn, now painted red. I'm told it was once the backdrop for the movie *Winter People*, but that evening it was the backdrop to about a dozen folks who were not out to hike but rather to party the night away. Fortunately, I was far enough away that I missed most of the sounds from what I suspect was a high induced by alcohol or some other substance. A young man who appeared to be about 25 years old was camped about 100 yards from me, but we had almost no conversation or contact as each of us cooked our supper and prepared for the night. The sun was setting behind me, and the shadow slowly crawled up the opposing mountainside covered with green trees. The view was magnificent and belied the sounds I would hear later that would wake me from my sleep three times.

I turned in at the "hiker's midnight" of eight o'clock. The soft sounds of crickets and a light breeze lulled me to sleep. It was the absolute picture of the perfect night, and I was soon sound asleep in my warm bedroll inside my comfortable, dry tent. Suddenly, I was awakened by a sound that undoubtedly came from a growling bear the likes of which I had no inclination to meet face to face, but judging by the sound, it must be only a few feet away from my tent. It was no easy task to find a flashlight, unzip a bedroll, roll over, unzip the mosquito netting, and then unzip the tent flap before throwing off the flap to expose the dark meadow around me. I climbed out of the tent as fast as I could, fully expecting to face a bear with nothing but a flashlight and a hiking pole that was stuck in the ground nearby.

The growling continued, but no bear was visible, even though I was camped some 100 yards from the nearest tree line or any other place a bear might hide. Slowly, I discerned the direction from which the sound came and realized it was coming from the tent 100 yards away where the other camper was sleeping. Unbelievably, the noise was his snoring! In my entire life I have never heard anyone snore that loudly. The snoring finally stopped, which indicated to me he must have turned over in his sleep, so I went back to bed and fell asleep almost as soon as my head hit the ground. Twice more, I was awakened by the "bear growling" and got out of my tent fully expecting to face a bear, only to realize again that it was the other hiker. The noise was so loud and sounded so much like a growl that I could not convince myself it wasn't a bear, so I got out of my tent to make sure.

The party at the red barn was what I had thought would keep me awake that night, but it turned out to be a "man" bear. Later I talked to other hikers who had the misfortune of tenting near Snorer; they were spreading the word along the Trail not to tent near him. In fact, several days later, I started to tent and another hiker informed me that Snorer was camped nearby, so I moved down the Trail another mile before tenting for the night.

The following evening, I camped near Mountaineer Falls Shelter. A light rain had begun to fall, and it was enough to give warning that more was in store. I awoke the next day to the rain still falling lightly, but the word on the Trail was that a larger storm was moving in and would take a couple of days to clear. Heavy rain could be expected, and the forecast did not lie! The rain fell all day and was moderately hard at times, which did not help the condition of my feet.

My feet had remained wet for several days, and I was unable to dry my socks and boots. I usually don't wear one pair of socks all day, so all the sweat from my feet doesn't remain in my boots and cause blisters and "jungle rot." Jungle rot occurs when damp or wet feet are continuously trapped in hot boots. Soldiers have suffered from this for years when spending continuous time outdoors in rain, water, and mud. Jungle rot is not easily cured and requires time out of the boots in a dry condition. Symptoms include itching that becomes painful; peeling that may be several layers of skin at once; raw, red skin; and blisters. I was showing most of the symptoms but was not aware of what caused it or how to treat it.

Late in the afternoon of April 26, I came out on Dennis Cove Road, and my guidebook showed a hostel two-tenths of a mile west.

I hiked down to discover Kincora Hiking Hostel, run by Bob Peoples. Downstairs is a small

Hikers share the woods with God's creatures.

kitchen with all sorts of old and broken cooking utensils, a few miscellaneous pots and pans, an old refrigerator, and an even older stove. Next to it is a small sitting area where as many as 12 or 14 people crowded in to talk and watch TV. Upstairs is a dimly lit sleeping area with 12 wooden beds without mattresses, and just enough room to squeeze between beds to an empty one that can be claimed on a first-come-first-served basis. Off the downstairs porch are a shower, two bathrooms, and a washer and dryer. And for the grand cost of $5 a night placed in an "honor box," anyone can stay the night and use all the facilities.

Once a day, Bob and a co-worker rounded everyone up, and we climbed into the back of a pickup truck and went to Hampton, Tennessee, over a narrow, winding road to Brown's Grocery, where we could purchase basic food supplies. Kincora wasn't the Hilton, but it was dry and comfortable enough. Enjoying the conversation and company of the other hikers gathered for two days to get out of the rain was a good way to pass the time.

Bob likes to tell folk stories. "I was once bitten by a large rattler," he said. "The snake was about five feet long and bigger around than most people's thighs, and he had fangs as long as most folks' fingers. The next five days were filled with all kinds of hollering and screaming and writhing that was heard all up and down the holler. In fact, everyone was preparing for a funeral. The sixth day, the snake died!"

Bob entertained us often with his old stories. He is also a member of one of the Trail clubs that maintains the AT and shared the wonderful work they do keeping the Trail open and safe.

'East' and 'west': The direction off the Trail is always referred to as either east or west. The Trail twists and turns so much that most of the time, hikers cannot determine which direction they are hiking, especially since the trees and surrounding mountains shield the hiker from seeing the sun. Therefore, rather than saying right or left, the hiking books will give directions in terms of east, meaning right, and west, meaning left.

I remember two hikers with whom I had some long conversations over the two days that we were stranded at Kincora. The first was a gentleman by the Trail name of Quaker. He had left his Quaker roots as a young man, gained an education as an engineer, and now was a true gentleman in his early 60s, still clinging to a strong personal faith in Jesus Christ. We immediately sensed a friendship as soon as we met and had several long discussions about our faith, lives, and families. I regret I did not get his real name or telephone number. Unfortunately, we were separated when I jumped into Bob's truck to ride back to the Trail, and I didn't realize that Quaker wasn't going. I would love to catch up with him again.

The second person I remember well was a Jewish man of about 30 years whom I will leave nameless. He, Quaker, and I sat up the second night until late discussing our faiths. He asked good, and sometimes difficult, questions about why I believed in Jesus Christ, why we Christians do not follow Jewish rules such as observing the many Jewish holy days, and what we mean by grace. We also discussed baptism and the role of resurrection. I couldn't tell if he was only curious about Christianity or if he was questioning his personal faith as a Jew and considering accepting Christianity as his faith. It was one of the deepest and most sincere, open, and meaningful conversations I have ever had. There was never a word or expression of hurt or "I can't believe you believe that" kind of tone. I can only hope and pray that our conversation was one step toward his confession of faith in Jesus Christ. I believe God was working on him that night and, at the same time, I learned a bit more about Judaism while witnessing to my own faith.

On the two trips into town, I bought a ready-made pizza that I baked in the oven, sandwich makings, hamburger meat, milk, and ice cream to supplement my dehydrated hiking food. The community of Hampton appears to be a sleepy little town where the basic values of life are practiced and time moves at a little slower pace than in the big cities, and it's a wonderful place to live. Hampton is named after Mary Hampton, the wife of Elijah Simerly, who established the community in the 1860s.

On the morning of the second day, the rain let up and cleared for a few hours. Rather than waste half of a day, several of us got into the back of Bob's pickup truck, and he drove us up the Trail about nine miles so we could slack-pack back to the hostel. It was good to get the miles, but I got my partially dry boots and socks wet once again. I put my boots in the dryer, but they made too much noise and kept knocking the dryer door open, so I stopped that. What finally made a difference was when I put newspaper into my boots and wore them for about 10 minutes before taking the paper out and putting in some dry newspaper. Then I rotated socks by putting on a pair and walking in my boots for 10 minutes, and then taking a pair out of the dryer and putting the wet ones in the dryer. That didn't totally dry my boots, but it helped. It took several weeks for my feet to heal, but I became much more serious about wearing dry socks.

Monday, April 29, dawned overcast but not raining, so Bob loaded us into his pickup again and drove us up the Trail to the point where we had gone south the day before. This time, we turned north. It didn't take a dozen hikers long to scatter out, and before long I was hiking on my own once again. Almost immediately, I came upon Watauga Lake, which was badly swollen by the recent rains. The Trail goes along the lake bank for several miles, but due to high waters, we had the option of taking the "high water bypass" route or continuing along the lake and occasionally wading through water that was up to six inches over the Trail. Most who had started the day with me opted for the detour, but I chose to stay on the original Trail. I didn't know if I'd have to turn back as the water might get higher than the six inches I was experiencing. As luck would have it, I made it on the original Trail, although I got my feet wet again in less than two miles after having worked to dry them out. In retrospect, and after learning more about jungle rot, I would opt for the detour now. The AT rule is that a hiker may take either route and retain the thru-hiker designation. Later I would learn that, when given the option, it was usually wiser to take the detour. Detours are not offered often, and then only when safety dictates their necessity.

I stopped briefly at the other end of Watauga Lake along with another hiker, and each of us took the other's picture by the dam. The dam was begun in 1942, but construction stopped during World War II and then was completed in 1948 to provide electricity for the surrounding area. The dam remains a source of power and provides a recreational lake for thousands each year. Unfortunately, construction of the dam displaced some 700 people from the town of Butler. The original site of the town is now under water, so a new Butler was built on higher ground.

I camped near a stream that night just before crossing the Holston Mountain Trail and rested well before an easy, primarily downhill hike for 16 miles followed by a rather steep, downhill, six-mile hike into Damascus. Arriving in Damascus is a bit strange in that the Trail goes from

Slack-pack: Hiking a section of the Trail without the normal heavy packs of bedrolls and tents. Usually, the hiker is taken up the Trail several miles by car, normally about a day's hike, and hikes back to either a pickup point or a base. This allows the hiker to hike faster, farther, and more easily without being burdened with his or her normal gear.

a steep, wooded forest, down between two houses, and then onto a residential street in front of the homes. I felt as if I were walking across folks' backyards, through their side yards, and on their front lawns out to the street. There is a path, so it really is the Trail, but it is so close to the homes that I felt like I should stop and apologize for walking through their yards and causing any disturbance.

About one-half mile away, along city streets, is Mt. Rogers Outfitters, and across the street sat my car, a bit dusty but no less a welcoming sight. I deposited my pack and poles in the car before walking across to Mt. Rogers Outfitters. I was a day ahead of schedule as far as getting home, so I arranged to get a ride from Damascus up the mountain to Summit Cut, where the AT crosses US 58. The cost was $30 for up to four hikers. Another hiker whom I had met at Kincora Hiking Hostel was already there and wanted to do the same thing. We agreed we'd meet back the next morning at seven and split the cost for the ride. When I got there the next morning, the driver informed me the other hiker had canceled. That was okay, as I had originally planned to pay the whole cost myself and had been pleasantly surprised when I found someone to share the drive.

After hiking into Damascus from Sam's Gap, I spent the night at the Holiday Inn Express & Suites near Abingdon, Virginia, where I'd been 10 days before. The continental breakfast there is included with the room, so I ate as big a meal as I could the next morning before driving back to Damascus to meet my ride.

The flip-flop hike from Summit Cut on Whitetop Mountain back to Damascus was relatively easy for three reasons. First, it was primarily downhill and much of it was a wide, flat trail. Second, I was slack-packing, so I only carried about 15 pounds instead of my usual 36 to 43 pounds. Third, it was my last day before going home, and I was eager to get back to my family.

The Trail starts out looking like the AT normally does: 18 inches wide, a bit rough with roots and rocks, with foliage parted about four feet so a hiker can easily pass. After about three miles, the Trail becomes what was once the Virginia creeper train bed, now without the train tracks and crossbeams, and smoothed flat.

The Virginia Creeper Trail gets its name from the Virginia creeper vine—which, ironically, is a fast-growing plant—and the slow-moving trains that once moved along the former railbed. The trail originally was for a commercial train to move coal and iron from the surrounding mountains. After several false beginnings, it became the main avenue for removing great quantities of cut timber, but the 1928 recession reduced the need for timber. Then the train carried passengers and light freight between Abingdon and Whitetop, Virginia. By 1977, rail traffic had stopped, the rails were removed, and the US Forest Service secured the trail as a recreational area. Today it is part of the Jefferson National Forest and is used primarily as a bicycle and hiking trail. The AT follows it off and on for several miles.

About halfway down, I was cruising! The trail was smooth with a small downgrade, and I was hiking at about the fastest pace I can go, somewhere around 3.5 miles an hour. I calculated how soon I'd be in Damascus and on my way home in the car. I almost didn't see a sign pointing off to the right and up into the mountains to a typical AT trail. I reluctantly turned right and up the Trail for an example of how bad the AT can be. The AT's winding, steep, rough, going-nowhere trail in the boondocks was an obvious comparison to the Virginia Creeper Trail, intentional or not! I hiked for several hours and suddenly came back out on the almost-level Virginia Creeper Trail, which I would hike on all the way back to Damascus. I had the feeling that if I'd stayed on the Virginia Creeper Trail, it would have been less than half a mile between where I got off to the point where I came back. This is one more example that shows the Trail is not meant to be the easiest or fastest way to get somewhere, but rather it is designed to be difficult and showcase all the sights, no matter how hard the path is to hike.

Flip-flop: Hiking a distance of the Trail in the opposite direction from the normal direction the hiker is going. This is done for several reasons, such as being able to hike downhill on a particularly steep section or in order to walk back to a location where a car is parked or a good place to stay such as in a local town.

The hike into Damascus from the north follows the streets back to Mt. Rogers Outfitters, where I found my car waiting for the second time in two days. The drive back to Jackson was difficult because I was tired and ready for a good night's rest, but the draw of seeing Judy, sleeping in my own bed, and enjoying home-cooked meals kept me going.

Legends related to balds and names

Cherokee legend: According to a display in the Roan Mountain State Park Visitors Center in Tennessee, "The Cherokee legend of the creation of the balds credits the Great Spirit. There was once a giant yellow jacket that terrorized an Indian village. The Indians finally tracked it down to its den by using scouts along the top of the mountain ridge, where they killed it. The Great Spirit, according to the legend, was so pleased that it rewarded the Indians' pleas for help by keeping the mountaintops bare of trees to serve as sentry posts if a need ever arose again."

Catawba legend: According to a display in the Roan Mountain State Park Visitors Center in Tennessee, "A legend from the Catawba Indians credits the Great Spirit for the beginning of the balds. The Catawba once challenged the Cherokee and other foes who were contesting occupancy of territories to a great battle on top of the Roan Mountain. The prize to the victor was being able to lay claim to the mountain. The Catawba finally won, and the Great Spirit, not wanting such a battle to be forgotten, caused the forest to wither from the spots where battles had taken place, creating the balds."

Rhododendron legend: An addition to the Catawba legend (above) is that in honor of the blood shed by so many good braves during the great battle on top of Roan Mountain, the Great Spirit colored the rhododendron red.

Legend of the origin of Roan Mountain's name: Legend says that Daniel Boone once rode over the mountain, and his horse, named Roan, came up lame. Boone set Roan free, thinking the horse would die a natural death soon due to his injuries. The next year, Boone came through that way again and found Roan had recovered and was fat from the vegetation on the mountain. To honor the mountain, Boone named the mountain Roan.

White blazes mark the route for AT hikers.

The old Virginia Creeper Railroad Track was converted to a modern walking (AT) path above Damascus, Virginia.

CHAPTER NINE

Missteps Can Ruin Your Whole Day

May 5 was a little over five weeks after I had come off the Trail at Rock Gap due to the IT pain in my leg and knee. Now I was back on the Trail, trying to accomplish what I hadn't been able to do before because of my injury: complete the section from Dicks Creek Gap to Fontana Dam. So much had happened that it seemed like months since I had been there, and then again it seemed like yesterday. The day before, I had made the long drive from West Tennessee to the mountains, going along the curving road called the Tail of the Dragon again.

I had left Decaturville as soon as the church service ended. As usual, I was afraid to eat much, as that might make me drowsy, and I hoped the caffeine-filled soft drinks I had iced down in the cooler would keep me awake. Late that afternoon, going through Maryville, I stopped and picked up a burger and fries to eat as I drove the last two hours. The chips and candy bars stashed in the passenger seat provided my dessert. Arriving at Fontana Dam, I parked on the Tennessee side beside a picnic table with a bear-proof trash canister nearby that reminded me I was back in bear country. Once again, I spread my bedroll in the back of the van and settled in for a night's rest.

The cold, dark morning came too quickly, and the constant ringing of my cell phone alarm clock rudely awakened me. Sixty minutes later, I had eaten my breakfast of Pop-Tarts, drunk hot chocolate heated on my little cookstove, and stuffed the last few items into my pack.

Jeff Hoch, who with his wife Nancy owned and operated The Hike Inn, picked me up promptly in the parking lot on the North Carolina side of Fontana Dam, where I left my car waiting for me to hike back, northbound, from Rock Gap. Our drive took about an hour, which gave us plenty of time to share some "war" stories about hiking in the Smoky Mountains. Jeff and Nancy were always wonderful hosts. I hiked in that area again in the summer of 2014 and stayed at their inn one night, where I again enjoyed their hospitality. Jeff dropped me in the same little parking area from which I had left weeks before. This time I had learned that, although I had some lingering pain in my leg, stretching exercises and a bit of Aleve would always drop the pain level to where I could hike 15 to 22 miles a day. Unfortunately, the Aleve would later mask other problems in my knees and shoulders that have led to some lifelong medical issues caused by the extreme difficulty of hiking the AT.

The Trail that day was well marked and well worn by the hundreds of hikers already on the AT that year. Each year, about 10,000 to 14,000 hikers start the Trail, but it's said that only about 2,500 will make it past the 100-mile point. I was now 106 miles from Springer Mountain and was building my confidence and stamina. I would continue to feel more comfortable in the wild and on the Trail, but I never lost my sense of caution and vulnerability. Weather, the path, animals, a fall, or any of a hundred other things on the Trail can change in an instant, placing hikers in life-threatening situations.

It was 19.5 miles to Cold Spring Shelter, which at the time was in dire need of repairs and would sleep only six people. One look at the old shelter reminded me of the numerous cases of norovirus along the Trail. Norovirus, which is easily spread by humans, causes nausea and flu-like symptoms. Each year, scores of hikers are afflicted by this virus, and signs in the shelters remind hikers to wash their hands well, dispose of food and human waste properly, and avoid contact with those who exhibit flu-like symptoms. One dangerous symptom is dehydration, which can strike quickly, leaving the hiker with little energy and unable to hold down food and water. Although the symptoms may only last three or four days, norovirus will leave the hiker too weak to do much hiking, including getting to a doctor, for a week or more.

I pitched my tent some 200 yards away in the tenting area and had a restful night. The shelter had bear cables, sometimes called "food hoists," which I used, and the water source was more convenient than in many places, as it was only a few feet from the shelter. The evenings were cold, so I still carried my winter bedroll, which is rated down to 15 degrees Fahrenheit, and I had gotten used to sleeping on the ground in my tent, so I slept well. The days were a different story, as the temperatures usually started at about 35 to 40 degrees, requiring several layers of clothes until I had hiked about 20 minutes and warmed up; then I had to pull off some layers as the temperatures climbed into the mid-60s. Immediately upon stopping for the night, I had to put on several layers of clothes until after dinner, and in my tent, long pants and long-sleeved shirts were again the order of the night.

Tuesday, May 7, was the first day on the Trail that I went through several good elevation changes. Later I would have much longer, steeper climbs and descents, but this was my first experience with drastic changes in elevation, so it built both my stamina and my confidence. I descended 1,200 feet and then climbed 800 feet before a steep, treacherous 2,800-foot descent into the Nantahala River valley. At one point, I stood on some steps about a foot square and looked off to both sides down into the valley below. In front of me was a view of the same valley, which appeared to be almost straight down several thousand feet. I was tired and carrying a loaded pack, and I knew any misstep or fall would be certain death. This rudely reminded me how dangerous the Trail is and that I had to take every step seriously. Years earlier, while learning to fly an airplane, I had an instructor named Wimpey Wimberley whose favorite phrase, when I'd overlook something while flying, was, "That'll ruin your whole day!" Missing any one of those steps that day, or any of two million others during those months on the Trail, could have ruined my whole day!

The Trail follows a winding stream down into the Nantahala River valley and the NOC, and I could hear the traffic and sounds of the small Nantahala Township wafting up the valley as I hiked. For about four miles, I kept thinking that I must be almost there, judging by the sounds. I was ready to get there. After the difficult hike down the mountain, I was tired and my legs ached. The Trail winds down, crosses the stream I'd been following via a metal bridge built for foot traffic, suddenly opens into the crossroads of the town, and then passes directly across the highway into the NOC. I passed the main building and followed the Trail across another footbridge over the Nantahala River to a small outdoor restaurant that overlooks the river. What a perfect place to arrive just in time for lunch!

The Nantahala River is 40 miles long, and through the centuries it has made a gorge thousands of feet below the summit. Nantahala is a Cherokee word meaning "land of the noonday sun." Next to the river is a road, now US 19, that was part of the Trail of Tears, and reminds those passing through that the Native Americans hiked and hunted in these mountains long before others even knew they existed. I can't imagine the Cherokees hiking through there on a forced march to Oklahoma, going 1,000 or more miles, carrying everything they owned, and taking everyone—young and old, sick and healthy! They didn't have dehydrated food, good hiking boots, Gore-Tex, and maps. I can't imagine how they felt leaving their home, the place where they grew up, and going to a place unknown to them. On the forced Trail of Tears, the muzzle end of army rifles would have been telling them to go faster!

I suspect neither the Native Americans nor the soldiers recognized that they had more in common than most would have expected, and amazingly it may have been in each of their own stories about how the earth, and all its beauty, was created. The Christian scriptures, in the first chapter of Genesis, tell us, "In the beginning when God created the heavens and the earth . . . God said, 'Let the water under the sky be gathered together into one place, and let the dry land appear.' " Cherokee legend tells of a time when only water existed and explains how the animals participated in forming dry land from the clay at the bottom of the waters. The larger animals were unable to bring the clay to the top of the water, but a small beetle was able to do the impossible—even make dry land where there was none before!

Both stories are about our God, who cares about His people and created us to care for each other and all creation. Today the road, river, and Trail that all cross at Nantahala are used by thousands who come to enjoy nature by floating and kayaking the river, fishing, bicycling, and hiking. Many may have little or no sense of anything outside of what they are presently seeing and doing, and they may have no idea that everyone was created by this same God, that we are responsible for nature and each other, and that our stories all have much in common.

That day, my mind was only on my own exhaustion, my aching legs, and how hungry I was. Lunch was fantastic! I ate a barbecue sandwich with chips and drank several Cokes, not Diet Cokes, trying to consume as much sugar and energy as I could. It's amazing how fast a sugary soft drink, especially one with caffeine, can revitalize you. I hope I didn't offend anyone by finding a picnic table and placing all my gear on top of it while I ate, and then going into the restroom, washing my feet, and coming outside to change my socks before hiking onward. The NOC has a constant parade of people enjoying themselves, so there are primarily young, outdoorsy people dressed in nearly anything one can imagine. I suspect I looked like most of the others, except they probably had taken a bath since I did and likely had a bit more hair, and not as much gray, atop their heads.

After lunch, I embarked on a memorable climb of some 3,300 feet over eight miles of hiking. I amazed myself with the ease in which I ascended the mountain and gained a good bit of confidence that, yes, I could make it to Katahdin! Near the top is Sassafras Gap Shelter, where I stopped for a break and a snack. While I was there, a pleasant young man from Texas hiked in, also coming up from Nantahala. He said he spent two weeks every summer hiking the mountains, and although his progress was slow, he had, over several years, hiked there from Springer Mountain. He planned to hike to Fontana Dam before returning home to his wife and his job in electronics. We took each other's pictures standing beside a sign stating that it was 144 miles from Springer before we parted ways and hiked onward.

Just 3.6 miles farther is Locust Cove Gap, where I tented for the night. My leg was beginning to hurt a bit from the IT injury, so Aleve was again my friend. I got up around four thirty, wanting to get an early start on the 18.5 miles to Fontana Dam both because rain was forecast for the afternoon and because I wanted to drive home that evening, if possible. My knee and leg began to hurt severely, and Aleve didn't help as much as it normally did, so I walked gingerly down the hills using my hiking poles to help take the weight off my right leg. It wasn't a comfortable or fast way to hike, but it was the only way off the mountain.

One risk of hiking the AT is that once you are on a mountain, you are pretty much on your own. Others will help you as best they can, including encouraging you and helping carry your pack, but they have packs of their own and are just as tired as you are. Only in the most serious events, such as broken bones and heart attacks, will rescue teams come up and carry someone down. Those teams are made up of volunteers who give up time at their own jobs or with their own families, and they risk injuring themselves, too, while helping others.

The view down the mountain parallels Fontana Lake, so I could see the water farther down and off to my right for several hours. The trees were not blooming yet, so the scenery wasn't as pretty as it had been when I hiked the same part of the Trail in 2012, but the view did help keep my mind off my leg. The way to Fontana Dam is a pretty one, hiking with the lake only about 100 feet away. I had planned to walk to the edge of the dam and look down at the view some 480 feet below the top, but I hurt too much to think about anything other than getting off my legs and into my car. I did take time to use the hot showers that are part of the dam and park. They are right next to the parking lot, so I didn't have to walk far, and a shower always feels good after several days on the Trail. Not only is it good to be clean again, but it also helps soothe the muscles, and changing into clean, dry clothes from the car can help you forget how tough the Trail was.

I left the dam around six in the evening, and I wasn't sure I could make the entire seven-hour, 350-mile trip to Jackson safely that night, so I decided to stop between Chattanooga and Murfreesboro and spend the night in a Holiday Inn Express before driving home the next day. Obviously, I spent a lot of time on the road and several nights in motels during my quest just to get the first 500 miles up the Trail from Springer to Damascus, Virginia. According to my quick calculation, I drove approximately 4,000 miles to support getting there and back.

One lesson I learned from hiking the Trail is that we take many things for granted in our society; we have become comfortable and assume we will have all the niceties of life until they are taken away from us. I came to appreciate life's comforts, such as hot meals; warm showers; clean clothes; soft beds with pillows; air conditioning; a comfortable chair rather than sitting on a log; the ability to ride in a car rather than walk even a short distance down the street; electric lights; turning on a TV to get weather and the news; cell service; almost immediate medical attention; and, most important, the comfort of conversation with loved ones.

Maps and sources for information about the Trail

I used three sources for maps and two sources for descriptions of the Trail and information about the towns near the Trail. The map I used daily is called the *Appalachian Trail Pocket Profile*, which is actually a series of 22 small maps, each showing about 100 miles of the Trail. The only thing shown about the Trail is in the form of a one-dimensional contour map with miles noted below, so I always knew how far I was from camping sites, water, and roads. Other cross-trails or roads were only noted with a dot or mile marker to indicate where they crossed the Trail. Hikers are expected to follow the white blazes for directions. This was great for quick, general information, but for details, I would turn to the descriptions given in the *Appalachian Trail Thru-Hikers' Companion* and *The A.T. Guide*. All of that put together was more weight than I wanted to carry, so I cut the pages out of the books for the corresponding upcoming 200 or 300 miles of my hike and would carry only those. Likewise, I only carried one or two of the pocket maps, which, all told, lightened my load by several pounds. Upcoming maps had been stored in my "supply room" to be shipped to me as I needed them. I threw away or burned each map or page of a book as I passed beyond what was covered so as to continually lighten my pack. Judy mailed me future maps and book sections as I would anticipate needing them.

Volunteers built these steps to prevent erosion and help hikers.

CHAPTER TEN
Leaving Tennessee Behind

    By Sunday, May 19, 2013, it was becoming routine: Get up early Sunday morning for my prayer and devotional time, which often looked more like sermon preparation. Eat a quick breakfast of oatmeal and lots of coffee before dressing for church. Then walk next door to the church, making sure everything was ready for this Sabbath's Sunday school and then worship.

    I had checked and rechecked my food and equipment the night before, so I had everything ready to head for the Smoky Mountains as soon as the worship service ended. I was waiting for my departure time of about twelve fifteen. I would hike 67 miles over four days from Newfound Gap, just above Gatlinburg, to Hot Springs, North Carolina, before returning either late Friday evening or Saturday by about noon. Now it was time to focus on the morning's worship.

    That Sunday morning, I continued a series of sermons on the "means of grace," or ways that God bestows His grace—love—upon us in special and unique ways. I specifically preached on the way that studying helps us discern and learn about God and how He wants us to bless each other. Often through the study of history, the Bible, ourselves, our condition in the world, and, yes, nature on a mountain or in a valley, God teaches us how to live for Him and for others. I preached from the 14th chapter of the Gospel of John, which includes Jesus's words in verse 27: "Peace I leave with you. My peace I give you. I give to you not as the world gives. Don't be troubled or afraid."

Yet, on several levels, I was troubled and afraid. Once again, for most of a week, I was leaving the church I pastored. There were people who relied on their church and their pastor to be there when they needed to hear again about God's love and care for them. What if someone needed me, and I was on a mountain in another state, and I didn't even have cell phone service to talk with them or know I needed to come home early? I was also troubled and afraid of what lay ahead of me on the mountain. I always had a bit of self-doubt and awareness that anything could happen to me even when I was being as careful as possible. The Good News of comfort and strength truly is to know that "My peace I give you" includes me and you, whether you are a believer in Jesus or not! He includes us all in His promises even when we don't desire it or understand it. That is good news indeed!

That afternoon, I headed up Interstate 40 through Nashville to Knoxville and on to Exit 407. From there, it was just eight miles to Sevierville and another four miles to Pigeon Forge, where I spent the night in another, you guessed it, Holiday Inn Express & Suites. I relished the last big meal before the Trail, so I stopped at an all-you-can-eat Oriental buffet restaurant that was far from the best I've ever had. The food was nondescript, but the server was a young woman who spoke little English but beamed a beautiful smile that made up for the poor food. It's amazing how much more a big smile can be worth than words spoken.

My alarm went off promptly at five thirty. I wanted to get out earlier, but the restaurant downstairs didn't open until six. Breakfast was more like a continental meal than the full meal I needed to furnish the calories for the day's hike. The local bus no longer ran from Gatlinburg to Clingmans Dome. I had planned to leave my car at the NOC, where it would be safe, and ride the bus up for $5. Again, the one constant you can expect on the Trail is change. The *Thru-Hikers' Companion* had reported that the bus ran regularly, but it no longer did. There were many other changes in the days ahead. Sometimes I couldn't find water where it was supposed to be, so I was unable to fill my water bottle or hydrate my food, and I missed several meals because of this. Other times, a bridge was out, so the Trail had been rerouted; a post office had changed its hours or closed; and more changes had to be accounted for on the fly.

Plan One didn't work, so I quickly conceived Plan Two. I would go to the NOC and find someone who would take me up to Clingmans Dome for a fee. However, the NOC didn't open until eight, and I had hoped to get an earlier start. Time for Plan Three, so I drove up to the visitors center for the Great Smoky Mountains National Park, which is located about three miles north of Gatlinburg on the way to the Dome. There, a local ranger told me he didn't know of any way to get up to the Dome except to hitchhike, and he strongly suggested I not leave my car at Newfound Gap due to some recent vandalism. I told him I was thinking of doing that, but my guidebook said it was illegal to hitchhike in that area. With a grin, he said, "It is, but we hardly ever enforce it, especially if they look like a hiker, which you do."

It took about 30 minutes for someone to pick me up. I'm sorry I don't remember his name, but he was a local photographer who enjoyed helping hikers, and during the thru-hikers' season, he took people up or down at least once a day. It's a 24-mile round trip over a relatively narrow road that requires a top speed of about 40 miles per hour. I offered to help him with his gas, but he was adamant that he never accepted any money for helping others. Another Trail Angel had cared for me!

The Trail leaving Newfound Gap is a good trail. It is heavily traveled by tourists and day hikers for the first three or four miles, so it is wide for the AT and follows the mountain ridge on which the Gap is located. The first three miles of the Trail ascend about 1,000 feet, but elevation changes are relatively minor after that, and the panoramic views are phenomenal. It is one of my favorite places to hike. The terrain drops off rapidly on either side of the Trail, thus allowing the hiker to see for miles on one side or the other most of the time. Near the peak of this section of the Trail is a short side trail called Bunion Loop that leads to a huge rock sticking up and overlooking the valleys below. It is a "must" for any hiker going that way to stop for at least a snack while perched on top of this huge slab. The view to the north is for at least 15 miles.

Two and a half years later, I was in Newport, Tennessee, with my wife, Judy, and while she was in a conference, I drove over to Clingmans Dome and again hiked the eight-mile round trip to Bunion Loop for the fantastic view. According to the orthopedic doctor, I wasn't supposed to be hiking at all because of problems in both of my knees, but it was worth the pain the short hike caused. I'd do it again tomorrow. Aleve can be my best friend! I also hiked to this wondrous place in 2019 to take pictures for this book.

Thirteen Trail miles from Clingmans Dome is Tricorner Knob Shelter, located on the south side of the Trail. The Trail runs along the ridgeline, as does the state line between Tennessee and North Carolina, which means I would spend the night in North Carolina. The shelter was built in 1961 and reworked in 2004. The unpainted wood inside and out is weathered and has its share of nicks and scrapes, as well as a few initials carved into it. The guidebook says it can sleep 12 people, but it is a bit crowded even when there are just 10 people, as there were the night I stayed. A reliable spring is a few yards from the shelter, and close by is the always-welcome privy. There wasn't a tent site because much of the surrounding area was roped off for protected vegetation, so I had to stay in the shelter this time even though the weather was good.

After breakfast the next day, I was doing the prescribed stretching exercises that my orthopedic doctor and physical therapist insisted I should do, when three of my "roommates" began to chastise me for stretching. They advocated just starting out hiking and then stretching in the evening. They said my way did more harm than good, and when I attempted to explain what had happened to my leg and the strained IT, they wouldn't listen to me or what the doctor and therapist had told me to do. For some reason that I've yet to understand, the three of them became rather heated in their arguments. That was one of the few times when I saw hikers use heated language with another on the Trail; there were also two occasions when a hiker got upset that I am a Christian preacher, although in those instances I suspect strongly the church had hurt those folks badly in the past.

I left not understanding why my stretching had upset them. Sometimes we just don't know the kind of "stuff" people carry with them and how it can affect their behavior at the least expected time. I suspect my stretching had nothing to do with the real reason for their ill tempers. I can only hope my calm, restrained response was helpful to them in some way.

The previous day's hike had minor ups and downs of mostly less than 500 feet, but this day's hike was the opposite. Over the first 17.6 miles, the Trail drops 4,930 feet into Davenport Gap before climbing 2,860 feet up the north side of the Gap. That day, I would only climb part of the way up from the Gap for about 1,500 feet. The Trail is a bit more difficult than previous sections, and severe drops in elevation are always tough on the legs and feet. That day would also end the time I had spent in the Great Smoky Mountains National Park, where camping was allowed only in designated locations and tent camping was frowned upon. Having the freedom to camp wherever I wanted would allow me to end each day at any point I chose rather than where someone years before had elected to build a shelter. After this, I would often hike into the late evening, even as late as ten o'clock if the terrain wasn't too rough. Until I reached Hot Springs, though, I stuck to my preplanned campsites, as I needed to cover a predetermined distance each day in order to arrive within four days of hiking and then get home on Saturday.

Late that afternoon, I came out on a gravel forestry road to be greeted by a 38-foot-long, fifth-wheel camper attached to a pickup truck. They were stopped on the narrow, one-lane, dirt service road, and two couples were standing outside the truck searching a standard state map that showed only the major highways. As I walked out of the woods, all four immediately turned to me as if I were a messenger sent from heaven. They had made a wrong turn off a secondary paved road and thought they could find a turnaround spot if they just kept driving. They now had driven four miles on this little road and had not found anywhere that they could turn a big rig like that around. Now, seeing me, they assumed I must be familiar with the area, and they turned and almost ran to me. One had his arms raised and open, and I thought for a moment he was going to hug me.

"We're lost and can't turn this rig around! Do you know if there's a road ahead we can get out on, or is there a place to turn around at? We want to get back on I-40 going to Asheville."

I explained that I, too, had no idea where I was and "was only following these little white blazes that went from Georgia to Maine."

"Surely," they asked, "don't you have a map?"

"Well, yes, but it doesn't show all the roads or turns along the way."

Can't you imagine how stupid that must sound to someone who has never hiked the Trail? It simply is impossible to explain. I left knowing that they must be asking each other whether, after they finally found their way out of the woods, they should report me to the nearest authorities!

About an hour later, I had hiked out to the Pigeon River, which runs parallel to Interstate 40, and was sitting on the north end of the bridge that crosses it, taking a break. I had my water bottle in one hand and a Snickers bar in the other when I saw the truck and camper coming across the bridge. The two couples were all grinning from ear to ear and waved as they

Hikers go around many scenic lakes like this one.

went by. One lady even threw me a kiss like I'd given them the exact information they needed to get out. Obviously, they had found another road or a turnaround spot. Either way, we all had found our way out of the woods and to a major highway.

All danger doesn't come from the woods or any other places you would expect. Almost immediately after the truck and camper had passed, a big yellow school bus full of kids came flying around the corner, crossing the bridge where I was sitting. My feet were sticking out a couple of feet, but the bus driver must not have seen me. Perhaps he was distracted by 30 or 40 screaming, yelling children, but for whatever reason, the rear tires came within six inches of my feet even after I had tucked them into the edge of the bridge as tightly as they would go. I was fortunate not to be run over that day, and since I was already halfway standing, I decided my break was over, so I hoisted my pack onto my shoulders and hiked onward.

Crossing any road, especially an interstate highway, can be difficult and dangerous, and it requires ingenuity on the part of the Trail planners and due diligence on the part of the hiker. Most often, the Trail goes miles out of the way to cross on an overpass or, in this case, an underpass of the interstate. On this day, I had to cross a secondary road next to the interstate exit, which meant negotiating a few crosswalks where traffic did not have to stop, but this was far out in the country so there was little traffic. After I crossed the road and under the interstate, the Trail went up a steep embankment on the left. Sitting on top of a large rock was a case of Cokes, obviously left by a Trail Angel. The Cokes had long since gotten hot, but I can't begin to describe how refreshing a sugary soft drink is to a hot, tired hiker even if it's not cold. I still give a daily word of silent thanks to all the Trail Angels who made my hike a bit more bearable.

Leading up from the gravel road is a flight of perhaps 30 steps built from locally found rocks. These steps help the hikers up the embankment, which goes almost straight up, but more importantly, they stop the erosion that results from thousands of hikers digging their toes into the earth while desperately trying to scramble up the dirt and rock. At the top, the Trail immediately disappears into the deep woods and up the next mountain. It was three miles and 2,863 feet to the Painter Branch camping area, and I was looking forward to a well-deserved night's rest.

The next afternoon, I crossed through Max Patch, a memorable hike for all who pass over it. I squinted from the strong sunlight after leaving the shaded trees and stepping out into the tree-free bald. The climb to the top is about three-quarters of a mile with a panoramic view that stretches for miles. I could see four mountain ranges when looking out at the horizon.

We know the history of this bald; years ago, early settlers cleared the land to graze cows and sheep. Later, the land was cultivated or burned to retain the "bald" effect. In 1982, the United States Forest Service bought the 392-acre grassy mountaintop, which continues to offer a panoramic view of the Smokies to the south and Mount Mitchell, which is 6,684 feet at the highest point, to the east. Today it is grassy, sometimes flowery and filled with blueberry plants, with masses of greenery stretching out to where the knoll gently disappears and falls into the valleys below. Max Patch is a favorite spot on the Trail for many hikers, and numerous day hikers park in a large lot and hike up the gentle slope for the tremendous view.

Bald: A low mountain or hilltop that is bald of trees and other tall vegetation but covered with grass and small bushes. It is unclear what caused the balding of these hilltops and mountains, but there may be many reasons, including lightning strikes that burned the trees, or farmers who have cleared the land long ago or raised cattle who ate most of the vegetation.

Two years later, Judy and I drove the 20 or so miles from Hot Springs up to Max Patch and hiked eight-tenths of a mile up to the top of the bald. The road is narrow and winding with almost no shoulders, but the view is worth the difficult drive. For the last four miles, it is a one-lane, bumpy, gravel road with lots of dust. Fortunately, we met only a few cars, but when we did, one of the cars had to pull way over and stop before the other car could pass. The blueberries were not ripe yet, so we didn't see any bears, but we did share the hike with about 20 section hikers. It was an easy way to experience the magnificent views and spend an enjoyable morning.

I tented near Walnut Mountain Shelter that evening, and the next day I climbed Bluff Mountain and descended 3,360 feet into Hot Springs, North Carolina. The Trail is particularly demanding there because of the steep descent and exposed tree roots, making it easy to hang a toe and take a long tumble down the mountain. I didn't discover I had lost my sunglasses until I reached for them as I was getting into my car to drive home. It was an expensive lesson,

$260 for new glasses, but one I learned well. I had previously kept them in a standard glasses case taped on a strap from my pack, but after that I bought a zip-up case, which I carefully tied and duct-taped to my pack. Another valuable lesson learned the hard way!

Arriving in Hot Springs, I stopped at Bluff Mountain Outfitters, where I found a woman who would drive me to my car for $80. Before she arrived, I walked 100 yards to the Smoky Mountain Diner, where I ordered a large hamburger with sweet-potato fries and lots of iced tea. What a way to end four good days of hiking!

I arrived at home late that night after fighting sleep for the last 100 miles of my drive. All is well that ends well!

Tricorner Knob Shelter in the Smoky Mountains of Tennessee is one of the nicer shelters on the Trail.

INTERMISSION ONE

Decision Time— to Go or Not to Go

 I had fully intended to start hiking again about two weeks after the Annual Conference for laity and clergy in the Memphis Conference of the United Methodist Church, of which I am an ordained elder. The conference meets once a year, usually in June, and as an ordained pastor, I am required to attend. Since ordination does not stop at retirement, I am supposed to go to the Annual Conference as a voting member for the rest of my life. I had to attend that particular conference because my official retirement as a full-time pastor was to be celebrated.

 We also had planned to go on vacation, perhaps to Panama City Beach, Florida, for 10 to 14 days before I returned to the Trail in late June. However, I was tired both physically and psychologically, and I was ready for a real rest. Part of this came from the pressures of pastoring for the past 16 years. But the second and perhaps the real reason to delay hiking was that the Trail is difficult and tiring in every way. I was somewhat ready for the physical toll on my body, but I was not ready for the isolation and lack of personal support from others each day. Judy and I talked almost every day when there was cell phone service, and we wrote notes and texted regularly when I was on the Trail, but none of that could take the place of being together.

I didn't make a conscious decision to postpone my return to the Trail. I continued to work out at The LIFT almost daily, and I hiked at Mousetail Landing State Park to stay in shape. But the longer I stayed off the Trail, the easier it was not to go back the next day or week.

We did go to Panama City Beach immediately after the conference in June. Then three of our four children and their families were at home for the Fourth of July. Denny, Leigh, and their daughter, Vivi, came home from Brooklyn, and Heather and Petar came from California. Kristi and Yancey, who live two doors down from us, were also there with their four children, Calvin, Ruthie, Mary, and Jack.

I didn't forget the Trail. I continued to work out, and on the first of August, Judy and I drove to Hiawassee, Georgia, where we rented a house on the hill on the way out to Dicks Creek Gap. We enjoyed driving around the community, and one morning we drove to the upper approach to Springer Mountain and hiked two miles up to the start of the Trail and back to the parking lot. Judy particularly enjoyed getting a feel for the Trail and seeing the shelter and camping area just north of the trailhead. I ribbed her for taking pictures of everything, including the privy.

I was definitely getting the "itch" to be back on the Trail. I knew that it was getting too late in the season by then to make it an official thru-hike, but I thought I'd rather go ahead and hike what I could that season and then do the rest the following year.

Each state welcomed hikers.

In this typical AT shelter, a backpack is hung from the ceiling to keep it away from mice.

CHAPTER ELEVEN
Saying Goodbye Is Hard

Summit Cut to Pearisburg

On Sunday, August 11, Judy and I went to church knowing it would be the last time for us to attend worship together for several months. The following day, Judy would drive me to Summit Cut, just north of Damascus, Virginia, which I had reached last May. At a minimum, I would hike to the New York state line, where I could stop until the next spring. If weather, Trail conditions, and my body allowed, I might try to make it a thru-hike. I'd probably have to do a flip-flop—stop somewhere along the way, find a way to Maine, and hike back to that spot from Mount Katahdin. A technical thru-hike is hiking the entire AT in one year, although not necessarily one calendar year, in any combination of north and south. However, the one consistency about the Trail is that plans will change!

Judy and I left early the next day for Abingdon, Virginia, which is a 430-mile drive on mostly interstate highways. I was a regular at the Holiday Inn Express, so I felt right at home. Judy and I dreaded the hardest thing about hiking—saying goodbye to those you love and knowing you wouldn't see them for several months. Knowing we'd have that final kiss and then I'd walk away was heavy on our minds. We couldn't bring ourselves to talk about it, as neither of us could trust our emotions.

Tuesday dawned wet and overcast, and the forecast called for light rain all day that would drop the temperatures to a bearable mid-70s. That was good because the day would start with a three-mile, 1,900-foot climb up Mount Rogers. We left the hotel around six that morning and drove into Damascus and then up winding US Route 58. I went by memory of what the AT crossing looked like and hoped I could pick the right one because the AT crosses the road in several places. Fortunately, I got it right the first time.

Our goodbyes were difficult. We held back our tears until I had walked up the Trail about 50 yards to the first turn. I lost sight of Judy and the car below on the road. I suspect Judy did the same as I did, letting the tears flow. We both are softies when it comes to goodbyes.

I was now 484 miles from Springer Mountain and felt somewhat like a seasoned hiker, although I still had much to learn. The climb up Mount Rogers was nondescript, as the Trail's tree canopy and high bushes kept me from appreciating the height and magnificence of the great mountain. It is the highest mountain in Virginia, at 5,729 feet, and is properly named after William Barton Rogers (1804-1882). He was a geologist; a professor at the College of William and Mary as well as the University of Virginia; and founder of the Massachusetts Institute of Technology (MIT). Rogers studied opportunities for economic development from the mountain's mineral resources, giving economic growth and business opportunities to many.

The Trail doesn't go directly over Mount Rogers but passes within about a quarter of a mile. A sign said there wasn't a good view, so I remained on the Trail and discovered a somewhat eerie scene nearby. About 40 yards off the Trail were two tents in disarray. Both were good tents that had been erected properly, but the poles had been knocked down, and some were bent; parts of both tents had been torn; camping gear was strewn about, and some equipment was broken; and a few pieces of clothing were on the ground. My first thought was that a bear had made a mess of the campsite, and the campers had fled the scene. But looking a little closer, I could see that a bear wouldn't bend poles in the way these were, and the tents didn't look like bear claws had ripped them.

Two other hikers were eating lunch nearby. I asked if they knew what had happened. Both said they didn't, and they were too afraid to go over and look. I threw off my pack and went to investigate. I thought that I might find someone hurt or dead, or the blood from a previous fight or animal attack. No blood or dead bodies were found, and I never did find out what happened. I went down the Trail wondering what could have caused such a mess. I saw abandoned tents, packs, food, and other camping and hiking equipment along the Trail almost every week, but those were obviously from a hiker who had gotten discouraged or too tired to go on, abandoned everything, and headed home.

Around noon, I came upon a parking lot facing a cow pasture. Since it was lunchtime and I didn't want to eat in the middle of a pasture filled with dozens of cattle, I stopped and ate my lunch with a light rain coming down. It was raining hard enough to be a little uncomfortable, and everything that came out of my pack got slightly wet, including my food. What I didn't know and appreciate at the time was that I was looking at Elks Garden, a high bald at approximately 4,400 feet in a saddle between two large mountains. At the top of the bald, which is only about half a mile away, is one of the most beautiful panoramic views on the entire Trail. In fact, it is a favorite of many hikers and gets a good bit of use by section hikers who climb up the rather easy trail from the parking lot to gaze for hours. The weather wasn't cooperating that day, so my view was limited, but I saw enough to make me want to go back.

The rain continued that evening, so I spent the night at Wise Shelter after a 16-mile day. Two other hikers came in after I had gotten into my bedroll, and I woke up, ate breakfast, and left before they ever moved in the morning, so I didn't get to meet them. It seems odd to spend the night within 10 feet of two other people and never get to know their names.

The sun came out bright and beautiful that morning, but that didn't keep me from making a wrong turn within the first 10 minutes. I was fortunate, though, as I only went about 100 yards before I came to a dead stop at a stream with no crossing. That made me realize I hadn't seen a blaze for a bit and caused me to retrace my steps to the Trail. So much for being a seasoned hiker, but it's easy to miss a turn in the Trail and quickly become lost. A number of hikers have done that through the years, and it has cost them their lives!

The Trail remained wet all day from the previous day's rain, but I felt good and made good time. When evening came, I found numerous semi-flat places to erect a tent, but nowhere could I find water. I hiked until well after dark, but rather than finding a place with water, I discovered the vegetation got heavier and the terrain a bit rougher. About ten o'clock, I stomped out a spot in the heavy underbrush, erected my tent, and slept on some rather uncomfortable rocks and brush. I didn't have enough water to hydrate my food, so I ate a candy bar and protein bar for supper. I had covered 20.5 miles that day but missed another important meal.

As I dressed the next morning while sitting on my bedroll in my tent, I realized I was sitting on something hard and tried to move off of it. I assumed I had dropped one of my belongings, so I began to feel around for it and put it back into my pack. I discovered I had slept on a broken tree stub all night, and hadn't felt it because I was so tired.

I still didn't have water, so I hiked on, assuming I would find water soon so I could eat breakfast and refill my water bottles. I had gone about three miles when I came upon Trail Magic at just the right time. In the middle of nowhere was a two-by-two-by-four-foot box filled with all kinds of goodies, including candy bars, small bags of chips, cookies, Band-Aids, hand lotion, tape, pencils and paper, Bibles, cans of soup and Vienna wieners, and all kinds of other items a hiker might need or want. On the outside were the painted handprints of an entire Sunday school class of children about 10 years old, with a note saying they hoped and prayed anyone coming that way would find and take what they needed. Beside the box were two ice chests filled with soft drinks and a thermos of cold water. I'd had a hard night without supper and now without breakfast until I came across this treasure chest of goodies. I refilled my water bottles, cooked my breakfast, and had a candy bar and Coke, thanks to these special Trail Angels. That evening, I tented near Trimpi Shelter at what is called Chatfield. I had hiked just over 20 miles that day.

Two days later, the 20-mile days caught up with me. I slept late and didn't start hiking until about ten thirty, which was unusual. I took it easy for the entire day and only hiked 11 miles, partially due to a long climb that afternoon. By five o'clock, fog had begun to roll in, so I was glad to find the most comfortable shelter I had experienced. Chestnut Knob Shelter is a former fire warden's cabin that was renovated in 1904. Today, it sleeps seven, has windows and a concrete floor, is weatherproof, and had no mice, at least the night I was there. Water is about a quarter of a mile away but manageable, the wooden bunks are relatively new, and a table is available for cooking and eating.

I woke up about daybreak the next day, looked outside, and found the visibility to be about 10 feet due to fog, which was dangerous because it would be easy to become lost. I went back to bed and slept until eight o'clock, when I found the visibility to be up to about 50 yards, so I quickly ate some breakfast, packed, and set out hiking. The fog was slow to lift, but it ended up being a nice day. I stopped for lunch at Jenkins Shelter, where I refilled my water bottles and then poured hot water into my hydrated noodles and beef bag.

While waiting about 10 minutes for the noodles to hydrate, I wandered around and began to look at the shelter and surrounding area. I had missed the notice on a large poster outside the shelter: "Caution: bear activity in this area. Use extreme caution." The small print said a bear in the area had shown aggressive tendencies in attempting to reach hikers' food and food bags. I was using a picnic table about 10 feet from the shelter and grew increasingly alarmed after I read the notes in the shelter notebook. The notes described a bear appearing in the middle of the night and at numerous times during the day. The bear became so aggressive that it threatened to get into the shelter with 8 or 10 men and women inside yelling and screaming while throwing rocks and hiking poles at the bear.

I picked up some rocks and branches nearby and placed them within reach, and then I ate my lunch quickly before traveling down the Trail. Better to err on the side of caution than be caught unprepared. I tented that night at Laurel Creek and took a fast bath in the cold water before hoisting my pack up on a rope hung from a tall tree for the night.

I was up at 5:30 and hiking by 7:10 into a fog that lifted midmorning, revealing a beautiful view of the surrounding countryside far below. I was glad to see the fog lift, especially because it had rained the night before, leaving me to roll up a wet tent. Nothing really dries on or inside your pack, but at least it isn't getting any wetter while you hike during the day.

Both of my knees began to hurt with what I assumed were my IT bands bothering me again. I took two Aleve pills and another at midafternoon. That was more than I should have taken, but it relieved the pain and allowed me to continue hiking. Two years later, I would suffer from severe knee problems that continue to this day. That time may have been the beginning of my knee problems, but I will never know for sure. I do know the Aleve covered up my symptoms, which led to bigger issues later.

I stayed at Jenny Knob Shelter that evening. Since I was the only one there and needed to dry my tent and other gear from the previous night's rain, I slept inside the shelter with my tent and gear hung out around the shelter to dry. I particularly had trouble keeping my socks dry even though I was cycling through four pairs each day and hanging them on the back of my pack to dry when I wasn't wearing them.

Good news that day: I had hiked 111.5 miles during my first week back on the Trail, and I still had another day and a half of hiking before I planned to take my first zero day.

Near Bland, Virginia, the AT crosses the highway about two miles north of the city. The Trail comes down a path between some older homes to an old building housing the senior citizens center, and in front is a wooden bench where I sat to eat a candy bar while changing my socks. People drove by and took a second look at the old man with a pack sitting on the porch, but none stopped. Across the street is a small church where I intended to stop inside for a minute of prayer, but the door was locked, so I kept going. It's a shame we have to lock our church doors!

The next day, I was close to Pearisburg, Virginia, where I planned to stay two nights and a day in a motel, when I fell and landed on one of my hiking poles, breaking it and rendering it useless. Hiking with one pole is difficult for me because I push hard with my arms, and when I'm only pushing with one arm, I tend to turn myself sideways, which slows me considerably. Also, the Trail was badly overgrown with brush and branches with thorns clinging to my clothes and sticking into my skin. Because the Trail was overgrown, I had trouble seeing it and finding the blazes defining where the Trail was. I came out on a road with no signage to point me into Pearisburg. More often than not, there were signs that pointed the way and noted the miles to town, so I would know whether to hike in or try to hitchhike. There was nothing that day, but nearby I found a friendly, helpful automobile dealer. Not only did he give directions, but he offered the use of his restroom and gave me information about Pearisburg. From there, I walked about a mile uphill into town to the Plaza Motel.

Pearisburg

Most motel employees in the many small towns I passed through were friendly and helpful, and the staff at the Plaza Motel was no exception. Although rather small, the rooms were adequate. Linda, the attendant who checked me in, offered to take my clothes and wash them for free, which she not only did, but she folded and returned them to me by late afternoon. I tried to pay her for the kindness, but she refused, saying she did that for all the hikers and never took any pay or gratuities for the service. It was Trail Magic again, giving of what she could.

I believe Jesus said something about caring for the stranger and the wanderer. Linda said I could hang my tent, sleeping bag, and any other items on the handrail outside my room to dry, and that if I placed my boots in the sun on the balcony outside my room, no one would bother them. She was so helpful and truly Trail friendly!

Later that evening, I walked across the street to a Mexican restaurant for supper. A few minutes later, a young lady of about 25 years of age came in and sat down to eat. I could tell she was a hiker because of the duct tape across an obvious tear in her pants leg, and she was wearing Crocs. After a few minutes, she came over to my table and asked if I was Preacher. She said Linda from the motel had told her about me, and she asked if I would mind if she joined me for dinner. She was hiking alone and wanted some company while she ate and to feel camaraderie with another hiker. She was a lovely young lady, although I have forgotten her name. I never saw her after that, as so often happens on the Trail.

My zero day consisted of walking down the street about 400 yards to the post office and getting the supply box that Judy had mailed me; taking it back to the motel room; and repacking my pack. Then I walked about three miles to Walmart and bought a cheap hiking pole for $14.95. I had lunch at the Lucky Star Chinese Restaurant, walked back to the motel, watched the news, planned the next two mail drops from Judy, and took several naps. I also took several hot showers, but the day's highlight was reading the letter Judy had enclosed in my box. It was so good to hear from home, as I already was a bit homesick after only 10 days.

Thru-hikers' prices: Many restaurants along the Trail that had buffets or salad bars posted notes on the buffet table or menu that thru-hikers would be charged an additional amount (usually $2 to $5). Thru-hikers have a reputation, and for good reason, of eating excessive amounts, especially when it is an all-you-can-eat meal. Note: The Lucky Star Chinese Restaurant did not charge extra.

August 23 dawned bright and sunny, a perfect day for hiking but also a perfect day to stay in bed. It's difficult to trade even a not-so-great motel bed for a bedroll and tent. After a long talk with myself, in which I reminded myself that the only way to go up the Trail was to first get out of bed and get dressed, I reluctantly rolled out of bed. I left the motel around six thirty and walked to Dairy Queen, where I had what equated to two breakfasts: a sausage and biscuit,

Hikers looked out for each other, leaving messages.

a platter of eggs, bacon, toast, a side order of hash browns, coffee, and two milks. Then it was time to hike.

I walked the mile back to the Trail. Vines, trees fallen across the Trail, tall grass, brush, and poor markings contributed to difficult maneuvering, but perseverance prevailed. In less than a mile, though, I came to the Senator Shumate Bridge crossing the New River via US 460. Fortunately, the bridge has a pedestrian walkway, so traffic wasn't a problem. Soon after crossing the bridge, the Trail turns up a gravel road and promptly goes left up into the forest on a poorly marked path. I missed the next turn and proceeded about 1.5 miles along the gravel road before realizing I had not seen a white blaze in a long time, so I finally turned around and followed the gravel road back to where the Trail had left the road. I was back on the Trail, but I'd lost a good hour hiking the wrong way.

I couldn't think about that long before considering a new obstacle, a 1,400-foot climb. Fortunately, the rest of the day was on a winding but relatively level trail on which I made good time. I camped that night near Pine Swamp Branch Shelter after hiking some 19 miles.

The hike the next day to Laurel Creek Shelter was relatively uneventful except that I had the pleasure of meeting nine students from Virginia Tech who were doing freshman orientation on the Trail. They spent five days hiking the Trail, getting to know one another, and establishing community. They hiked about five miles a day, carrying everything they needed, and it was particularly tough on them because they didn't have lightweight camping equipment, nor were they carrying dehydrated foods. One carried a cast-iron skillet that must have weighed somewhere around 20 pounds. They all appeared to be in good health but not in good shape athletically, but they were having a good time, and that's what counts. Surely if they could survive five days on the AT with all that, they would be able to make it for four years at VT! As for me, I was feeling good that I might make it to Cloverdale in five more days.

We are creatures of habit. For breakfast one morning, I had planned on a meal of dehydrated ham and eggs, which are rather tasty when seasoned with plenty of salt. I inadvertently opened the wrong package, and there are few ways to reseal a package of lasagna, so I could either throw it away or eat it then. I didn't have enough food to be throwing any away, so for the first time in my life, I had wonderful lasagna for breakfast, and ham and eggs for lunch. We are a people of habits and routines, but when on the Trail, plans change!

The rest of the day went about the same way. There was heavy dew that morning, so my boots were already wet on the outside, but I took the wrong step into a puddle that was deeper than I thought and spent the rest of the day drying my boots and swapping out socks to dry. Then there was a long, steep climb of about 1,300 feet, which was taxing, and some tough rocks to go over. It wasn't one of my better days, but it improved when I met two southbounders named Lefty and Hush, a delightful couple. Their Trail names were because he was left-handed and she was very quiet. They had some bad news, though. The next water was two miles away, but then there was no water for the next 10 miles.

I didn't think I could make it that far before nightfall. Tired and frustrated, I elected to stop at Niday Shelter for the night. By three o'clock, I had my tent up and my bedroll in the tent, so I decided to take a nap before supper, and the next thing I knew it was five thirty in the morning. I had missed supper and hadn't filtered my water for the day, but I was rested and rejuvenated. The news from Lefty and Hush changed my plans for the next three days. Due to a water shortage from an ongoing drought, I would have to carefully plan my days based on where there was water rather than how far I could hike.

Cloverdale

Three days later, I hiked 19 miles into Cloverdale, Virginia, without any real difficulties. The Trail doesn't go into Cloverdale proper, but it crosses US 220 near the Interstate 81 intersection. The Trail comes out suddenly onto a four-lane highway and crosses it diagonally. I turned right toward a BP market, and beside that is a Howard Johnson's motel. I stopped at the BP market and bought two Cokes and a quart of milk before heading to the motel and checking in. I had previously made reservations there, and Judy had sent a supply package three days earlier, which arrived on time.

The motel was adequate. I stayed in a typical motel room with two queen-size beds, a desk with a straight chair, and a bath that miraculously would spout hot water from the little silver thing called a faucet each time I turned a small handle mounted in the wall. Oh, what a joy it can be to experience again the little things we take for granted back home!

A washer and dryer were downstairs, and a Mexican restaurant was across the street, which was convenient. Farther down the highway was a shopping center with a Bojangles' fast food restaurant and an outdoor outfitter. For lunch the next day, I walked down for some greasy chicken at Bojangles', which was fabulous, and bought a spork made of titanium for $12 at the outfitters. I had broken my plastic spork several days before and had taped the two short ends together to make an eating utensil that, when handled with just two fingers, was long enough to reach down into the little pouches containing my hydrated food. It was good to be able to eat again on the Trail without getting my fingers into my meal, and especially to know that my fork wouldn't bend, break, or melt. Several years later, I still have that titanium spork in my pack.

I spent some time repacking my pack and planning where I would stop for my next supply drop—Buena Vista—and what supplies to tell Judy to ship there. One problem I had was that I would ask Judy to send the maximum number of meals needed for the next section, but then I would miss some meals or hike faster than I had anticipated. This built up an extra supply of food in my pack, so eventually I would have to throw away some food packets or give them to other hikers. I hated to waste them as they cost $8 to $10 each, but they also took up a lot of room in my pack and added weight. After my typical two nights and a day as a "zero," I went back out on the Trail.

Buena Vista

The hike from Cloverdale to Buena Vista is 78 miles and took four days. In the early morning mist of the fourth day, I began to see the James River from several miles away. Its beauty and the magnificent way it twists through the valley below made me pause and try to imagine how many centuries it had taken a little stream to become a huge river that stretched for miles and eroded the valley. At one time, the Trail crossing was along a railroad bridge and was quite nerve-racking when a hiker and a train decided to cross at the same time, I'm told. Bill Foot, a thru-hiker in 1987, made a hiker bridge a reality after seeing that hikers needed another way to safely cross the river. Today it is the longest hiker-only bridge of the AT. It's made with concrete pillars supporting steel crossbeams that form the outline. Wooden crosspieces provide the floor to walk on, and steel and wooden handrails going up six feet keep the hikers safely on the bridge. The hiker bridge is approximately eight feet wide and 150 yards long. I had the pleasure of watching a train cross the river on its own bridge several hundred yards away as I walked across with the morning mist rising from the water and slowly fading into the blue sky above.

We follow blazes no matter where they lead.

Later that day, I had a decision to make. I had been hiking close to 20 miles a day for several days and found myself 24 miles from the road going to Buena Vista, where I would next zero. I could either make it an easy day and a half, or try to make it in one day. I decided to do the latter. It was a tough day, but I had a goal and a "carrot." If I arrived by dark, I could take a hot shower, eat a good meal, and sleep in a real bed in a motel, so I hiked hard and steadily, although I was tempted to slow down several times. Once was when I came across two does that were just off the path. I wanted to stop and watch them for a while but chose to hurry on down the Trail. The second time was when I heard several wild turkeys and wanted to see if I could sneak up on them but, again, Buena Vista and the comforts it offered called me onward.

The sun had set and darkness was creeping in when I finally reached US 60 heading into Buena Vista. I was just one hitchhike away from a good meal and a bed. I stuck out my thumb at each car that went by, but none slowed down or gave me a second look. Time dragged on, and soon it was nine o'clock. Cars weren't coming steadily then. In fact, there was only one about every 15 minutes, and still no one stopped to pick me up. By eleven o'clock, I gave up and pitched my tent 15 feet from the road, which was the only semi-flat spot I could find. It was a tough night because not many cars came by, but lots of trucks drove past all night. Fortunately, a man picked me up about seven the next morning. He was going to work and offered to let me ride in the back of his pickup truck. The ride into town took about 15 minutes, and the wind in the truck bed was cold even though I was almost lying down in order to stay out of the wind. The man dropped me at a fast food restaurant and informed me that the motel where I planned to stay was about three blocks away.

I walked to the motel, which didn't look appealing from the outside, and tried the office door. It was locked, so after a short time I decided that since no one had answered, I'd go across the street to a little nondescript restaurant for breakfast. While eating there, I asked the waitress, "Do you know when the motel office across the street is open for the day?"

She immediately said, "You don't want to stay there!"

Two customers chimed in, "Don't stay there. It's dirty and a lot of shady people stay there, including people with lots of drugs."

I was in a small town where everyone knew one another's business—I wish all towns were like that. They told me to go to the Buena Vista Motel on the highway. I had ridden past it a few minutes earlier about a mile out of town, but it was the only alternative to the one across the street.

After breakfast, I walked across the street and found the proprietor in the motel office. I had called the day before and made a reservation but did not guarantee it. Judy had sent a supply box, which was waiting for me, so I certainly had full intentions of staying there until my conversation over breakfast. Now I just wanted my supply box.

I walked in, told the lady my name, and asked if I had a package waiting for me.

"Yes," she replied, "Do you want your room?"

"No," I said. I explained I'd been unable to get a ride into town the night before. I decided it was best not to tell her I was looking for a room that coming night.

"You no stay with me, you no get package," she said in broken English.

Again, I tried to explain what had happened, but she said, "You no stay here, no package."

I explained it wasn't my fault I couldn't get there the night before, but I needed my package. She wasn't listening.

"I no give you package. Package belongs to me now," she said.

It quickly became obvious I was not getting my package, and she told me to leave. I tried to remain calm and as nice as I could be under the circumstances, but I wasn't leaving without my package. I needed it, and I thought, but was not sure, that it came under federal law since it had been mailed through the US Post Office.

I said, with what little authority and conviction I could muster, "I would ask where the local sheriff's office is, but this is federal, so can you tell me where the post office is, please? They won't have anyone there, but they will call the FBI or whoever handles this, and they will be here quickly to get my package." I wasn't sure what the law said or who to contact, but I figured a threat to call the law might work, especially if what I'd heard across the street was true.

The lady immediately changed her tune and said, "No want FBI here. Give me $10 and I give you package."

I replied, "You've helped me get my package, and you should get something, but I think $10 is too high. I'll give you $5."

She quickly said, "Okay," and she gave me my package. I went up the street to the only other motel in town, still carrying my pack and hiking poles, but now I had my supply package.

The gentleman at the Buena Vista Motel was as courteous as the woman at the other motel had been discourteous. My stay there could not have been better. He gave me a map of the town, told me where I could wash my clothes and where to eat, and arranged for a man who charged only $15 to take me back to the Trail the next day.

After checking in and spreading my tent, bedroll, boot socks, and other equipment around the room to dry as best they could, I gathered all the clothes I wasn't wearing, tucked them into a small canvas bag, and headed out the door for the 1.5-mile walk to the local laundromat, aptly named Buena Vista Coin Laundry. It was on the other end of town, but the walk was pleasant and on a concrete sidewalk. Washing and drying my clothes took a better part of an hour and a half, but I enjoyed sitting and watching what little traffic went by.

I had realized I was missing my water bottle when I unpacked back at the motel earlier, so I went to a dollar store and bought a bottle. It wasn't what I wanted, but it was better than nothing.

I stopped for lunch at the Foot of the Mountain Cafe, where I met a couple who noted my hiking attire and promptly asked every question they could think of about the Trail. It was nice to have a real conversation with someone, even if they were strangers at a sidewalk cafe. Three years later, Judy and I visited Buena Vista while researching for this book and ate lunch there. The food was good both times.

Late that night, the motel phone rang. A male voice said, "Are you the hiker from Tennessee that I picked up this morning and gave you a ride?"

I said, "Yes."

The man said, "I found the water bottle you left in the back of my truck, and I wanted to get it back to you. When are you leaving?" Now how nice is that? Surely I was talking to another Trail Angel!

"I have a guy picking me up at six in the morning and taking me up to the trailhead," I said.

"I don't go to work until after that," he replied, "so tonight I'll leave your bottle on top of the post beside the Trail that has a sign pointing north, and it will be waiting for you in the morning." The guy obviously was familiar with the Trail and must have realized how important something like a simple water bottle is to a hiker.

I thanked him for finding me and putting the bottle where I could get it the next morning.

After we hung up, I realized he had not known my name and had thought I'd be at another motel, so he had made some effort to find me. Most people would have forgotten about an old, beaten-up water bottle and thrown it away, but not this Trail Angel.

When I got to the trailhead the next morning, I found my bottle and two store-bought bottles of water. What a nice guy, and I never got his name, nor will I ever see him again to thank him. I'm not sure it's possible to hike the entire Trail without people like him who don't know you, will never see you again, and will never receive a "thank you," but don't expect anything in return. God is so good, and so are His people.

This stranger to me was certainly living out the instructions from Hebrews 13:2, which says, "Do not forget to show hospitality to strangers, for by so doing some people have shown hospitality to angels without knowing it."

This Trail Angel showed hospitality, rather than receiving it, and I am very grateful, although I'm no angel!

Buena Vista to Waynesboro

Over the next several days, I had two unrelated experiences that demonstrate the variety that can be found on the Trail. First, I met a young couple about a mile from a trailhead. They were about 30 years old and had two small children with them. The older child was a three-year-old boy who was "hiking" slowly up the Trail beside Mom and Dad. He had a hiking stick, cap, and boots, and looked all grown up. The younger one was a six-month-old girl riding on her dad's back in a backpack made for carrying children. She was asleep without a care in the world but was as cute as they come. I stopped and talked with the parents, who said they often came on the Trail with the little ones and walked as far as their son could go, and then Mom and Dad carried him back to the car. They looked forward to when the children were old enough to hike with them on overnight trips, and they even wanted to hike the entire Trail, but that would be a long way off. They were letting the children get used to the Trail and become comfortable with hiking. What a joy to talk to two wonderful, obviously caring parents who were enjoying their children and God's great outdoors.

The other experience is what I thought was Trail Magic. It was like any other day. I was hiking and came across a parking lot for section hikers where two cars were parked. Getting out of one car were three men in their early 20s who were totally self-absorbed. They were getting their packs out, and did they have a lot of gear! At one end of the parking lot, a Trail Angel had left a thermos of water with white paper cups for whoever came along, so I stopped to fill my water bottle just as the three young hikers came by within 10 feet. I spoke, as all hikers do when we pass, but none of the three responded in any way. It was as if I wasn't even there. I didn't think too much about it, but they must not have been seasoned hikers or they would have spoken to me.

Two hours later, I stopped at a beautiful little stream where I spread out my gear, heated water to hydrate my food, and then began to look around. Right where the Trail crossed the stream and about three feet from me was a six-pack of German lager beer. "Trail Magic," I said to myself. I don't drink beer, so I left them alone. I hadn't had a beer in 15 years.

Judy had tried to find some different types of dehydrated food because I was tired of the same old stuff, so she had sent me a new flavor package, but when I tried it, it tasted like boiled cabbage and roots from a tree, not good at all! I didn't have food to waste, and I needed to eat all I could. I was losing weight fast, and it was getting to the point where I was taking my weight loss seriously. I tried to eat the cabbage and roots, but it just wouldn't go down, so I had an idea. I'd take a bit of food and force it down with a swallow of beer. I tried that, but both the cabbage and the beer tasted bad, and I couldn't get either of them down. As a last resort, I poured the beer out and washed the cabbage down the stream, ate a candy bar, packed up, and walked on without lunch, thinking it was nice of some Trail Angel, anyway.

I walked about 100 yards and rounded a corner, and camped beside the Trail were the three men I'd seen in the parking lot below. Immediately, I realized what had happened. The beer wasn't from a Trail Angel, but rather these men had put the beer into the stream to cool. And I had drunk one of their beers!

At that moment, I had to make a hasty decision. My first reaction was to go over, tell them what I'd done, apologize, and offer to pay for it. My best judgment told me these three would not see this as funny or be glad they could provide me with a beer, so my better, and maybe defensive, judgment took over, and I walked right past them and on up the Trail. They never looked up or spoke, and I never saw them again. So much for showing honor and etiquette on the Trail!

Waynesboro

Three days and 65 miles from Buena Vista, I hiked up a slight grade and had to step over the guardrail beside the road leading to Waynesboro, Virginia. Posted on a typewritten piece of paper tucked into a clear, protective sheet of plastic was a list of telephone numbers for perhaps 25 Trail Angels who would be happy to pick up hikers and take them wherever they wanted to go in Waynesboro. I looked on the list and thought everyone probably calls the ones on top, so I called the one on the bottom. The pleasant lady who answered took my information and told me her husband would be there in about 20 minutes.

Shortly I piled into the vehicle with my pack and poles with a nice man whose name I've forgotten. He handed me a bottle of cold water, a sandwich bag filled with chips, and a map of Waynesboro showing all the places a hiker might need. He explained some folks had organized a shuttle service for hikers, and he and his wife had signed up. Their son had done some hiking "up north" and experienced the hospitality of strangers who gave him a ride, and they decided the shuttle service was a "pass it forward" opportunity. Fifteen minutes later, I was dropped off at The Quality Inn, a motel he suggested, and he insisted that despite my early morning departure time of six thirty, he would take me back to the Trail. At six fifteen, he was waiting in the parking lot. He was so hospitable and such a good representative for the community.

According to the Waynesboro Visitors Guide, Waynesboro evolved from Joseph Tees's purchase of 465 acres in 1739, and a settlement developed sometime around 1797. The city was named in honor of the Revolutionary War hero General "Mad" Anthony Wayne. It was the site of the Battle of Waynesboro in 1865, which resulted in the defeat of Confederate forces, but is now a quiet little town that is exceptionally hiker friendly.

After checking in at the motel, I got a cold drink from the machine down the hall and headed for a shower. I always had the same question about showers along the Trail: Did I want to take a cold shower first and then a hot, soapy shower, or the hot, soapy shower first and then the cold shower? No matter what the order was, the showers were always long!

I walked across the street to get a large pizza to go from Ciro's Pizza, and then a gallon of milk from a drugstore nearby, before returning to the motel and collapsing on the bed, eating supper, and watching TV before dropping off to sleep. It wasn't a zero day, but a night off the Trail with a shower, "real" food, and a soft bed is next to heaven for a hiker.

Shenandoah

After a short hike the next morning, I entered Shenandoah National Park. A sign on the Trail pointed to a sign-in book where hikers could enter their name, home address, telephone number, date and time, and whether they are going north or south. The book has two purposes: to give the park rangers information and a contact telephone number in case a hiker doesn't show up as scheduled; and to help the park service track the number of hikers, where they plan to go, and what they plan to do so the park can provide future services. I signed all books along the Trail, knowing they might direct help to me if I got lost or hurt.

Shenandoah quickly became one of my overall favorite places. The terrain is generally about 3,000 feet above sea level, so the temperature is comfortable; the Trail has continuous ups and downs but few long climbs or descents; there are numerous outlooks and vistas; and the animals are not hunted, so deer, bears, and other wildlife are not afraid to be seen.

We owe many of our national parks to President Woodrow Wilson, who signed the National Park Service Organic Act into law on August 25, 1916. Established in 1935, Shenandoah National Park covers more than 300 square miles and has 1,400 vascular plants, 100 species of trees, and 300 species of animals. The Trail runs more than 100 miles through the park and passes through three campgrounds that include camp stores, restaurants, and bathhouse facilities.

By now, I was hiking a steady 18 to 20 miles a day. I had my Trail legs and could make good time over almost any terrain. In fact, I had reached the point where elevation changes were unnoticeable, which made my days much easier and more enjoyable. Also, I had gotten used to carrying 40-plus pounds in my pack, so I was filtering more water at each stop and didn't have to stop as often. Life was good!

At midday about two days later, I stopped at Loft Mountain Campground, which is run by the National Park Service. The camp store had a variety of microwaveable foods such as hamburgers, pizzas, and sandwiches. Not wanting to miss a "real" meal, I ate a lunch of two hamburgers, a hot dog, chips, and a large serving of ice cream. Adjacent to the store was a shower that cost $2.50 for a shower and a towel. While eating, I decided to use the washer and dryer to wash all the clothes I wasn't wearing, and to talk with the other hikers who were resting there for a few minutes or hours.

Soon after leaving Loft Mountain Campground, I met two lovely ladies out for their daily stroll through the park, and they gave me a quick lesson on observing bears.

"Have you seen any bears?" one lady asked me.

"No. Not recently."

To which she replied, "Look up."

At first, I thought she meant there was one in the tree overhead, but she went on, "The bears hear you coming, and most of the time they will climb a tree and stay there until you pass."

About two hours later, some bark dropped a few feet from me. I thought it was from squirrels playing above me but, remembering what the lady had said, I looked up. Way up in the tip-top of the tree were a momma bear and her cub. They were so far up I had trouble seeing them through the leaves. Remembering what I'd been told about bears, I didn't stop right there but moved on about 50 feet and got out my camera. I couldn't see the bears through the trees, so I decided to move back closer, only to find the momma bear was coming down the tree headfirst, walking as easily as I do across a clearing. As she was already about halfway down, I quickly decided this was not a good situation, turned, and eased away as fast as I could without appearing to be running from the bears, although inside it felt like I was crawling when I should have been running!

That evening, about a quarter mile from where I spent the night, I again noticed bark falling from the tree I was under and, again, it came from a momma bear and a cub. This time the momma wasn't quite so high up, and I could see her clearly. I paused as I looked up only to see firsthand just how big a grown bear's teeth are! She was showing me her big teeth and growling, so I decided it was best to move on and not pause for pictures.

I sheltered that night at Hightop Hut. There was a place to tent, but after seeing four bears that day, including two very close to where I would sleep, I thought it best to sleep in the shelter. Shortly after I got there, a southbound hiker Trail-named Fireman showed up with a dog Trail-named Smoky. In the middle of the night, Smoky began barking wildly, and although we never saw or heard a bear, Fireman said his dog had only barked like that once, and that was when a bear came into camp one night. That was the only time I know of that a bear may have come into camp while I slept, but then again, I doubt I will ever see a bear while asleep and in an enclosed tent!

The Trail is not always easy.

The next morning, I rose cautiously and looked around as I stepped out of the shelter in case a bear was lingering, but it was all clear. By about eleven o'clock, I had gone nine miles and was still feeling strong when I came upon Lewis Mountain Campground, complete with a camp store that had food, showers, a washer, and a dryer, all the comforts of home! So I had to stop, eat, shower—that was two in two days—and wash the clothes I had not washed the day before. Then it was time to hoist my pack and hike nine more miles up the Trail to Big Meadows Campground, which had everything a hiker could possibly want, including a young bear, perhaps a year old, who ran out of the bushes ahead of me. I could see him darting through the woods, and I whipped out my camera and got several pictures, but none turned out to show a bear anywhere. Bears and my camera just never seemed to cooperate!

Near the entrance is a full-service restaurant, unusual in the middle of a great forest but, oh, so welcome! I left my pack outside on the sidewalk, due to its mystical hiker aroma, and sat in the restaurant's back corner so as to not offend others who were dining. Two large hamburgers, fries, and several Cokes later, I was ready to hike to the campground for the night. I saw perhaps as many as 20 deer near the Trail that seemed to be as comfortable with me as any animal I have ever seen. I'm sure that being in a park camping grounds caused them to become comfortable with humans.

When I checked in, I asked if they had special rates for thru-hikers and was told there were no special rates but the ranger, "if he wanted to," could comp the nights camping. The going rate was $20, which seemed a bit high for just my little tent, so I asked the ranger if he could comp my night. He didn't answer me straight out, but rather began to ask me questions, such as where I was from and if I had much money. All that told me was that he could do what he wanted to do, so I just stood around for about 15 minutes, before he suddenly turned around and told me to go down the roadway about 100 yards and pick out a site. I got one right across from the bathhouse, so I had clean water for my drinking bottle, a shower with hot water, and a "real, indoor, sit-down-on toilet that flushed." It doesn't get any better than that.

The next morning, eight miles down the Trail and 200 yards to the left, I saw the Skyland Resort and its restaurant. I joyfully dropped my pack at the door to the restaurant, where I was going to get a great big breakfast with all the trimmings—only to be told they had closed for breakfast and would be open for lunch in two hours. I stated my case to one of the waitresses that I was hiking and really hungry and needed to go on down the Trail rather than wait for lunch. A twinkle formed in her eye.

She asked, "Would you mind eating from the buffet line that hasn't been picked up yet? Most of it is still hot and good. And would you mind sitting in a corner of the restaurant where other customers would not see you are getting special treatment?"

Of course, that was fine with me, and about 30 minutes later after my three trips to the buffet table, she got a big tip. I met some nice people on the Trail, and most people do want to give others a hand! I left the Trail knowing it was now my turn to give a hand up to others along the trail of life.

I ate lunch at the Pinnacles picnic area, which is a great place to stop, whether by foot or in a car. The area has picnic tables, fresh water, restrooms, and a nice grassy spot to enjoy lying in the sun or watch children playing ball. As usual, I "cooked" my lunch by boiling water, pouring it into my dehydrated food, and waiting 10 minutes for it to become fit to eat.

After I finished my lunch and filled my bottle with fresh water, another hiker came by and identified herself as Pencil; she was a retired schoolteacher. She asked, "Do you know anything about a homeless guy who is on the Trail ahead of us? A southbounder told me about him. Are you going to camp at Byrds Nest Hut No. 3, the next shelter?"

"No, I haven't heard anything," I said. "I'm not planning on staying there tonight, but I'm going on another three miles beyond and catching a ride into Luray for a zero."

She obviously was afraid to be by herself, and for good reason. There are homeless people on the Trail, and most are perfectly harmless, but everyone should be alert and take no chances anywhere on the Trail. Caution is always the key to a safe hike.

About a mile later, I came across a Ridge Runner.

I told him about Pencil, who was behind me. "She's worried about a man at the next shelter."

The Ridge Runner had already seen the man and was a bit concerned himself, but he had an alternative place for Pencil to stay that night.

Ridge Runner: A Ridge Runner is a volunteer who hikes the Trail to help others when needed, offer information, and report problems on the Trail such as downed trees and landslides.

"I'll tell her when I see her later," he said.

"Is it difficult to get a ride from the trailhead into Luray?" I asked.

To my surprise and good fortune, he offered to pick me up and take me in if I'd wait about 30 minutes at the trailhead. He had to hike back to the Pinnacles picnic area to get his car and then would drive around to where I would be.

The Ridge Runner picked me up just as promised and drove me eight miles into town. I found out after he picked me up that he had planned to go in the opposite direction from where his car had been, but he had called his wife and told her he'd be late. He was so generous to go so far out of his way to give me a lift. He was another example of how good and kind some people can be, and how good God was to send them to me when I was tired and exhausted, needing someone to point the way. This man did just that, not only by giving me a ride, but also by suggesting that I stay at the Best Western motel rather than the one I had picked out of a trail book. I knew it was a good suggestion after I saw the motel I had picked.

Luray

I zeroed at Luray, Virginia, on the nights of August 9–10. The motel room was adequate, although the air conditioner was less than desired and, even though it was turned up all the way, the temperature inside during the day got up into the 80s. The motel had a small restaurant and a place to do my laundry, so I didn't have to go out much. The waitress in the restaurant, I could tell, was used to serving hikers. She knew immediately that three eggs, sausage, and two pieces of toast would never be enough. She kept me in extra toast and extra milk, as well as pancakes and syrup. Even with all that, I still got up feeling I could eat another full breakfast each morning. I said the bill was perhaps not enough, but she simply smiled and said she was glad to be able to help me up the Trail. It seemed that everywhere I went, God's people were helping as best they could with no expectation of a reward or extra pay. God has created so many wonderful people.

I did have one problem that I thought could be symptomatic of something serious. I broke out in red bumps that itched terribly, and nothing seemed to stop the itch or reduce the rash. I thought at first it was some type of allergy; Denny, our son, thought perhaps it could be bedbugs; and someone else suggested a bad case of chigger bites. After trying several remedies, I finally walked down to the dollar store and bought two tubes of diaper rash ointment, which helped tremendously. I could feel a real difference even after the first day. I decided I had a heat rash and continued with the ointment twice a day for about a week. The next few days after I went back on the Trail, I splashed water on my chest and back whenever I came to a spring or other clean water to help cool me off, which seemed to help. The rash went away, but each time something seemed to itch, I got out the diaper rash ointment and applied it, just to be on the safe side.

My supply box from home came a day late at the post office but didn't cause a hiking delay. It was torn on one corner and wet. The postman asked what was in it, and I told him I thought it was mouthwash. I don't think I was supposed to be mailing that, but he chose to ignore it, fortunately. Also in the box was another hiking stick to replace one I'd broken, so I now had a matched set of poles again. The box contained all the other routine items I needed in addition to dehydrated food, such as toilet paper, hand sanitizer, vitamins, candy bars, wet wipes for my glasses, maps for the next 100 miles, and toothpaste. I was set for another week on the Trail.

Past Luray

The morning of August 11 arrived way too soon. My zero day was over, and it was time to hit the Trail again, eight miles away. Hoisting my pack, I stepped out onto Main Street and stuck out my thumb, hoping for a ride, but no one at that early hour of six thirty seemed to be in the mood to pick up a hairy-faced stranger carrying a large pack and holding two hiking poles. I walked down the street for about a mile before a man in a white service truck called out to me from across the street. He was coming out of a store with a cup of coffee in his hand and motioned for me to get into the truck.

As we talked on the way up to the Trail, I discovered that he was on his way to work, and this was taking him in the opposite direction from where he needed to go.

He explained, "I'm teaching my eight-year-old son about helping others, and it seems to me if I'm going to teach about helping others, then I need to do it myself."

He dropped me at the Trail right where I had left two days before. Again, the kind act of another person going out of his way had helped make my day easier and, collectively with all the other Trail Angels, made my hike possible. I will never know or be able to thank these people, but possibly I can pass it on to others. Thank God for those who help others.

Elkwallow Hut is a wayside for automobiles traveling the Blue Ridge Parkway and has a small store that sells hamburgers and soft drinks. Hikers never pass up an opportunity to eat, and I was no exception. After two hamburgers and a couple of soft drinks, I was on my way again. Shenandoah is a favorite among hikers because it's the only place on the AT where hamburgers and drinks are available twice a day.

I tented near Compton Peak that night before leaving the park the next morning. It's obvious when you exit the park, as the Trail leaves the nice, smooth, well-kept paths and suddenly dives down a long, rocky path that, at first, doesn't even look like a trail.

Psalm 121:7-8: The Lord will keep you from all harm—He will watch over your life; the Lord will watch over your coming and going both now and forevermore.

Two days later, I encountered the beloved Roller Coaster, a series of approximately seven rises and falls of the Trail of about 500 feet each. Each one by itself is not particularly taxing but, put together over 9 or 10 miles, they become a bit grueling. At the end is Bears Den, a hostel run by the Appalachian Trail Conservancy (ATC) for long-distance hikers. For $30, I got a bunk, laundry, two Cokes, a pizza, a pint of Ben & Jerry's ice cream, and good company.

Bears Den, according to a pamphlet published by the hostel, was built in 1933 as a summer home for a Washington, DC, physician named Dr. Huron Lawson and his wife, Francesca Kaspari, an operatic soprano. The beautiful building has medieval-looking architecture, is made of stone, and fits the natural mountainous surroundings.

I arrived after dark; on the way, I had passed several men from a church group who came out each year for a retreat. Most were hiking 5 to 8 miles and were not prepared at all. Many wore street shoes, most had on jeans and cotton shirts, and only a few were carrying water. I enjoyed the little conversation we were able to have between their gasps for air on the inclines, and I looked forward to accepting their invitation for a short worship service after dinner. By the time we got to Bears Den, they had become so strung out over several miles that the worship service didn't happen, as the pastor was one of the last to return. One of the men had serious health issues and didn't arrive until about one in the morning, and then only with the help of several others. He was taken to the hospital for observation and was thought to be either dehydrated or having some heart issues.

As several of us gathered to pray for a man I had not met, but whom others in the group knew personally, I remembered a passage from Psalms that reminds us of the presence and constant care God provides for all of us.

I left at six the following morning. I have often remembered this man whom I never met, and I've wondered what became of him. The Trail can be fun and enjoyable but should always be taken seriously, and no one should go unprepared or underestimate its difficulty.

Harpers Ferry is near the halfway point of the AT.

CHAPTER TWELVE

Meeting Place of South and North

Early the morning of September 14, I crossed into my fifth state, West Virginia, and I arrived in Harpers Ferry by midafternoon after hiking 20.5 miles that day. Harpers Ferry is a historic town that played a key role in the Civil War and early American expansion to the west. Judy and I went back three years later and spent most of a day walking through the town and exploring several of the older historic sites and buildings.

Numerous signs and plaques tell of Harpers Ferry's rich history, which includes battles fought in and around the town; the struggle between the iron horse—the railroad—and riverboats traveling in the canal built alongside the river as to who would ultimately win the nation's transportation business; stories about John Brown's raiders, who, in the killing of Heyward Shepherd, helped bring the issue of slavery before the nation; and Father Michael A. Costello, who flew the Union Jack flag over his church, thus informing both Northern and Southern forces that the church was neutral so it became one of the few buildings in Harpers Ferry to avoid heavy damage by cannon fire from both sides during the war.

My first stop upon reaching Harpers Ferry was the ATC office on Washington Street, not far from the downtown historic area. I gathered some information about the town and the Trail before walking several blocks to the Econo Lodge. In the lobby were two brothers whom I had seen at the ATC, and as we waited for the desk clerk to check us in, we began to talk about the Trail and the equipment I was carrying. They were taking their first hike on the AT and planned to hike about 50 miles over the next few days. As they asked questions about my gear, they began to describe their equipment and ask what they should or should not take. We checked in before long, and they invited me to their room to look at their packs and make suggestions regarding the Trail and everything they intended to take.

We talked for perhaps an hour and ended up in my room looking at my equipment, and soon they invited me to go to dinner at the Bisou Bistro Restaurant. We enjoyed a fine meal and then, to my surprise, they insisted on buying dinner. Nice of them and wonderful Trail Magic.

I left early the next morning, but the brothers hiked south while I hiked north. I met them again a day or two later as we passed on the Trail. They were adjusting well to the Trail, although they were carrying lighter packs after our conversation back at the motel. One of the men and I kept in touch for about a year via email, and he said they hiked another section the following year and hoped to continue their summer excursions together. He was having marital problems and later shared in one of his emails that his wife had left him and expressed how hurtful this had been for him. As a pastor, I offered words of hope and encouragement, which I hope and pray made his life a bit better.

The hike from the Econo Lodge took me back to the Shenandoah River bridge and then around by the river passing Jefferson Rock; St. Peter's Roman Catholic Church, built in 1833; the historic downtown area with buildings dating back prior to the Civil War; and then to the railroad bridge crossing the Potomac River. The bridge has a walkway separated from the train tracks by a chain-link fence. The views were beautiful with the morning mist coming off the rivers and the rays of the rising sun bursting through, casting a mosaic of shadows and brilliant colors on the water. This magical walk reminded me of America's grand history and the thousands of men and women who had walked this way before, and who had left such treasures for us to remember them by and to remind us of who we are.

The Trail drops down from the railroad tracks by way of metal steps to the "tow trail," which is the remains of the old trail where oxen pulled barges up the canal dug beside the Shenandoah

River. The "tow trail" goes for 2.8 miles along the river. It is flat and about 15 feet wide, and it is the most ideal walking trail imaginable. That morning, bicycles were flying by in both directions, carrying bikers out for a morning ride. On the canal's other side is a modern-day railroad, still running on the old railroad beds carved out of the side of a mountain in the early 1800s. From the flat riverside, the Trail suddenly turns left and goes up a moderately steep 600-foot climb to a peaceful walk through the woods for about a mile where numerous day hikers were strolling.

The Trail in West Virginia is just 17.3 miles long. Oversimplified slightly, there is only one elevation rise of about 1,000 feet over approximately two miles, not difficult by Trail standards. I spent one night in the state of West Virginia, and that was in a motel.

The Trail through Maryland is about 41 miles long with no difficult climbs that I can remember. In fact, there is a "four-state challenge" in which people try to hike from just inside the Virginia state line, through West Virginia and Maryland, and then to just inside the state of Pennsylvania, or about 58 miles in one day. Needless to say, I neither accepted nor completed the challenge.

Maryland offered several places that are noteworthy in my memory. Please note that when hiking 20-plus miles a day, eating dehydrated food, and sleeping on the ground in heat that reaches 90 degrees, my memories are not consistently reliable, so I may have walked right past some otherwise noteworthy sights and places without seeing or remembering them. With that disclaimer, I will relate two that I do remember.

Gathland State Park contains a huge monument to war correspondents, most notably George A. Townsend, who reported the events of the Civil War and the news surrounding the assassination of President Abe Lincoln. A nearby museum displays plaques about events in the area during the Civil War. The park gave me a place to stop under a covered pavilion, eat lunch, and replenish my water bottles.

Seven miles farther is the Dahlgren campground, whose claim to fame is a bathhouse with a sink and showers for use at no charge. Other amenities include bear poles for hanging your pack and food, campfire rings, and hammock rings for those who prefer a hammock to a tent. A short walk of two-tenths of a mile, or approximately 1,000 feet, is the Old South Mountain Inn, where many hikers go for a delicious meal in the evenings after they have taken a shower, as instructed by a notice on the restaurant door. I came through this campsite at midafternoon and took advantage of the shower but hiked on to Pine Knob Shelter, where I tented for the night after 22.9 miles that day.

The water I used that evening and for filling my bottle for the next day came from a piped spring near the shelter. Many thanks to the Trail Angel who did that, most likely someone from the Trail club that maintained that section of the AT.

I came upon Washington Monument State Park at midafternoon. I was caught by surprise and had no idea what it was. I met a man and woman who, by the way they couldn't take their eyes off each other, were obviously madly in love, and asked them what this place was. They said, "We were just out driving and came upon this park and decided to stop and walk around. Sorry, but we don't have any idea." I met another couple taking pictures, so I guessed that surely they would know where we were. Again, I got about the same reply!

I figured I wasn't the only "crazy one" out that day so, after a quick picture of the monument—which stands about 50 feet tall and looks like an upside-down beehive—I went on my way, still not knowing what this monument was and why it was there. It wasn't until three years later, when Judy and I visited and took time to read all the signs and plaques, that I learned the park was a tribute to President George Washington from the people of the surrounding county for all he had done for them. It also was used during the Civil War as an outlook for both the North and the South.

The state line between Maryland and Pennsylvania was indicated by a post announcing I had reached the Mason-Dixon Line. I was 1,058.2 miles away from where I had started the Trail at Springer Mountain in Georgia, and I had 1,126 miles to go to reach the top of Mount Katahdin in Maine. I was closing in on the halfway point.

West Virginia and Maryland had been good, but Pennsylvania was coming, and it is rocky!

Following white blazes to the edge is only for daredevils.

Rocks came in every size on the AT.

CHAPTER THIRTEEN

Crossing the Halfway Point

 Hikers know Pennsylvania as the state with all the rocks, and that is certainly true! The state of Georgia has roots and a few rocks to step over on the Trail, but that doesn't hold a candle to both the number of rocks scattered on the Trail and the rock castles, as I call them, found in Pennsylvania. These are large layers of rock poking up out of the sides and tops of mountains that can be any size, even up to a thickness of 500 feet, and as long as a mile, and they can lie at an angle of most any degree.

 Typically, the rock formations are rough and lie at an angle nearing 45 degrees. The hiker has to climb over, up and down, and even under these rocks, often looking down the mountainside for 1,000 feet. In some places, the Trail even follows the knife edge of the rock formation, so the hiker has to walk carefully to keep his or her balance. One slip and the hiker either slides down the rock or falls over the edge. It's slow going and treacherous, where one slip can ruin your whole day!

 Added to that, I often had trouble finding the white blazes indicating where the Trail was, and in a number of places, hikers had left paper notes held down by small rocks indicating the presence of rattlesnakes ahead so other hikers would know to be vigilant. Progress over the rocks was often slow and frustrating. Adding to the frustration is the fact that the Trail is routed over the rock castles when a smooth path runs alongside it only a few feet away. In some places, I easily could have gone down and hiked on the footpath below and made better time with much less energy. If I had done that, however, then I would not have hiked the Trail but rather some other trail. It would get worse, though: I wasn't in the White Mountains of New Hampshire yet!

I spent my first night in Pennsylvania at Deer Lick Shelters, after hiking 22.7 miles. I arrived well after dark to find two shelters about 40 feet apart, rather than the usual one, but no campers at the entire site. The shelters appeared clean, and since no other campers were there, I slept in one of the shelters rather than my tent. My water came from a small creek about 50 feet away, which I had difficulty finding in the dark. My Trail guide said it was there, so I hunted until I found it. I was surprised to discover that I had walked right past it on my way into camp. After 20-plus miles of hiking, I wasn't as alert as I often thought I was.

I was now an even 300 miles from Greenwood Lake, New York, where I planned to stop for the summer. Judy and I had decided she would fly into New York and spend a day with Denny, Leigh, and Vivian—our son, daughter-in-law, and one-year-old granddaughter—before she and Denny drove to the Trail to pick me up. Then we'd spend a few days with them before flying home. I was counting the days!

Each day, I would calculate the miles to New York and divide that by how many days it would take to get there if I could hike one more mile each day. For instance, I could make it in 15 days if I averaged 20 miles a day, but I could get there in 13.5 days by hiking only one more mile a day. I was tired of the Trail; I was ready for real food and a real bed, clean clothes, air conditioning, and sitting in an easy chair for days at a time. I was pushing myself to the limit, attempting to go just a few more miles each day. Anything less than 20 miles a day was unacceptable in my mind.

But a new issue was slowly developing, and initially I ignored it. I had noticed that my clothes didn't fit the way they used to, but I failed to pay attention to my body, as I was intent on hiking more miles each day. I didn't have a mirror, but I began to realize I was losing enough weight that I could be hurting my health. That fact hit home one day when, as I sat on a log to rest, I looked down at my thighs and saw how thin they had become. It disturbed me, as I could tell I was losing not only fat but also muscle, and that could be dangerous, especially in my legs, which were propelling me up the Trail. I couldn't do much about my weight loss except slow down my hiking and try to eat more. I wasn't willing to slow down, and eating more when you are hot and tired isn't easy. I tried to be intentional about resting periodically each day and eating more candy bars and peanut butter energy supplements, but I wasn't successful. I hoped I'd get to New York before my body gave out, but I recognized that my body was starting to wear down, and I had to pay more attention to the signs of fatigue and loss of energy. I also noticed that the more fatigued I got, the more I risks I took by not being careful enough about where I placed my feet and not looking out for critters such as snakes and bears.

On September 18, I reached Pine Grove Furnace State Park. Located just off the Trail are the remains of the Pine Grove Furnace, which was built circa 1770. Over parts of two centuries, it produced iron for items such as cast-iron cooking pots, stoves, and Civil War supplies, but it has not been a working furnace in more than a hundred years.

Iron was produced by pouring iron ore, limestone, and charcoal into the top of the furnace. The charcoal heated the ore and limestone to approximately 3,000 degrees Fahrenheit, combining the limestone and iron ore. Purified iron is heavier than limestone or charcoal, so it dropped to the bottom of the furnace, where it was drained out into "pigs" to solidify, while the slag (impurities) floated on the iron and was drawn off through a hole in the furnace. These types of furnaces were built before railroads became common, so they were located in areas where the iron ore and limestone could be mined nearby and timber was available to make charcoal.

Also located close to the Trail are the Appalachian Trail Museum, several other buildings, and a must-go place for hikers—a small restaurant where, if a long-distance hiker can eat a half-gallon of ice cream, it is free and the hiker joins the "half-gallon club." I was so focused on getting up the Trail that I walked right past everything and remember none of it. I know about it now because Judy and I visited three years later, and after walking around, I told Judy I couldn't believe that I had walked right by and missed it all.

Interestingly, Pine Grove Furnace State Park claims to be the halfway point on the Trail. According to the *Appalachian Trail Thru-hikers' Companion (2012)*, the park is at the 1,096-mile point, which is one half of 2,192 miles. Depending on when and who you ask, the Trail is said to be 2,160 to 2,196 miles. The number I've seen that seems to be the most reasonable and consistent is 2,186. Remember, though, the Trail itself has to go around trees that have fallen and rivers that sometimes are overflowing out of their banks; other detours are due to forest fires, landslides, bridges that have collapsed, new construction such as malls, and changes in leases that allow hikers to cross people's land. In reality, the length of the Trail changes daily. For this reason and maybe others, I found three or four places that signs indicated were the halfway point. I do think Pine Grove Furnace State Park is, rightfully, the closest to the midpoint.

I hiked into Boiling Springs that evening. For the last several miles, I hiked beside cornfields that seemed to go on forever and, becoming complacent, I missed a turn and walked down the wrong road for about a mile. After not seeing a blaze for all that time, I stopped and talked to a man mowing his yard, but he had never heard of the AT. I figured he would have seen hundreds, if not thousands, of hikers going by over the years if that area was on the Trail, so I walked back to where I'd seen my last blaze and finally found I had turned left instead of right. After two more miles through acres of crops, I came to a small stream with a bridge over it and stopped to watch several trout, which weighed about two pounds each, swimming below. Just past the bridge was an abandoned iron furnace dating back to the 1800s, which, when you're tired and hot, doesn't take long to observe.

The Trail suddenly bursts out of the woods, through a parking lot for fishermen and hikers, and follows alongside the Boiling Springs Children's Lake for half a mile. Amazingly, even as tired as I was, I had my longest daily hike of the entire journey at 29.4 miles. I hadn't set out to hike that far; it just happened. Even though my body was tired and I had lost a lot of weight, my stamina and strength had increased significantly. I can't remember being in that kind of physical shape since my days at Lambuth College, when I ran on the track and cross-country teams and held the college's distance records for the 880-yard race; 1-, 2-, and 3-mile races; and its cross-country course. Even an old man can regain some of his stamina, or perhaps the truth is that an AT hiker will either get stronger or fail to complete the Trail. But the trouble is that I can lose my stamina quickly when I get off the Trail.

As I came into town that evening, the view and the wildlife were eye-popping. Several types of ducks, geese, and swans inhabit the lake and have little fear of all the people who come to walk around the lake. The birds have grown accustomed to swimming toward people rather than away from them. I have pictures of scores of ducks, geese, and fish swimming just a few feet from me.

I had called from the Trail and made reservations at the Allenberry Resort Inn and Playhouse, located about a mile past the lake and well out of town. It's an old homeplace that converted stables, servant quarters, and a pool house into an inn. On the weekends, they have plays that draw people who come by the busload. I zeroed there for two nights and a day, and although I had to walk into town twice, once to eat and another time to explore the lake with its "boiling spring," I enjoyed my time off the Trail. I ate lunch the following day at Caffe` 101 and sat outdoors, where I could see the lake and the historic homes that surround it, before ordering the biggest strawberry shake I have ever seen. I walked around the lake after lunch before heading back to the inn and still had not finished the milkshake, but I did eventually! It was tough, but someone had to drink it. The inn has since been sold.

I left early the next morning for a hike of 25.7 miles to Duncannon. I had to carry extra water because southbound hikers whom I had passed told me water was scarce all through Pennsylvania and especially in this area. They were right, and I was so glad I had carried the extra water and that other hikers had cared enough to warn me. We never hike the Trail alone even when it seems so, and we never walk through this life on earth alone, even when we feel lonely and maybe even like the world has deserted us. God is always with us and often shows His love for us through other people. And we should never forget that we may be God's instrument for someone else along the way.

The Trail that day was easier than I had often experienced. I only had one easy ascent of 700 feet over two miles and another almost-as-easy ascent of 1,000 feet two miles before I came down a steep path into Duncannon a little after dusk. I had put on my headlamp while in the woods, and I would need that light while walking through town for two miles. I looked for a motel but found none, so I kept walking. The Trail goes directly through town along the sidewalks, first through a small downtown area and then through an old residential section with the houses built right up to the sidewalk. I could see people in their homes comfortably watching TV or, perhaps, finishing their evening meal. A few sat on their front porches and spoke as I went by. I stopped at a pizza restaurant for dinner and then kept walking. On the far side of town, I came upon what I had planned to use as a last resort, a nondescript camping ground for small campers, most of which belonged to weekend fishermen. I arrived so late that no one was at the office, so I went in and found a spot near a rustic, poorly maintained bathhouse, put up my tent,

This walkway offered safe passage over rocks and rapids.

and rolled out my bedroll before passing out for a well-needed night's rest. I got up as usual at four thirty and hoisted my pack by six. I stopped at the office, but the owner had already left to carry some canoeists up the river. Another man in the office said the rate for camping there was $20. I paid but felt that, considering the condition of the park, it was highway robbery. However, considering all the other places where I stayed for free or for very little, I was maintaining a low average for the cost per night to tent.

The hike out of Duncannon first goes over a narrow bridge that is about 100 yards long. Every car that went by made my heart skip a beat as they came within inches of me. Then there is a long bridge over the Susquehanna River, but it has a pedestrian walkway. The view of the river is beautiful with all the rocks, swirling waters, and the occasional duck that flew by. The climb out of the valley quickly reminded me I was back in the mountains, as it starts rather steeply before it eases back for a total climb of about 1,000 feet, but then everything levels out again. It's still the Trail, though, with lots of rocks but not much in the way of ascents and descents.

Due to the scarcity of water in the area, I decided to stay at Clarks Creek, even though I had only gone 18 miles that day. I made up for it the next day by hiking 26.7 miles to the William Penn Shelter. Since there was no water there, the next morning I stopped 4.1 miles up the Trail for breakfast beside a small stream. I stayed that night at an old shelter called the Eagles Nest, which was built in 1988 and appeared as if it had not been maintained since then. I made a note not to stay there again, even though I did not ever plan to go back to that area.

On September 24, I hiked down a steep trail descending about 1,000 feet in less than a mile into Port Clinton. I came out of the woods into a railroad yard and crossed four or five tracks with railroad cars on both sides where a few men were working on the track. Turning left toward the small town, I first decided to find a restaurant, but the one on my map was closed, so some ladies in a little candy store directed me up the road to 3C's Family Restaurant, where I got a wonderful breakfast with excellent service. I had to walk at least half a mile out of my way to eat there, but it was well worth it. Then I also had to walk back past where the ladies had directed me to the local post office for my supply box. The post office is in an old building with a front porch that is devoid of any paint. It reminds me of something built in perhaps the 1930s and never painted since then. However, the postman was exceedingly polite and helpful. I asked whether he minded if I sat on the front porch and opened my box. He was fine with that and told me to leave the empty box and any trash I had to put in the box, and he would dispose of it for me. What a gentleman. I wish I had gotten his name.

After a late breakfast and resupplying, I hiked out of town on a road that leads under Pennsylvania Route 61. I was rested and content after having my fill of a real breakfast, and I enjoyed walking on a paved road so much that I missed the blazes indicating that the Trail split out to the left under the highway overpass. Consequently, I walked on the unmarked, paved road for about three-quarters of a mile before I realized I hadn't seen a blaze in a long time and backtracked to the underpass where I'd made my mistake. I hiked some 2,200 miles, but I can only remember four or five times when I missed a blaze that required me to hike more than 100 yards or so before I realized my mistake and turned around. Considering how tired I often was and how many side trails and roads I crossed, I am amazed I didn't have more trouble following the Trail. I give credit to all those wonderful Trail clubs and Trail Angels who maintain the AT, and keep tens of thousands of blazes painted and repainted, for preventing me from wandering off the Trail more often.

An email I sent to Judy that day notes that the Trail goes "straight down with boulders the size of cars." The maps show an almost-flat hike at an elevation of about 1,500 feet, but the Trail is always filled with the unexpected.

By late afternoon, I had hiked 23.8 miles to the Eckville Shelter, which is two-tenths of a mile down Hawk Mountain Road. The shelter is an enclosed bunkhouse that sleeps six hikers. I got there after dark and met the caretaker, who is a man of few words. I attempted to ask a few questions such as where the water supply was, and he said, while pointing with his entire arm to a sign hung from the side of the building, "Read the sign." I remember asking one other question and got the same reply, so I decided to do exactly as he said. The sign pointed out a few rules for using the shelter such as keeping it clean, where the bathhouse and shower were, and when the quiet time was. The little I did get from him was a warning not to use any more water in the shower than I had to, and he pointed out that the water came from a 55-gallon barrel mounted on the bathhouse roof and was the same temperature as the surrounding air. I said I would take a shower in the morning, to which he said simply, "It'll be even colder in the morning!" I took my shower that night!

The Blue Mountain Eagle Climbing Club owns the shelter, I am told, and the caretaker who runs it lives in a house right in front of the shelter. A building housing a real, "flushing" privy and shower is nearby. The shelter features six bunks built of two-by-fours and plywood, a table on which I cooked my supper and breakfast, a couple of metal folding chairs, and glass windows. Good water comes from the faucet on the side of the caretaker's home. It is one of the best shelters on the Trail, without a doubt.

My alarm sounded promptly at four thirty, signaling the time to begin my morning ritual of boiling water to hydrate my breakfast and then changing into my hiking clothes before rolling up my bedroll. It takes about 10 minutes to hydrate each bag of food and another 10 minutes for it to cool enough to eat. That's plenty of time to pack and be ready to hike after breakfast.

The days always seem to start with a climb of 1,000 to 2,000 feet because most campsites and water sources are at lower levels. That morning was no different, so after a climb of 900 feet, I settled into the day's hike. I went 24.2 miles before reaching the George W. Outerbridge Shelter, an older shelter that sleeps six and is perched on a mountainside facing the valley I would descend into the next morning. Two section hikers, both high school-aged boys, had arrived before I did. They were spread out over most of the shelter but quickly made room for their new roommate for the night by moving their bedrolls and cooking gear enough that I had plenty of space. They were nice young men who were out for two nights but were, shall we say, "experimenting" a bit. They tried to hide their bottle of liquor but did not attempt to hide their marijuana. I think they assumed that an "old man" wouldn't recognize the smell, nor would I notice what they occasionally did when turning their backs to me while holding a glass that always seemed to be filled more than it was a moment before.

One thing I hate about almost every shelter is the number of mice that have lost their fear of humans. That evening, one such mouse played peekaboo with me while I was cooking my dinner. His home was behind a rock just a foot from my cookstove, and although he stuck his nose out every minute or two, he didn't come out while I was standing nearby. However, I found some of his leftovers on the floor the next morning. I also was aware he had run over my sleeping bag during the night. My tent was always my preference, but there wasn't an area big enough for the tent, which is the reason I chose the shelter that night.

Rising early, I ate breakfast, slipped out before my companions woke, hiked down 500 feet in elevation, and crossed the bridge over the Lehigh River near Slatington, Pennsylvania. I had trouble finding the Trail on the river's north side, as it is just a sliver of a trail behind a guardrail next to the highway. It rises steeply up 900 feet in less than three-quarters of a mile over jagged, exposed rocks. The climb was difficult because of the steepness and lack of footholds, and because of the almost-vertical view down to the highway and the river on the other side of it. Still etched in my mind is a vision of the long fall I would have taken if I had slipped.

Near the top, the Trail takes a "blue trail," or detour, around the Palmerton Zinc Superfund Site. The Trail follows a nearly level construction road for several miles around the site, giving hikers a wonderful panoramic view of the river, manufacturing plants, town, and barge docks along the river. It belies what has been done to the forest that once thrived there and the amount of pollution left on Blue Mountain.

From 1912 to 1980, the New Jersey Zinc Company produced zinc on the mountain and left 33 million tons of slag that caused the deforestation of 2,000 acres of land and a cinder bank 2.5 miles long, 100 feet tall, and 500 to 1,000 feet wide. From this giant pollution nightmare, rainwater has run off, carrying pollution into the Aquashicola Creek and then into the Lehigh River, and eroding the countryside. In 1983, the federal government added the site to its Superfund National Priorities List as the Palmerton Zinc Superfund Site. The AT once went across the mountain but now skirts the site on a somewhat permanent basis.

Later that day, after I had hiked 21.3 miles, the Trail suddenly opened up to a two-lane road near Wind Gap, where it took me under a major highway, Pennsylvania 33, and then immediately back into the woods. That was the Trail's way of crossing a major highway while avoiding the danger of traffic. It was late evening, so I quickly decided to spend the night in town and go on first thing in the morning. The first car that came by picked me up and took me to the far side of town to the Travel Inn. After a hot shower, I walked about a quarter of a mile to a nice restaurant for dinner, where I splurged with a big steak, potato, and side salad.

Thinking of how I would get back to the Trail at five thirty the next morning, I asked the waiter if there was a taxi service in town. He wasn't sure, so he suggested I ask the bartender if he knew. It was a small bar with only about six people there, so after I approached the bar, everyone joined the conversation when I explained I was a hiker and needed a ride the next morning. There wasn't a taxi service, but two people offered to give me a ride, which I refused because I was getting up so early. One gentleman, who was sitting on a bar stool and had obviously had too much to drink, got in on the conversation after someone asked what my Trail name was and then asked if I was a "real" preacher.

I said, "Yes, I was, but now I'm retired."

"Well, Preacher, preach me a sermon in 60 seconds or less," replied the gentleman who was "three sheets to the wind."

Suddenly, this preacher was at a loss for words. I can't remember anyone ever asking me to preach a sermon in a bar, nor do I remember exactly what I said. I believe it was something about how the Good News is that Jesus Christ loves him and all of us. I've since wondered how many times I've had the opportunity to tell the Good News to someone but missed it because my mind was somewhere else. That night, I was thinking about getting a taxi and perhaps missed helping a child of God.

The next morning, still looking for a ride to the trailhead, I went half a block to the Gap Diner for breakfast. At that time of morning, there were only five or six other customers eating breakfast and one waitress who gave me excellent service. I ate course after course of food: two eggs over easy with bacon, toast, and fried potatoes; a waffle; another order of toast; two large glasses of milk and an orange juice; and then more, all of which I have forgotten. When I had finished, I got up and approached the same waitress at the cash register.

"What do I owe you?" I asked, expecting a bill of maybe $25 or $35.

"How does $10 sound to you?" she answered.

"That sounds fine with me, but I think I must owe you more than that."

"To tell the truth, I couldn't keep up with all you ate, but $10 sounds good to me, if it's okay with you."

I gladly paid the bill and then went back and left a healthy tip. Just as I got to the front door, I turned and addressed the small group of customers who were finishing breakfast and said, "I'm an AT hiker and need a ride back up to the trailhead. I understand there isn't a taxi service here, so would anyone be so kind as to give me a lift up the road to the Trail?"

A gentleman who was on his way to work lifted his hand and said, "If you'll give me about five minutes to finish my coffee, I'll be glad to drive you up there."

A small town with people who have big hearts! Rev. Don Thrasher, pastor at Northside United Methodist Church in Jackson, Tennessee, where I attend church, is a good friend of mine, and

Trail Magic of water was left for hikers during a dry period.

he has said several times from the pulpit, "Serve God every day by loving the person right in front of you." I believe those people in Wind Gap had heard that already and are daily living that out, and I was fortunate to be the one in front of them.

The Trail rises steeply out of Wind Gap for 500 feet before leveling out for 16 miles, and then it drops 1,000 feet into the Delaware Water Gap. The Trail comes into town through a dirt parking area that has a sign warning hikers against leaving their cars there overnight due to a high rate of auto theft at that location. Four or five cars were parked in the lot, but I had no way of knowing how long they had been there. The Trail exits the parking lot by the driveway and then goes onto a narrow, paved road that becomes a neighborhood street.

The Trail only goes through an edge of the town before the street dead-ends and passes through the manicured grass to a sidewalk that is part of the Delaware River bridge. The Trail guidebooks that most hikers carry inform us of restaurants, motels, and grocery stores in town, but I was well supplied, so I crossed the river after a quick break sitting on the edge of the sidewalk and consuming a candy bar. The sidewalk runs beside the four automobile lanes of the bridge, separated by a metal rail. Those riding in cars don't feel the bridge sway as large trucks cross, but I could feel the bridge moving under me as I walked. It's a strange sensation, especially while looking down several hundred feet at the river below. The wind was strong that day, so I walked across holding my hiking poles in one hand and hanging onto my hat with the other.

I was now in New Jersey, my eighth state, and 1,287.8 miles from Springer Mountain, with only 75 more grueling miles to Greenwood Lake, New York, where I would stop for the summer. I was exhausted and growing weaker every day, putting one foot in front of the other but steadily making my way north. I had only a few more days until I could rest. I was ready for this part of the journey to be over, but I was determined I would not quit before I got there!

A hiker's dream trail is one that is flat, cleared, and easy walking.

CHAPTER FOURTEEN

Almost Finished, or So I Thought

 I entered New Jersey on Friday, September 27, midway across the Delaware River bridge. I had already hiked 15.7 miles that morning and was looking forward to reaching Greenwood Lake, New York, where our son, Denny, would pick me up. Judy was to arrive in New York the following Tuesday, and I wanted to be there to surprise her when she stepped off the plane. I was 75 miles from Greenwood Lake, so I figured I needed to average a little over 21 miles a day to get there, and I planned to hike another 10.7 miles for a total of 26.4 miles that day. I could make it, but I had to stay focused and not waste any time. Any delays would mean Judy would get to New York before I did and ruin my surprise.

 For about two weeks, I had been sending Judy false information about where I was. I didn't want her to know I might be waiting for her when she got there. Each day I had to remember where I had said I was the night before and then calculate where I needed to tell her I was. I had been telling her I'd come in two days later than I really would, or the day after she was scheduled to arrive in New York. I hesitated a couple of times when she asked me where I was, and once I thought she got suspicious about what I was telling her. I managed to change my story, but that only made it worse as she worried that maybe I was confused about where I was. She had the same charts at home that I carried with me, so she was keeping track of everything I told her. But right then I just needed to hike as long and as far as I could each day.

I hiked into the Mohican Outdoor Center at about eight thirty, just as it was getting dark. Judy had sent a package there so I would have plenty of supplies to finish that section of my hike, and, yes, it was waiting for me. The camp is a rather nice one made to accommodate all kinds of groups. Most people who stop there are not long-distance hikers, but rather are groups that come for various outdoor activities. The cabin I stayed in had private rooms and several community baths nearby, a common sitting area, and a kitchen. I was fortunate to have only one other person stay in the cabin, which had about 10 bedrooms on a long hallway, and that person was with a group and didn't come in until later.

Judy had sent the supplies I wanted, but I ended up with way more than I needed. First, because I had told Judy I'd be on the Trail for two more days than I really would be, she sent two days' worth of supplies that I didn't need. I also had not been eating all of my food, as I was often too tired to eat, so I had about three and a half days' worth of extra food.

A group of teens from New York City was staying there for several days. They had never had the opportunity to visit the countryside and several, I was told, had never been outside the city, so they were experiencing the outdoors for the first time. One of their leaders told me about them, and she described one young lady who, because of the bright lights of the city, had "never seen the stars." I was blown away and still can't imagine someone who has never had the opportunity to experience God's magnificence displayed in the sky. I was told the youth were asking questions about my experience hiking the Trail, what I ate, and where I slept, so I took the opportunity to share with them the extra supplies Judy had sent me.

One of the leaders sent me a card after I got home telling me that the youth had eaten every bit of the food I gave them and expressed their thanks for sharing my supplies. The truth is that I shared out of my abundance, giving what I really didn't need and because I didn't want to carry the extra weight in my pack. I wonder: How often do I give what is "left over," things I don't need, or after I'm through with something, rather than giving until it hurts or giving what I really need myself?

Scripture calls for us to give "first fruits," or the best of ourselves, not just what we don't need.

Rather than throwing something away, we give it to the "needy." Generosity is not just giving what we don't need or want.

I left early the next morning before I got a chance to meet the youth and have wished since that I could have talked with them about the Trail and how God can be seen so readily in nature.

The Trail goes back and forth for a number of miles between New Jersey and New York, and I usually didn't know which state I was in. I was still climbing over rock castles, which were sapping my energy and slowing me down considerably, and in my deteriorating physical condition, I was an accident waiting to happen. Fortunately, even though I had a few minor falls, I was not hurt.

I made 20.6 miles the next day. I had hoped for a few more, but the next camping area was almost six miles farther and I had been told there was no water there, so I settled for what I could get. The shelter at Gren Anderson is old, but the surrounding area is flat and somewhat open, so it afforded me a good place to camp, and water was just 200 yards behind the shelter. I was ready to get off the Trail and spend some time with my feet up and eating "real" food, but again, it was the same old stuff for supper and breakfast.

Hebrews 13:2: Do not forget to entertain strangers, for by so doing some people have entertained angels without knowing it.

The next morning, I started before daylight and was rewarded in several ways. First, the squirrels and birds were out with a flourish. Their chirps and calls to each other sounded to me like all of nature was enjoying the morning. Then, suddenly, I topped Sunrise Mountain and unexpectedly saw the arrival of the new day as the sun peeked over the horizon. What a way to start a day!

I was now only two days' hike and one night from getting off the Trail. I was tired; I was dirty; I was exhausted; mentally, I was depleted. I was ready to call it a summer! But wait—I still had 43.9 miles to hike before I could take off my boots and pack for the summer, and I told myself I could do it.

Exhausted, I tented near the Pochuck Mountain Shelter after a grueling 25.4-mile day. Again, it had been rock castle after rock castle, but I kept repeating to myself what other southbound day hikers had told me: "The big rocks end in New Jersey." I kept thinking, "Surely this is the last rock castle I'll have to climb," but they just kept coming. That night was one of the few nights I didn't sleep soundly. All I could think about was finishing the next day with only 18.8 miles left and then just under a mile to hike down into town.

The day started with two climbs of about 600 feet each and the familiar rock castles. However, my feet were moving! I was on my last leg, and "I was never going to hike again," or so I thought. I'd had my fill of the Trail and seriously thought I would never go back. I was tired and every muscle in my body felt like I had run a marathon, which, in a way, I had every day for months. As a long-distance runner of yesteryear, I can say that hiking 20-plus miles a day for weeks on end, with only a few days off, is like the worst workout you can imagine but having to repeat it every day for the next month. That day, I would never have dreamed that eventually I would finish the Trail all the way to Katahdin.

The Trail down into Greenwood Lake is a narrow side trail primarily used by local hikers. It isn't particularly well marked and was a bit overgrown because of the lack of traffic that late in the season. It opened into what appeared to be a school bus storage and repair site, and a short walk down city streets took me to Murphy's Tavern & Restaurant, where I had told Denny via cell phone earlier that I'd wait for him. I celebrated with buffalo wings and several Cokes (no Diet, please) until Denny arrived about an hour and a half later and drove me back to his home in Brooklyn, and was he ever a grand sight! I had missed my family and friends more than I'd ever anticipated, and a couple of hours later, it was just as good to see our daughter-in-law, Leigh, and our granddaughter, Vivi. There is nothing like hugs and kisses from a little one!

I had made it. My body was worn (a lot) but in one piece, and most of what hurt would heal in a couple of months, I hoped! I'd lost 23 pounds and three inches in my waist, which I didn't have to lose, being a small guy of normally only 162 pounds, but I had hiked 1,363 miles while carrying my food and equipment over the roughest mountains in the eastern United States. Or so I thought, as I hadn't been in New Hampshire yet!

Judy arrived about eleven the next morning, as scheduled. She was bringing my street clothes and shoes, but right then, all I had to wear were hiking clothes that I had washed the night before. I wanted to surprise Judy, so I went incognito. I borrowed an old shirt and a cap from Denny, put on my sunglasses, and got a newspaper to hide behind. When we got to LaGuardia Airport, Denny and I went to the baggage claim to wait. I sat far away from where the bags would be claimed, and Denny met his mother as she came into the room, greeted her, and walked with her to the baggage carousel. As Denny and I had previously planned, I called Denny on my cell phone and talked with him for a moment, and then he gave his phone to his mother.

After a brief "hi" and "how are you," Judy asked, "Where are you?" She assumed I was still on the Trail and wouldn't be in until that evening or the next day. I walked up behind her without her seeing me, so when she asked me where I was, I said, "Turn around." She did, and was she surprised! Denny told me later it was a good thing I didn't carry on the conversation any longer because two of New York's finest had spotted me hiding behind my newspaper and, in their eyes, I was acting suspiciously, so they were "closing on me fast." I had not noticed them and was fortunate Judy was glad to see me because, as Denny related, "They obviously meant business, but when they saw you two embracing each other, they looked at each other, shrugged, and went the other way." It makes me wonder which would have been more comfortable: another night on the Trail with dehydrated food or a night in jail with bread and water?

Judy later texted our other three children: "Boy, was I surprised. Dennis met me at the airport today. He and Denny pulled a fast one on me as I thought I was still on schedule to meet Dennis at five. He has lost 25 pounds. So good to have him here in person."

I had asked Judy to bring me some clothes to wear home on the plane. Knowing that I had lost a good bit of weight, she brought jeans that had been too small in the waist for me to wear before. I had outgrown them and kept them, thinking someday I'd lose weight and they would fit again. Now they were too big! So we went downtown to Macy's, where I found a new pair to try. It wasn't until after I'd tried them on and was changing back into the pair Judy had brought me that I realized I'd just loosened the belt and my pants had fallen off without me even unzipping them or undoing the waist button! I ended up buying a pair of jeans with a waist size of 29 inches. It wouldn't be long before I would be back in my old size 32-inch jeans, though, especially after I got home to Judy's good cooking.

Most long-distance hikers get used to eating so much at each meal while on the Trail that it's hard to stop eating those large portions at home. Almost every long-distance hiker has told me that even six months and 20 to 40 pounds later, they were still fighting the urge to eat more than they needed at every meal and to snack heavily between meals.

Judy and I spent two days in New York before flying home, where it was good to go back to

Often trails start easy but can change quickly to difficult.

the yard work. The past few months had been tough, and it took a few more months before I decided I would go back and finish the Trail as I originally had planned. I can't describe what days that turn into weeks and then months on the Trail can do to your body and mind. Perhaps the most difficult part for me was being away from family and friends. The loneliness and isolation can't be described. Indeed, we have been created by our living God to be creatures of relationship, and we need companionship. Both of these are two-way streets. We need them, and we need to give relationship and companionship to others. I had heard that Christianity is more about a relationship with Christ Jesus, but it wasn't until I had time to digest my thoughts and feelings that the reality of that became even stronger for me. Jesus desires a relationship with each of us based on love and forgiveness, and He invites us to share this relationship and love with others. For this reason, and others, we call Jesus "Love."

Deuteronomy 7:9: Know therefore that the Lord your God is God; He is the faithful God, keeping His covenant of love to a thousand generations of those who love Him and keep His commands.

Shelters come in many forms but are almost always three-sided. This one is near Damascus and one of the oldest.

INTERMISSION TWO

Time to Pause for Family

I returned to Jackson, tired, worn out, and ready for a few months of rest and relaxation. I had mixed feelings about whether to go back to the Trail come spring. I wanted to finish the Trail, but I was tired and wanted to relax. I was fully retired now and ready to work around the house and garden, do a little traveling, and spend time with my family.

Judy and I continued to go to the gym and work out, as I needed to gain my weight back and wanted to be sure it returned as muscle rather than fat. I mostly worked on weights for my upper body and walked, usually approximately two miles three days a week.

In January 2014, I started working part time at Northside United Methodist Church in Jackson as a pastoral care pastor, making hospital visits and visiting our sick and homebound members. One condition was that I would be able to take time off that summer to finish the Trail. The fact that I was a retired pastor and now serving again as a pastor is evidence that God works in mysterious ways. I felt called to be a pastor while in high school, and I accepted that calling and even enrolled at Lambuth College as a pre-ministerial student at age 18. However, during the summer of my sophomore year, I decided my real natural talents lay in math, chemistry, and engineering, so I changed my major, tried to forget about my call to be a pastor, and went the ways that I thought were best for me. After graduation from Lambuth, I attended the University of Tennessee as an engineering student and then worked as an engineer, manager of engineering in manufacturing, in industrial sales, and as a sales manager, and expected to retire having lived "the good life." We had a good home and a good income, I was part owner in two airplanes, and we pretty much did whatever we wanted. But God had other plans still, and an even better and more fulfilling life.

In 1994, I was on a spiritual retreat called the Walk to Emmaus when God spoke to me again. I wasn't sure where He was calling me to go or what He was calling me to do, but I told God during that retreat that I would go and do whatever He directed me. No matter how many times I had said "no" or "maybe later," God still was calling my name and wasn't finished with me yet.

Finally, in the fall of 1996, I took two courses at Memphis Theological Seminary with the intention of being a "well-educated layperson." I told myself I was an engineer. I thought as one, talked as one, and related to people more with a "black or white" mentality of what is right or wrong. I saw few areas of gray in life, and frankly offered little grace to others who didn't live up to what I thought was right. Besides that, what do you say to someone facing death or serious health issues? How do you offer words of hope and encouragement to someone whose child just died? Yet, during that first semester at seminary, I heard God still calling. After class one night, I sat alone in my car while God and I had a long "conversation," during which I told God I wasn't sure where He was taking me, but I would go, although I couldn't do that on my own. My greatest weakness, as I saw it, was in the pastoral care of people in crisis and life-changing situations. I would have to lean on God to lead me, and He did and still does.

God does work in mysterious ways! I served two small churches in Chester County, Tennessee, while attending seminary and obtaining a master of divinity before being ordained as an elder in the United Methodist Church. We had three of our four children in college while I was in seminary, so it was a rough five years financially, and it took many long hours, but I finally made it with the help and support of my lovely bride. I served six churches before I retired, and in each of those churches, I was told that my strength as a pastor was in—you guessed it—pastoral care! Then in retirement, I was called to work part time in pastoral care. I've often wondered if God doesn't have a sense of humor for Him to call me, of all people, as a pastor! I am convinced that

God wants us to lean on Him for our direction and power, and that is when He can use us the most. I am living proof that "He doesn't call what He doesn't enable!"

During the winter, I worked out and made plans to hike again in the spring. I had hoped the weather would be good enough that I could start back in New York sometime in May, but that might put me in the midst of the swarms of flies in New Hampshire and Maine come June, so I was debating about whether leaving in June was a better idea.

However, a phone call in January 2014 was a showstopper! Our daughter Heather Renshaw-Vucetin and her husband, Petar Vucetin, were expecting. Heather was almost 40 years old and the doctors said there could be as many as five babies; it was deemed a high-risk pregnancy. There was no way I was going to be on the Trail while all that was happening. They live in San Francisco, which is a long way from our home in Tennessee and the mountains of the AT. We already had five grandchildren, but none of them had been difficult pregnancies, and no matter how many babies there have been in the past, this granddaddy is going to be there!

On July 28, Heather gave birth to twin boys, Marko and Luka. They were born a month early, and it had been a rough time for Heather. Now five years old, the boys are healthy and developing well. Their father, Petar, is originally from Bosnia and now an American citizen, and Heather and Petar wanted the boys' names to be common to both cultures and languages, so they chose Marko (Mark) and Luka (Luke).

In April, however, I was able to hike from Dicks Creek Gap near Hiawassee, Georgia, to the Nantahala River, a distance of approximately 66 miles. It felt good to be back on the Trail, and the weather was good until I got to the Nantahala River. I had planned to go on to Fontana Dam, but the weather was threatening and I'd done that before, so I stopped there. My strongest memories of that section hike were, first, that the mountains of Georgia are not as high or as steep as they seemed to be the first time I hiked them; and, second, I was amazed at the amount of hiking gear left beside the Trail by well-intentioned thru-hikers who go out unprepared for the difficulty of the AT. If I could have carried them, I am sure I could have brought back a dozen hatchets, a tent or two, a lawn chair, a whole wardrobe of cotton shirts, an iron skillet, and much more!

> **John 14:13-14:** And I will do whatever you ask in my name, so that the Son will bring glory to the Father. You may ask me for anything in my name, and I will do it.

I resumed mild workouts at the gym while wearing a 40-pound pack and my hiking boots, hoping to replicate what I'd be doing and carrying on the Trail. Fortunately, most people at the gym got used to me, and after the initial questions to me or to others in the gym, those doing more conventional exercises strongly supported me. My workouts primarily consisted of climbing approximately 50 flights of stairs, walking 4 to 10 miles, and lifting a few weights. At least once a week and sometimes twice, I drove 45 miles to Mousetail Landing State Park, where I would hike 16 miles over the trails while carrying all my equipment. I was getting into shape, although I knew I wasn't really in the kind of shape the Trail requires, but I'm not sure if anyone is ever ready for the AT! Before I had thought I was in shape, but this time I knew I wasn't.

By the end of April 2015, I was planning to leave for New York in a week to 10 days. I was in as good a shape as I was going to get; I had ordered all the food and supplies I needed to get to Maine, and they were stored in my workshop as I had done before. All my gear and equipment had been weighed piece by piece in order to lighten my load as much as possible and now were either in my pack or ready to go, and spare equipment such as hiking poles and extra socks had been stocked, ready for Judy to ship them to me as I needed them. I was ready. All I needed to do was buy an airplane ticket to New York. Denny would pick me up at the airport and take me to the Trail. I just had one more thing to do before I left, and that was to spend time with Judy.

Judy and I had planned to take our fifth-wheel camper out for four or five days before I left. It's really not a camper, though. It's a 40-foot-long portable home! Inside is a king-size bed, a full kitchen with a microwave and stove, a full bath including a shower and two sinks, two large TVs, a couch that opens out into a queen-size bed, and everything else that anyone could possibly want. The only thing I wish it had is the ability to follow me on the Trail.

We were ready to leave the next morning, and I had already gotten into the bed and was watching the late news on TV. Judy was taking a few items out to the camper so she wouldn't have to do that in the morning when the unthinkable happened to her. She had an armload of blankets and sheets and was walking down a dimly lit path to the camper when she missed the last step of some stairs, fell, and badly broke two bones in her leg and ankle, causing a compound fracture. To make matters worse, no one was around to see or hear her. At first, she crawled to our truck, which was already hooked up to the camper, and dragged herself up high enough to honk the horn for several minutes. The truck is a Ram 2500 Diesel and has a loud horn, but we live in the country and I am hard of hearing, was in the back room of the house, and had the TV on, so I didn't hear her. She then crawled back off the truck, across that driveway, up about 40 feet to an asphalt driveway, across that, and into the garage, where her car was parked. With difficulty, bleeding badly with a compound fracture, she climbed into her car and honked the horn repeatedly. I heard something, but I wasn't sure if it was the TV or we had a visitor late at night. Anyway, I climbed out of bed, walked down the hall, and heard her screaming my name. Long story short, we called an ambulance and went to the hospital, and she had surgery and now has a plate and 12 screws in her left ankle and leg.

Judy's recovery would take several months. The first month, she was on crutches and was not allowed to put her foot down. The second month, she was allowed to use a walker but could put only limited weight on her foot. It was tough going for her; it was painful and frustrating not to be able to take care of herself or do the things she wanted to do. Obviously, even though she insisted I go on and hike, there was no way I was going to leave her like that.

1 Corinthians 2:9:
. . . However, as it is written: 'No eye has seen, no ear has heard, no mind has conceived what God has prepared for those who love Him.'

By the first week in June, five weeks after her fall, Judy was moving around rather well and driving after the doctor gave her permission to use crutches and put a little weight on her foot, which helped with her balance and gave her a great deal more confidence. Getting on crutches allowed her to be somewhat independent, so I began to make plans to head to New York. Our daughter Kristi Pettigrew, her husband Yancey, and their four children—Calvin, Ruthie, Mary, and Jack—live almost next door to us, so Judy had family watching out for her and we felt she would be okay with me gone.

I flew out of Memphis to New York on June 16. I was on my way, but with Judy off her feet for more than a month, I had not been able to work out much during the last five weeks. I had to start a little slower than I originally planned and get into better shape while hiking. I just didn't know how much slower I'd be!

My intermission of a year and a half was over, and now I was back to the Trail.

Early morning starts have you hiking in the fog.

CHAPTER FIFTEEN

Plans Can Change in a Flash

The trip to New York, with a change of planes in Chicago, wasn't bad. It felt good to be going toward the Trail, and I was excited to get back. Denny picked me up at the airport, and I spent the night at his home. Leigh was concerned because I had to sleep on the floor in their small apartment and, although I explained I was comfortable on the floor with a blowup mattress, I never convinced her it was much better than what I would have on the Trail. I was glad the only "bear" to contend with was our three-year-old granddaughter, Vivian—what fun.

Denny put me on the Trail early the next morning on the outskirts of Greenwood Lake, New York, where I had come off the AT over a year and a half before. Words cannot tell of the joy and honor it was to have my grown son, whom I had helped teach to pray, stop me before I turned to go into the woods and say, "Dad, I'd like to pray for you before you leave." And he prayed a wonderful prayer that only a son can pray for his father. I will always remember that.

The "blue" side trail up to the AT wasn't as steep or long as I remembered. My memory was that it had seemed steep, and that I kept sliding and almost falling when I was coming down the Trail. Perhaps I had trouble getting down before because I was so exhausted, which tells me I had been in much worse shape than I had thought. I made a mental note to be more alert to my body and listen more intently.

I only managed 14.5 miles the first day, but my Fitbit indicated I had climbed the equivalent of 349 stories. I had started hiking several hours later than I normally do, and the Trail was a little tougher than I anticipated. When I looked at the charts, it was relatively flat and seemingly only deviated plus or minus 50 feet from the 1,150 feet above sea level where most of the Trail runs. Some rocks seemed to be pointed or sharp, and several times I could feel them through my boots, which was unusual. At one point, I went down an old landslide with large rocks piled up, and I had to climb down over them, being careful not to get overbalanced with a pack full of supplies for the week. What I wouldn't know for several days is that apparently I bruised my right foot that day, and it would become a major problem later.

Trail markings (blazes): The AT and most trails crossing it are marked by a painted area about 3 inches wide and 8 inches long that is painted on trees, rocks, signs, other posts, and even buildings. Different colors are used to identify specific trails. The AT's blazes are always white. Other trails may be any color but white, and trails to water are normally blue. They are not directional so hikers must determine for themselves which way to hike on a blazed trail.

I camped that night just off the Trail in grass that was about a foot high with a few trees nearby. My charts indicated I should only camp in designated campsites, but there were none, so I did what I had to do; I pitched my tent and spent the night even though something about the area looked like it should be bear country. I don't know why I thought that, but I knew I was vulnerable. The trees were not suitable for hanging my food and pack, so I put them in my tent and hoped no bears were in the area. There was no water nearby; I used a little water from my bottle for supper and ate breakfast at the first water hole I came to the next day.

Early in the morning, the first thing I came to was the Lemon Squeezer, a set of rocks with a narrow passageway between them that squeezes hikers when they pass through it. I couldn't fit through the passageway while wearing my pack. I'm five feet eight inches tall, and my pack came to just the right (wrong) height to get stuck. I'd have to back out, take off my pack, and hold it over my head in order to pass through; the whole thing is only about 15 or 20 feet long.

I'm small enough that except for my pack, it's really no squeeze to go through there. The Lemon Squeezer is just something that someone decided was needed to make the Trail more interesting. The rocks are somewhat by themselves; it's easy to walk around them. In fact, there is a well-used trail around them, and I know it's not the purist's way, but I didn't want to go through the effort of taking off my pack, so I simply walked the 20 feet around them. Confession made—I'm not a purist hiker!

I stopped for lunch at the William Brien Memorial Shelter. Sitting on the ground outside the shelter was an almost-full can of Off! mosquito repellent. That reminded me that I had not sprayed myself that day with DEET, so I used the Off! instead. I discovered it was much easier to use than the little bottles of DEET that I had been using, so I put the can into my pack and used it the rest of the trip. When I ran out, I bought some more.

The whole area was suffering from lack of rain, and the water holes, streams, and springs were drying up or already gone. By midafternoon, I was running out of water, and I had several miles to go before there was even a chance of finding more water. By evening, I was thirsty and had less than half of a cup of water, with which I would occasionally wet my mouth. By the time I came to Bear Mountain, I was at risk of dehydration, which is dangerous. Dehydration can cause dizziness, confusion, disorientation, and physical weakness, any one of which can be dangerous no matter where you are but can be deadly on the Trail!

It's about a 700-foot climb up Bear Mountain, and the last part has steps that someone put there because of the steepness. After what seemed like hours, I dragged myself up to a grassy area and collapsed. My stomach was cramping, but nothing would come up. I lay there gagging and wondering if I could make it to the closest water. Nearby was the tower atop Bear Mountain, but my charts did not show water there. Half an hour later, I made it into the parking lot near the tower and saw no water but did find a Coke machine. Fortunately, I had enough change to buy two Cokes, which I drank immediately. Although I knew I needed to drink slowly, I couldn't make myself do it, but someone was looking after me because I kept them both down.

Jeremiah 29:12: Then you will call upon me and come and pray to me, and I will listen to you.

Isaiah 65:24: Before they call I will answer; while they are still speaking I will hear.

The Perkins Memorial Tower atop Bear Mountain is a four-story building some 20 feet square and constructed of rock from the surrounding area. I didn't go up because I was too tired to climb another 40 feet for a view that didn't interest me at that point. The drop from the peak is about 1,300 feet to the Bear Mountain Inn and was a surprisingly good trail, about 8 feet wide and smooth. I was still dehydrated, which also made me somewhat weak, but I made it down with no problems. I wasn't in the mood to tent, so I splurged and stayed at the inn. There I would find plenty of water and a good restaurant, or so I thought, because by the time I got to the inn, checked in, and splashed some water over my head, the restaurant was closed for the night. I should have asked when I checked in, so I suffered from my own mistake. There was nothing else nearby, so I fired up my little stove and heated water to hydrate my supper. It was good to get a hot shower, lots of cool water, and a comfortable bed for the night, though.

But it wasn't in the cards that I'd get a full night's sleep. There was a wedding party on the second floor with a loud band that played until one thirty in the morning. I complained about the noise and the fact that I could even feel the drumbeat.

The obviously frustrated clerk said, "We've asked them three times already, and they refuse to turn down the music."

I slept well between one thirty and five thirty! The good news was that although my foot was getting sorer by the day, and I had run out of water and missed a good supper, I had hiked 18.5 miles the day before.

The hotel's continental breakfast that came with the room wasn't what I expected. I was hoping for something hot but found it to be fruit, cold cereal, and pastries. I have become way too spoiled by good Southern breakfasts of eggs, bacon or sausage, and biscuits with butter and jelly. However, the waitress was nice and offered good conversation while I ate. There are nice people everywhere. Perhaps that's because God created all of us, and as the little boy said, "God don't make no junk."

The evening before had not gone well with the lack of water and the restaurant being closed, and the morning didn't start well, either. I left the inn immediately after breakfast and went out to the sidewalk. It was marked as a white blaze, but I missed a turn and hiked a half mile before I realized my mistake and turned back. To add to the confusion, the Trail then crosses under the road through a tunnel to a zoo where the gate opens at ten thirty for hikers. This is the only place where the Trail goes through the middle of a zoo; if the zoo is closed, as it was that morning at seven, the Trail follows a blue trail around beside the zoo. I was aware of that from my hiker's guide and was looking for the blue blazes but, unfortunately, I walked right by the blaze and continued all the way down over the railroad tracks to the Hudson River, where the only choice was to swim in the river or turn around. On the way back, I was walking beside the tracks when I heard a train coming. I made sure I was well away from the tracks, but that didn't keep the engineer from blowing the air horn as he went by. I must have lost about 10 years of my life right then! I'm not sure if he did it to scare me or if that was where he blew the horn every day, but he sure got my heart pumping!

Past the zoo is the Bear Mountain Bridge, which crosses the Hudson River. I texted Judy: "I crossed the Hudson River again today. Two days ago, I crossed it by going under it in New York City. Today I crossed on top." Of interest, perhaps, years ago hikers had to pay a nickel to cross over the bridge, but today only vehicles pay a toll.

The weather starting out that day was nice, but clouds started to build later. Word on the Trail was that a bad storm with heavy rain of two to four inches and the possibility of flooding was coming in that night, and to take shelter. Hikers get used to a bit of rain or a mild storm, but when the word is out that a bad storm is coming, everyone takes notice. The saying on the Trail is "No pain, no rain, no Maine!" and there is a great deal of truth to that. Most times I hiked on and endured the rain, sometimes for what seemed like days at a time. I would put on my rain jacket, rain pants, and gaiters that go over my boots and up around the ankles to keep water from running down into my boots; pull my hat down hard over my neck and face; and keep on hiking. The extra clothes made it more difficult to move, and they became hot quickly. I sometimes wondered whether I'd be drier if I didn't wear the rain gear that caused me to sweat so badly and just put up with the rain.

The rain made the Trail muddy and slippery with large puddles, and caused the creeks to rise, and there was always the possibility of water suddenly rushing down a deep valley or ravine, fed by the rain up above. Even more dangerous was the possibility that a small creek that I was sleeping by would suddenly swell, flood, overflow its banks, and wash me in my tent down the mountain. For that reason, I was always careful to camp above a creek or river when rain was expected. Needless to say, I didn't have any way of knowing the weather forecast, so it would be easy to be caught unaware of any rain coming.

When I reached the shelter at the Graymoor Franciscan monastery, even though I'd only gone 7.3 miles, I stopped and got a place in the shelter for the night. It's not really a shelter but a small, concrete picnic building with a metal roof where the walls only come up about 30 inches, leaving room for wind and rain to come in. It's part of the baseball field owned by the Graymoor monastery, and hikers are welcome to spend the night there at no charge. There are electric lights and plugs to charge cell phones, a shower house with cold water, and two portable toilets nearby. I was the second person there, so I pitched my tent in the middle of the floor and put my bedroll inside so the rain couldn't get to it. By dark, there were about 15 people in the shelter and several in tents outside as hikers piled in to escape the weather. It only rained a little that night, and the wind was light. So much for weather reports on the Trail, although in the mountains the weather can be bad in one valley while the sun is shining in the next. There isn't an easy way to predict weather there.

Graymoor is the headquarters for the Franciscan Friars and Sisters of the Atonement, part of the Roman Catholic Church. The Franciscan order was started by Saint Francis of Assisi, who lived in Europe from 1181 until 1226. He is known as the patron saint of animals and the environment, so how appropriate it is for the AT to go through the grounds of the monastery! Hikers and visitors are welcome to use the facilities at the ballpark when the community is not using them. The friars' and sisters' policy is to care for every stranger who passes through. Their emphasis is on the poor and the hurting, and no pay or compensation is expected from those in need. Everyone is invited to participate in the daily prayers and worship services. According to Matthew 19:14, Jesus said, "Let the little children come to me, and do not stop them; for it is to such as these that the kingdom of heaven belongs." In this case, "little children" can mean children, as in small or young people, or it can refer to those who are small and immature in faith and in understanding of God, or those belittled by the world.

My foot was getting worse and I limped slightly, but some part of your body hurts all the time on the Trail, so I tried to ignore it and thought the pain would go away soon. I didn't see anything on the bottom of my foot, although I couldn't get a good look at where it hurt, so I hiked onward.

Twelve miles later, the Trail suddenly opens onto New York State Route 301. It took me a minute to place where I was, but it looked vaguely familiar, and then it hit me. This was the place near Canopus Lake where Camille and I had gotten onto the Trail three years earlier. I rested there, and another hiker took my picture with my camera. As I sat there, I wondered if the Trail would seem as hard as it had before, but in no way was it as difficult as I had remembered. What a difference three years of hard training and hundreds of miles of hiking can make in one's physical stamina and strength.

I camped that evening near the RPH shelter where Camille and I had stayed before. I had hiked 18.8 miles that day, while we had hiked 7 miles three years earlier, and I had thought that was a lot back then! In fact, it took only a day and a half for me to hike the section Camille and I had taken three days to hike before.

As I described in the first chapter, this building is not what I typically call a shelter. It is more like a one-room house. It has four walls made of painted concrete blocks with a door on one end, and is open on the other end; it has bunks to sleep six, although four or five others could easily sleep on the floor; and a writing desk and chair are available for those who wish to sit at a real table. Outside on the concrete pad is a nice picnic table with a real awning for cover from the sun and rain, and 15 feet away is an old-fashioned hand pump for water. A road passes by about 100 feet away where deliveries can be made from a local restaurant, so I used my phone to order a large pepperoni pizza. Life was good!

I shared the shelter with five other hikers, and another showed up late that evening and tented nearby. I awoke the next morning to the soft sound of a ukulele playing ballads outside and found it was the latest guest to the shelter. He was hiking southbound, carrying his musical instrument on his back, and somehow kept it safe and dry. I didn't get the man's name but remember he was hiking somewhat aimlessly on the Trail in the general direction of Harpers Ferry, enjoying the Trail perhaps as it should be.

The Trail continued to be relatively flat and a good, easy trail with only a few rock formations that were easily traversed. The woods were somewhat open, so I could see the vegetation around me for about 50 yards, and there were a few vistas overlooking the surrounding countryside and rivers below. This area was 500 to 1,000 feet above sea level, so the temperatures were running a bit warmer than I had previously experienced.

Volunteers built this walkway to protect the environment from hiker traffic.

I hiked only 17.5 miles that day, partially because that was the distance to the next good camping spot and partially because my foot continued to hurt and slow me down. I did everything I could to keep my weight on my left foot and stepped down or over logs with my left foot. When I got to water, I took off my right boot and tried to cool my foot in a stream. I still couldn't find anything that looked like a cut or a blister, so I assumed I had a deep "rock bruise" in the ball of my foot and perhaps under my toes where I couldn't see it.

At midafternoon, I came to what a small sign called the Swamp River Boardwalk, which is a long, winding boardwalk over a small river and marshy area with grass and cattails growing up to 10 feet over the semisolid marsh. Walking across the 600-foot-long structure, I could only imagine the many types of snakes, birds, and other animals that called this home. I remember giving silent thanks to the volunteers who had braved the deep mud, snakes, and all the other critters while building the boardwalk. What a gift so many have given to us hikers without knowing our names or thinking they might one day meet us, and we hikers now receive that gift, sometimes without considering that others worked hard so we might safely continue hiking. It takes a community to hike the AT, but most often when hiking the Trail, it looks like there's no one else in the whole world. The Trail can feel lonely even when we are not alone, and especially so when we really are alone.

Life can be a bit like that. It always takes a family and a community to raise us up, train us, and support each of us, but sometimes we forget there are others who love and care about us, and we can feel alone. Sometimes we even forget about God or feel abandoned by God. But God never leaves us alone. He is always present and always loves us no matter what we have done, who we are, or even what we may be planning to do or not do. As the prophet Zephaniah said in the Old Testament, in Zephaniah 3:17: "The Lord your God is with you; He is mighty to save. He will take great delight in you; He will quiet you with His love; He will rejoice over you with singing."

First John 4:10 in the New Testament says: "This is love: not that we loved God, but that He loved us and sent His Son as an atoning sacrifice for our sins."

At the other end of the boardwalk, I came to a railroad track, which is not uncommon on the AT, but this one is different. Just a few feet to one side is a wooden platform bench affectionately known as the Appalachian Trail station. This was where Camille and I had waited for the train to take us into New York at the end of my first hike on the AT. This time, I barely noticed the little platform or the railroad tracks as I limped to a plant nursery about 100 yards down the highway where I spent the night.

Pete Muroski, a hiker himself, owns Native Landscapes and Garden Center, and it is hiker-friendly. He doesn't have a specified camping area, but I was directed down a small service path to an area surrounded by small trees and plants for sale. I found a spot at the farthest end of the nursery directly in the middle of the service path. The grass there was about a foot tall, but it was semi-level and beat most of the camping spots I usually found elsewhere. Six or seven other hikers had already set up their tents there, and several had gone up the road to Tony's Deli to buy supper. I set up my tent and soon found myself at the deli ordering a Coke and a huge hoagie, half of which I ate there. I ate the other half for breakfast the next morning. For a hiker, "real food" is always worth the distance hiked and any associated pain such as a sore foot.

Located behind the nursery and only a few feet from the railroad track is an outdoor shower with just a small wall jutting out, so there is privacy from two sides but the other two sides are open to the railroad and all who ride by. Trains passed by at different intervals, so the trick, I surmised, was to guess when the trains were coming and try to take a fast shower between them. I laid out my clean clothes, waited for a train to pass by, and then quickly got a shower. Even though I could hear the next train coming, I wasn't quite fast enough to be fully dressed when it passed. In fact, I was closer to undressed than dressed! I figure that with a train coming by six feet away at a speed of about 60 miles per hour, anyone who happened to be looking out probably didn't have time to focus. At least I hope that everything, and I do mean everything, was a blur as they came by!

Judy had sent a supply box to the nursery, but as usual, I had asked for far more food than I needed. For instance, that night I didn't need a food pouch, nor did I need one the next morning, because I ate the hoagie. After I'd gotten all the food and supplies I needed, I set the box in the middle of the path with a note saying, "Grab box—get all you want." The next morning, all the food and the box were gone.

As soon as I finished repacking my pack with the new supplies, I hit the sack. I couldn't miss the trains coming by on the railroad tracks I had crossed before getting to the nursery, but I wasn't ready for trains to pass only 20 feet from my tent. They raced by at an average of one every 15 to 20 minutes until about two in the morning, and then they came by less often until about four, when they got really busy with the New York morning commuters. I would hear them coming, and suddenly my tent would bow in from the wind of the approaching train, and then just as suddenly the engine's bright headlight would shine into the inside of my tent before the light and noise would diminish quickly.

To make matters worse, on the other side of me was the highway with its traffic noise. That didn't bother me until I realized that, for some reason, 18-wheelers were stopping some 100 feet away from me and idling their engines. The next morning, I walked by there to discover a truck pull-off where truckers had been stopping to rest during the night. It had been a restless night, to say the least! Amazingly, though, I was so tired that I did get some sleep, despite all the noise, bright lights, and wind periodically bending my tent.

The next day was even tougher—not because of the 20.8 miles on the Trail, but because my foot was seriously painful! Early in the day, it was only sore, but with 10 miles to go, I was using my poles as crutches to take the weight off my foot with each step. I had to leave the Trail and find out what was going on, and I'd probably have to get off for two or three days at a minimum.

About noon, some hikers I passed going south told me about a store near the Trail that was a must. I took their advice and walked the half mile or so there despite my sore foot. On the way is an old, covered, wooden bridge with a history going back to 1740, when the Bull family built the first version of it; thus, it is named Bull Bridge. In the mid-1800s, a second bridge was built to accommodate additional traffic out of New York City. Today, it is a beautiful, one-lane, early American bridge where hikers must walk cautiously to avoid the few cars that compete with them for space on the narrow passageway. On the sides of the bridge are open windows where I stopped and took pictures of the river and the nearby waterfalls. It crosses the Housatonic River, which I would cross again going into Kent that evening. Lunch at the little store wasn't worth the mile-long hike to and from it, but the beauty of the picturesque

Grab box: Many hostels, outfitters, and campgrounds provide a box for hikers to throw excess equipment and supplies into so others can rummage through and grab whatever they need. Often found there are partially used butane tanks, excess clothing, discarded equipment, and lost and found items.

bridge was well worth the detour. A year later, Judy and I traveled by car over the bridge, and I enjoyed it the second time as much as the first.

My afternoon hike grew increasingly painful. When I crossed into Connecticut, my 10th state, I was too concerned about walking to notice. I wanted to get to Kent and put up my foot. I noticed in my hiker's guide that there was only one hotel in town, so I began to call about noon to get a reservation. My cell phone service was intermittent, and when a call did go through, I reached an answering machine, so I called Judy and asked her to stay on the phone and find me a room for the night. Apparently, the lady at the Fife 'n Drum Inn was calling me back, but I wasn't getting her calls because I didn't have service. Judy reached the hotel and confirmed I did have a room for the night. By that point, I knew I had more than a stone bruise and needed serious medical attention. The pain was excruciating.

The Trail comes out on a two-lane, paved road about a half mile from Kent. I had hoped to catch a ride, but no one stopped, so I ended up hiking into town. The hotel was at the far end of town, or another half mile. I was now trying to walk on my right heel and couldn't put any weight on my toes, but I made it to the hotel. Business was slow apparently, because no one was in the office when I got there. I called Judy to confirm our earlier conversation that I had a reservation, and she said to look on the door to the office, and I found an envelope with my name on it that had the room number and a key. Fortunately, I made it to my room and collapsed. With difficulty, I was able to get my foot up on the countertop in the bathroom where I could get an angle in the mirror to see the place on my foot. I couldn't tell what was wrong, but there was a red place about three inches round, the skin was broken up between my toes, and it looked infected. Not good news for someone who wanted to put his foot back into a hot boot and hike another 723 miles.

The only medical service was a doctor's office at the other end of town, and it was already closed, so I limped next door to the Fife 'n Drum Restaurant for a large order of hot wings and a Coke. The next morning, I hobbled down the street to the Villager Restaurant before going to the doctor's office. The doors were still locked, but the desk clerk was kind enough to unlock the door and let me sit in the waiting room, where a nurse came out and got a little information from me. I am so very sorry I don't remember her name because she was the key to getting me medical help. She explained that the facility had stopped serving hikers because, first, they had all the business they could handle. Second, hikers usually didn't pay their bills even if they had insurance, so the office referred all hikers to a doctor in another town.

The nurse took pity on me and helped me beyond words. She said the doctor wasn't in, so she had the say as to whom they served, and she could see I was in considerable pain and needed help right then, so she took me to an examination room over the desk clerk's objections. When the doctor came in, she also decided to overrule the policy, and they were so nice and helpful. Their first opinion was that I definitely had an infection, but they didn't know, and I still do not know, which came first. Was it a blister that got infected, or was it a small wound that became infected and looked like a blister?

The doctor took a swab to send to the lab and correctly diagnosed it as a staph infection. She guessed at what type and the necessary antibiotic, telling me we might have to change the type of medicine when the lab results came back, but we had to do something. This was serious, and we had to take immediate action before the infection spread into the bone. Besides the medicine, the first necessary action was I had to get off my foot until it healed. The doctor said we would have to wait three days to see how my foot responded, but she thought I would be off my foot for several weeks.

The following emails outline the next few days:

6-24-15:

I wrote to Denny: "Hiking is never without its problems. Appears I have initially bruised the sole of my foot the first day out. Have mild pain but nothing visible until last night. Had increasing pain until yesterday when I could barely walk. Last night I found a huge blister that had split open. At doc's now. Will have to take several days off for it to heal. So much for plans but it happens out here. Treating for possible infection. Took culture so will know in a few days. Wet hiking boots will not be ideal once back on the Trail and probably fewer miles starting back per day. Will have to check out local library. Local guy saw me limping and gave me a ride here. Kent . . . about 96 miles from where I got on. Had plans to zero here . . . just not this long."

Denny wrote to me: "Kent is 78 miles or two hours if you need me to come get you."

I wrote to Denny: "Right now I have redness and swelling in most of my foot and can only bend toes a little. Hope it's just irritation from all the hiking on a bruise. Amazing the bruise came through the boot sole."

I wrote to Judy about staying at the Fife 'n Drum Inn: "Has a frilly bedspread on one bed and a day bed in the room. When I got there, they had the hotel key taped to the gift shop door with my name and room number on it. It looks like my grandmother's bedroom."

I wrote to Judy: "Go back to doctor on Friday. She mentioned possibility of wound clinic but hope it heals now with antibiotics and soaking to clean and keep dry. Must stay off foot and keep elevated so it's a wait and see for Friday."

6-25-15:

I wrote to Judy: "Foot a bit better. Definitely infected and think Denny may get me tomorrow for R&R with him. Can only walk on my heel with some discomfort. See doctor tomorrow."

I wrote to Judy: "Denny is picking me up tomorrow so will stay with him for a couple of days. Hope to get back to the Trail soon."

6-26-15:

I wrote to Judy: "Appears I have a staph infection in foot and doctor wants me off the Trail (no hot, sweaty boot for 10 days). Afraid infection could go into the bone. Denny picking me up this afternoon. Thinking seriously of coming home for two weeks to heal."

I spent four nights in Kent before the doctor confirmed I had a staph infection and recommended that I not hike for two to four weeks. I had thought I would have to decide how to wait out a week off the Trail, but now there wasn't much of a decision. I needed to call Denny to come from Brooklyn to pick me up and put me on a plane for Tennessee. It was cheaper to fly home than to stay in a hotel all that time, and it certainly was more appealing to go home to Judy than to sit in a hotel room watching TV and to hobble around town to restaurants at mealtimes.

Denny picked me up about three that afternoon, and we drove back to his home. We stopped at a Walgreens in Brooklyn, where I bought a pair of crutches, and I wondered why I hadn't done that several days before. I guess I was hoping I'd be able to continue hiking, but now I had resigned myself to going home for a few weeks. I still didn't realize how serious a staph infection can be, even though the pain was tremendous each time I put my foot down.

I was grateful for the opportunity to wash my clothes in Leigh's washer before flying out of LaGuardia at midafternoon the next day. I'm sure Judy was also thankful when she picked me up at the airport in Nashville, not to mention the poor folks who had to sit by me on the plane for two hours. Although I couldn't smell it myself, Judy had previously made me aware of the lingering odor that my clothes had from days on the Trail without daily washings.

I'm reminded of a story about two strangers on an elevator together. The aroma in that small elevator became almost overbearing, which prompted one man to say to the other, "I believe someone's deodorant in this elevator quit working." The other man quickly replied, "Not mine! I don't wear any!"

I arrived in Nashville about eight in the evening, and as both Judy and I were exhausted, we elected to stay at the Radisson near the airport. We got several looks as we checked in and out, with both of us on crutches and each trying to pull a small suitcase behind us, but we were just glad to be together. I was glad to have some normal clothes to wear. But mostly I was glad to be home with Judy, and in a car instead of walking on my sore foot.

When trees are green and thick, they obscure the beauty and dangers of the Trail.

INTERMISSION THREE

Falling Isn't a Failure Unless You Don't Get Up

The time back home went fast even though I was there for a little over a month. I had hoped to be there only about 10 days, but a trip to the doctor quickly squelched those thoughts. He confirmed the same diagnosis I had gotten previously, but he was not nearly as optimistic about how soon I could "put my foot back into a hot, wet boot." He was right. I was on crutches for about 10 days, but then had to wear an open shoe and walk gingerly for another two weeks.

The first Sunday I was back, Judy and I went to church and sat on the back row since we both were on crutches. About halfway through the service, we grew uncomfortable, and we propped our injured feet up on the pew, Judy's foot sticking out to the left and mine out to the right. Then we leaned against each other with our backs together. We were a sorry sight, and yes, we did get ribbed about how we sat, but fortunately, no one took a photo.

I told myself I would go to the gym and work out regularly, but I never did. At first, it was too hard to get to the gym on crutches, and then I asked myself what I could do there that would really help me hike. Of course, there were strengthening exercises for my upper body and legs, but I convinced myself that what I really needed were endurance exercises. Also, Judy was still on crutches and had a hard time doing a lot of things, which further helped convince me to become more of a couch potato than anything resembling a long-distance hiker or exercise enthusiast. Sometimes any excuse will do when you don't want to go to the gym.

Deep down, I also thought that perhaps I wouldn't be able to complete the Trail. Neither the doctors nor I knew how much damage had been done to my foot and whether it might adversely affect on my hiking. All I could do was stay positive and hope my foot would heal quickly.

After about three weeks, I felt reasonably ready to go back on the Trail and began to plan to return, but the staff at church realized all four of us pastors were scheduled to be out of town for a week and I was the only one with a flexible schedule. One part of me wanted to head out to the Trail, and the other part said I really wasn't ready and was needed at church. As I said previously, I am officially retired but work part time at the church, and my job description did not include preaching or anything regarding regular Sunday worship. When I offered to preach the two Sundays the others would be gone, Dr. Don Thrasher, knowing how much I wanted to get back to the Trail, initially turned down my offer. After I insisted I could wait another 10 days, he accepted my offer. I knew I still had plenty of time, at least theoretically, to finish the Trail before October 15, the day the Trail up Mount Katahdin closes. Judy's leg was also taking longer than expected to heal and, although she encouraged me to go, she was having more trouble getting around than she liked to admit.

Isaiah 30:19: How gracious He will be when you cry for help! As soon as He hears, He will answer you.

I waited until Wednesday, July 22, to fly out of Memphis and return to New York. Denny picked me up at the airport, put me up for the night, and took me to the Trail early the next day.

I knew I had been lucky to reach Kent, some 1,461 miles from Springer, with only one serious injury, and now to be healed and headed back to the AT. I had reflected on this for over a month.

I had called on God to carry me safely over the mountains and through the valleys. I had called on God to get me off the Trail safely when I hurt my foot. I had called on God to heal me and set me back on the Trail. Now I called on God to be with me all the way to Maine.

Surely God was with me!

And surely God would walk with me for the rest of the journey!

And God was with me . . . and still is . . . as He is with us all!

The AT often followed the ridges of the major mountains.

Freebyrd and Preacher enjoyed the abundance of water at the waterfall.

CHAPTER SIXTEEN

Someone Looks Out for Me

On Thursday, July 23, Denny dropped me at the Trail crossing on Connecticut Route 341 where I had limped off nearly a month before. During the pleasant drive up there, I enjoyed spending a few hours with him without any interruptions except the occasional checking of road maps, even though he had a good GPS to guide us along the way. Just before reaching Kent, we drove over the old, one-lane Bull Bridge, which I had hiked over on the way to get lunch on an afternoon that seemed like just a few days ago.

After hoisting my pack, I paused briefly on a ladder over the fence beside the road. It was a wooden stepladder in the style often used to go over fences that cross the Trail so that hikers don't damage the fences. Standing atop that ladder, I knew this likely would be the last time I saw any family or friends until I had summited Mount Katahdin. It was a moment I won't soon forget. There was our son, now fully grown and with a family of his own, taking a picture of his dad and wishing Godspeed for me. There was no going back for me, and so, with a final farewell, I turned toward Maine, hoping he didn't see the tears in my eyes.

My foot was as good as it was going to get, with little or no discomfort, and I was more than ready to resume my pilgrimage to Katahdin. During my time off the Trail, I had not exercised or done any walking that resembled a workout or any kind of training. I expected that the next week would be another adjustment to the physical difficulties of the Trail and that I had lost some stamina. I was excited to hike again and anxious to put more miles between me and Springer Mountain.

In less than 50 feet, I was reminded to be vigilant at all times on the Trail, as a "harmless" green snake almost ran over my boot, startling me back into the reality of how fast accidents can happen on the AT. Although a green snake is not poisonous, any snakebite requires a trip to the emergency room because of the nasty germs all snakes carry from having eaten field mice and other small animals, not to mention what it does to my heart rate when those little creepy-crawlers suddenly fly across the Trail only inches from my feet!

The first five miles were relatively easy, giving me some time to acclimate to my pack and hiking again, but the Trail changed slightly as the terrain became a bit more difficult with climbs over ridges and then down into shallow valleys. The rivers and creeks were full from recent rains that had allowed the mosquitoes to hatch en masse, reminding me to use plenty of insect repellent and cover every inch of any exposed body parts. Several blue trails were necessary to cross minor rivers, adding more miles, but I covered 14 miles even with the detours and late start before stopping at the Caesar Road campsite for the night. Fortunately, the temperatures were mild for that time of year, running in the low 80s during the day and low 60s at night, so it was a comfortable evening and I rested well.

As I neared Falls Village the following morning, the Trail detoured due to construction around the Housatonic River bridge, and the blue Trail went for about three miles along a paved road sporadically lined with homes on one side and the river on the other. In the yards of the houses were hand-painted signs apologizing for the inconvenience and added miles to the Trail during construction. To further show their concern and hospitality, the homeowners had put out everything they thought we hikers could possibly need. One person even placed a child's red wagon near the road filled with cucumbers, zucchini, and bottles of water with a sign inviting hikers to take all we wanted. Another yard had a table set up with homemade brownies wrapped in plastic as Trail Magic! I was amazed at the concern and hospitality offered by these strangers, who didn't know any of us coming by and never would but were concerned their construction had inconvenienced us. And they expected nothing in return. Knowing they had helped us up the Trail was enough. Truly, that is the heart that Jesus Christ has asked of each of us, to show hospitality to one another.

That afternoon, for the first time, I met two southbounders coming from Mount Katahdin. They were full of stories about how hard the Trail had been in New Hampshire and Maine, and how bad the bugs were. At that point, I didn't believe the Trail could get any harder, and I remember thinking to myself, "Just wait until you get to North Carolina!" Forgive me; I was definitely wrong. I was still learning about this thing called the AT.

Late that afternoon, after 18 miles, I came across four other hikers tenting on the Trail in an area not normally used for camping, but they were making the best of what the Trail offered. Since my maps indicated the next several miles would not be likely camping spots, and there was company to be had here, I pitched my tent in their general vicinity. That turned out to be an exceptionally good decision as I met four fellow hikers with whom I would hike, camp, and zero in the coming weeks: Coffeeman, known for his freshly brewed coffee that he shared with all who were present each morning and evening; Freebyrd, who felt he was free from his career and long work days, and with whom I would summit Mount Katahdin later; and Low Priority and Mado—I never learned the origins of their Trail names.

1 Peter 4:9-10: Offer hospitality to one another without grumbling. Each one should use whatever gift he has received to serve others, faithfully administering God's grace in its various forms.

My charts showed Salisbury, Connecticut, was about a half mile off the Trail, so I detoured into town the next morning for a "real" breakfast. I hadn't yet realized how much time we would spend together and assumed these four were like all the others I'd casually met and may never see again, so I rose early and hiked into town, leaving my four new friends still packing. But no one else was up yet in Salisbury, and the stores and the only restaurant were closed for several more hours. The local grocery store was open, so I bought a large milk and two ham and egg sandwiches at the deli, and I ate sitting on the curb outside.

On the way out of town, I passed a large cemetery with a sign that said: "Water faucet beside small building in center of cemetery. Hikers are welcome to get water." I experienced numerous invitations of hospitality along the Trail, but that is the only place I remember being invited to visit the dead. Seriously, the hospitality along the Trail was phenomenal!

The day turned out to be challenging with three mountains to climb and descend: Bear Mountain, Mount Race, and Mount Everett. All are rocky and steep at times, with some climbs up a 60-degree angle on bare rock, which was like walking on glass when it was wet, and elevation changes of up to 2,500 feet.

Fourteen miles later, at Glen Brook Shelter, I found Coffeeman and Freebyrd had already made camp and there was plenty of room for me. I was pleased to find a privy and a metal bear box, but the water supply was dry. To add to our comfort, Trail Angels had left about 10 one-gallon jugs of water on the camp table for whoever came by. Like so many times before, strangers had made our stay safer and more enjoyable. I often felt alone, but at other times I felt there was a whole invisible community looking out for me.

For some reason, a lot of section hikers were on the Trail on Saturday, and there were no fewer the following day despite the steep climbs. I saw perhaps as many as 75 hikers each day. Maybe it was because the weather was getting cooler, which always makes hiking more enjoyable. School was starting soon, so people may have been trying to get some hiking in before the fall.

It started raining during the night and rained off and on all day. The Trail became slippery and grew worse throughout the day, with rain running off the rocks in sheets that were sometimes several inches deep. Hiking was tricky with wet rocks and occasional mud, and I fell four times within an hour, but luckily I wasn't hurt. My clothes, shoes, and all my socks became soaked with no chance to dry. In the afternoon, the rain and clouds grew so dark that I had to use my headlight to see clearly along the path. I spent the night in the Mount Wilcox North Shelter, but since everything was wet outside and the shelter was three-sided, nothing dried overnight.

Dawn broke with drizzling rain and temperatures in the low 60s. That always makes it difficult for me to get out of my sleeping bag, let alone boil water for hot chocolate and to dehydrate my little packet of eggs and ham for breakfast. After that, I had the chore of pulling my pack out of my tent and filling it with all my belongings while trying to keep the inside dry. Next, I had to take down my tent, which exposes the inside to the rain; I never did discover how to do this while keeping the inside from getting wet. Not only did this mean my tent weighed about a pound more from the water, but it also meant the inside would still be wet when I got into it that evening. That meant my bedroll and some of my clothes also would get wet and could remain that way for several days unless the sun came out so I could stop and dry them during the day.

The weather cleared overnight, and I was glad to see the sun again, although my feet, socks, boots, and everything else were still soaked. The storm had left obvious damage, including trees blown down across the Trail and parts of the Trail washed down the mountain, which slowed me down considerably. I met four men from the local hiking club going up the mountain carrying shovels, axes, and chainsaws to repair what they could. Mercifully, the Trail was not as difficult as the day before, and I stopped and spread most of my clothes and boots out in the sun to dry for an hour while I lunched. After 16 miles, I was relieved to reach the Upper Goose Pond Cabin, which is two stories high with bunk beds upstairs and a living area and kitchen downstairs. Goose Pond is really a lake near the cabin. I looked around and, seeing no one, as is often the case while in the wilderness, I stripped down and took a much-needed bath in the lake. Fortunately, no one came near while I was bathing, but if they had, I'm sure they often did the same.

The cabin is owned and operated by the Berkshire Chapter of the American Mountain Club (AMC). For a non-specified donation, all long-distance hikers can spend the night, relax on the porch or in the living room, and enjoy a pancake breakfast in the morning. Additionally, canoes are available for those who have energy left from the day's hiking and want to cruise the lake. I am grateful to the volunteers who made my stay comfortable and refreshing, and furnished my breakfast the next morning.

Low Priority and I had hiked together off and on for five days. Somewhere he had heard about the Cookie Lady who lived near the Trail, and we would be hiking nearby the next day, so we decided to visit her. In the afternoon, we reached a gravel road where a hand-painted sign pointed down the road advertising "Granny's Cookies." We found three other hikers who had been patiently waiting for Cookie Lady to return for more than an hour. Fortunately, she arrived soon after we got there. She is an older lady with a wonderful smile, and she came out and greeted us and then took our order. We had the choice of a chocolate chip, oatmeal, or raisin cookie. I chose chocolate chip and, just as she said, she came out of her home again 15 minutes later carrying a small basket with large, warm cookies. For a dollar, we could help ourselves to the canned Cokes in the cooler beside the porch. I had been told Cookie Lady never would give anyone two cookies, but after considerable flattery and compliments, I found her bringing me a second cookie. I felt truly honored and am appreciative of her Trail Magic.

We finished the day after 19 miles by stopping at the Kay Wood Shelter, where 14 tents were set up for approximately 25 young men who were working on the Trail. Their project was to hack a path from the shelter down to a small stream about 40 yards away. They were cutting steps into the mountain and placing stones into the cutouts so campers could safely get water from the stream. Some rocks were the size of a large chair and probably weighed nearly 400 pounds. I don't believe I have ever met such polite, hard-working young men before. They were spending a month doing community service during their summer vacation, learning at 14 or 15 years of age the importance of giving back to society. Their expenses were paid, and they would receive a small amount of pay for their hard work, but no amount of money could really repay them for the service they were doing for us. I don't know if they knew the scripture about cheerful giving, but they were certainly living it.

Matthew 25:40: The King will reply, 'I tell you the truth, whatever you did for one of the least of these brothers of mine, you did for me.'

2 Corinthians 9:7: Each man should give what he has decided in his heart to give, not reluctantly or under compulsion, for God loves a cheerful giver.

Early Wednesday, July 29, six days after Denny had dropped me off near Kent, Connecticut, Low Priority and I hiked three miles into Dalton, Massachusetts, for a zero day. Before finding a motel, we stopped at Angelina's Subs for a "real" breakfast. Next door is the Shamrock Village Inn, where they were kind enough to allow us to check in early, and we stayed for two nights, during which time we did what all hikers do while zeroing—eat, take hot showers, sleep, and wash clothes.

The motel room was typical for Trail towns. It was an older motel with older furniture, two queen-size beds, and a small dresser with a TV on top that got a few of the cheaper cable stations, but the room was clean with an air conditioner that worked. Also, located just off the main lobby were a clothes washer and dryer, an ice machine, and the all-important soft drink machine. The inn served its purpose, as we only cared about lots of food, good rest, and marginally clean clothes.

Low Priority and I shared a room to cut expenses. Mado and Freebyrd shared a room just down from us, and Coffeeman, who came in late, had his own room, but we all hung out together and enjoyed one another's company. As usual, Judy had sent a package with all my supplies for the next week, which would add about 15 pounds to my pack, but it was always a welcome sight, especially with the cards and extra goodies she always sent.

Friday morning dawned clear and beautiful. We got a slightly later start than usual as we waited for Angelina's Subs to open for breakfast and coffee. Coffeeman, Mado, and Low Priority wanted to sleep in, so Freebyrd and I hiked together that day. We hiked at about the same pace and enjoyed one another's company, and both of us appreciated having someone to "watch our backs" and be there if an emergency occurred. Thereafter, we hiked together as much as possible but got separated a couple times. The first time was when Freebyrd had a friend come up for a few days and they were only going to hike about 10 miles a day, and the second time was when Judy came to visit me for four days in New Hampshire. Each time, we got back together, and we later decided that after all we had been through together, we wanted to summit Mount Katahdin together, which we did.

What I wouldn't discover for several weeks was that Freebyrd had some issues he wanted to talk to someone about. He had prayed that God would send a preacher to him on the Trail, and then I, "Preacher," showed up. Freebyrd was facing a time in his life when he felt the need to separate himself from the family business where he had worked since he was a teenager. His wife supported him in that decision, but it put a strain on his two brothers, who worked with him. He didn't want to leave them with all the work and responsibility, and he wanted God to be a part of his decision. We would have hours and days together to discuss those issues, which I will keep in confidence except for the things he shared publicly.

The Trail from the motel followed about a mile of city streets and sidewalks before it suddenly turned into the woods for a climb up Mount Greylock, which is 3,491 feet at the highest point. From the top of the mountain, I had a beautiful view of the Green Mountains, the Catskill Mountains, the Taconic Mountains, and the surrounding towns. Around noon, we passed through the outskirts of the small town of Cheshire, where we happened upon Diane's Twist, a small building housing a business that serves ice cream and various iced drinks. I got a large vanilla shake and sat in the shade of a big tree, resting against my pack. It's amazing how many

Volunteers build steps over fences on private land in hopes of hikers leaving no trace.

small surprises there are on or just off the Trail that can revive you and change your whole outlook for the day.

Late that afternoon, after hiking 18 miles, we reached Bascom Lodge, complete with several bunk rooms that slept about six per room, a full "working" bathroom with showers, and a dining room with a sit-down, four-course dinner. I was surprised to find such luxury in the middle of the woods. Bascom Lodge, according to its website, is "a rustic arts and crafts mountain lodge built in the 1930s by volunteers from the Civilian Conservation Corps. Constructed of local stone and old-growth red spruce timbers, the lodge was designed in an architectural style that would later become the blueprint for America's national parks. Nestled on the summit of Mount Greylock, the state's highest mountain, the lodge is the centerpiece of a 12,500-acre wilderness park and has been in continuous operation for over 75 years."

Coffeeman, Mado, and Low Priority had decided not to stay at Bascom Lodge because it cost $20 for a bunk and $5 for a shower and towel, so we had left them several miles back. I had expected to eat my usual dehydrated, packaged supper but was surprised to find a four-course, semiformal meal was provided in the dining room for $46. I had a hard time justifying paying that amount for supper when I already had a meal in my room, but after first declining the invitation while checking in, I couldn't resist the opportunity to eat "real" food in a nice restaurant. Sleeping arrangements weren't quite as nice, as it was a bunk room that slept eight, but there were only four of us in the room, which certainly beat sleeping on rocks in a tent.

After a wonderful meal, I wandered out onto the summit to view the moon and stars. Fully visible was the second full moon, the blue moon, of July; it was especially beautiful with the lights of homes and towns clearly visible below in the valleys. As I looked up at the sky and the moon, despite my tiredness and need for a night's rest, I was overcome with the beauty of God's earth and His eternal care for us all. In that moment, although I couldn't recall it all then, I remembered the beginning of Psalm 121:

"I will lift up my eyes to the hills
From where will my help come?
My help comes from the Lord,
Who made heaven and earth.

He will not let your foot be moved:
He who keeps you will not slumber.
He who keeps Israel
Will neither slumber nor sleep.
The Lord is your keeper:
The Lord is your shade at your right hand.
The sun shall not strike you by day
Nor the moon by night.
The Lord will keep you from all evil;
He will keep your life.
The Lord will keep
Your going out and your coming in
From this time on and forevermore."

I went to bed that night with a clear understanding that I was not alone and that God indeed was caring for me along the Trail in the mountains and on the trail we call life. It was a sweet and comforting time.

Saturday, August 1, dawned clear and cool, and the view of the sunrise from Mount Greylock was as spectacular as the full moon had been the night before. The lodge served a continental breakfast, and the freshly brewed coffee was a treat. Waiting to eat breakfast at seven, getting confused by Trail signs, and doubling back several hundred yards to check my direction caused me to get a later start than usual, but I was headed toward Katahdin, and that was what was important. I was hiking alone again, as Freebyrd was going to meet a friend that morning, so it was just the wild animals and me for most of the day.

Typed signs attached to trees at road crossings advertised that the North Adams Trail Club would serve a hamburger lunch for all hikers starting around eleven in North Adams, Massachusetts, and I was determined to be there. The six-mile hike from Bascom Lodge was relatively easy. I arrived about an hour before they started serving food. Clubs often provide meals as Trail Magic to help long-distance hikers along the way. That day, they had a real treat for us: hamburgers, hot dogs, several types of salads, desserts of all kinds, and cold, iced-down soft drinks. Along with the food came the good company and encouragement of Trail Angels sharing the magic of love for others. All of this was provided at no cost to us hikers.

Coffeeman, Low Profile, and Mado showed up while I ate lunch, so we hiked together that afternoon and crossed into Vermont, our 12th state. We now had only 592.5 miles and two more states until Katahdin. They stopped sooner than I wanted, so I left them and tented after dark farther up the Trail in tall grass beside a pond. It was a small area even for one tent, so I was surprised when another hiker wandered in about midnight, wearing bells on his shoes to alert the bears in the area (and me) of his presence.

"May I pitch a hammock near you?" he asked.

I said hesitantly, "Of course."

I got up and moved my camp stove and boots so he could have a place for the night. It's just what you do on the Trail: make room for one more, whether it's to camp, eat, or join a conversation. Most hikers are accepting of others, especially knowing we may have to depend on each other one day in an emergency. I had no trouble going back to sleep.

John 13:34-35: A new commandment I give you: Love one another. As I have loved you, so you must love one another. All men will know that you are my disciples if you love one another.

Matthew 6:1-4: Be careful not to do your 'acts of righteousness' before men, to be seen by them. If you do, you will have no reward from your Father in heaven. So when you give to the needy, do not announce it with trumpets, as the hypocrites do in the synagogues and on the streets, to be honored by men. I tell you the truth, they have received their reward in full. But when you give to the needy, do not let your left hand know what your right hand is doing, so that your giving may be in secret. Then your Father, who sees what is done in secret, will reward you.

The following morning, my alarm went off at four thirty as usual, but that day and several after it would not be normal at all! I woke up with severe vertigo, worse than the bout I had dealt with way back in Georgia. I carried medicine for vertigo, as I suffer from it about twice a year, and it can almost completely disable me. I took one pill, hoping it would help me make it to the next shelter, where other hikers could help me by getting my water and preparing my meals as needed. I was about four miles from the nearest shelter, but the good news was that it was primarily downhill. The truth is that you fall farther when going downhill than when going uphill.

After taking down my tent and packing up my gear, I tried to hike. The stranger who had come in late the night before was still asleep, and I decided not to wake him, as I wasn't sure he could or would help me because he was heading in the opposite direction. I could stagger about a quarter mile before I collapsed wherever I was and had to rest. The effort simply to stand took a large part of my energy, and the vertigo itself left me exhausted. I would immediately go to sleep, still wearing my pack, and wake up about 15 to 20 minutes later; struggle to stand up; and then stagger another quarter mile before I collapsed and went to sleep again. It was a long four miles, but I got to the Congdon Shelter, where I crawled into my bedroll and went to sleep.

Low Priority came through later and, after several tries, woke me up to make sure I was okay. I assured him I was and, with my encouragement, he proceeded up the Trail. I felt better by midafternoon and hiked another seven miles, where I found my four fellow hikers already tented and ready for bed. They helped me put up my tent, and I fell into my bedroll, exhausted. I still had some vertigo and functioned only at perhaps 70 percent. Nature called during the night, so I got out of my tent to take a few steps into the woods but was so dizzy that I fell over my tent, bending several support poles. I straightened all but one pole, which still is bent and now reminds me of that night each time I put up my tent.

I awoke the next morning to find my tent floor covered in water. I had left the valve to my water bladder open, and water had run out of it, getting my sleeping bag and most of my clothes wet. I used a wool sock to push out as much water as I could and used the other sock to dry the tent floor, but I wasn't successful with either effort. I have a picture of my campsite that evening with all my equipment, including my tent, spread out on rocks and hanging from bushes in an attempt to dry everything out, at least partially, before I went to bed. Unfortunately, it took several days for everything to dry and for my vertigo to go away.

Misfortune must come in threes, as later that day I stepped on one end of a loose board on a bridge. Not only did I fall, but the board came up and hit me hard across my nose. I lay there in the mud, weighed down by my pack and trying to roll over or push myself up, but initially I was unable to do either. It startled me to think I couldn't move, but either I gathered my strength or recovered from being initially dazed, and finally I rolled over. Realizing how hard I had hit my head, I felt first to see if I'd broken my nose, but it seemed okay. Then I checked my mouth, knowing I must have lost a tooth or worse, but there was no blood there. Next, I felt for my glasses, which had been knocked off, and when I found them, I was surprised to see they weren't broken. I still cannot believe that after I fell that hard and took such a forceful lick to my nose and face, I didn't have anything to show I had fallen, not even broken glasses! Surely an angel must have softened my fall and kept me from serious injury. I thank God for that, as such a fall could have easily ruined my hike.

The day wasn't an easy one. My vertigo continued, and my fall took its toll with a few bruises. The climb up Glastenbury Mountain, with a peak elevation of 3,748 feet, was hard, but the day wasn't over yet. It started raining about five that evening while I was putting up my tent, and then came the most prolific lightning storm I have ever experienced. Lightning strikes were coming every three to five seconds, and the storm lasted for over 30 minutes. I was camping near the Story Spring Shelter, so I took shelter in it during the worst of the storm, thinking I was safer there than in my tent in the event of a direct lightning strike or a tree falling. I couldn't help but be aware of how vulnerable I was, with nothing but a small shelter protecting me from such a potentially deadly natural event, and how our natural life can come to a sudden end. It certainly reminded me of who is ultimately in control of our lives and the entire universe.

Psalm 121:7-8: The Lord will keep you from all harm— He will watch over your life; the Lord will watch over your coming and going both now and forevermore.

After the storm passed, I strung a cord between two trees and hung my wet clothes out to dry. The storm wasn't over, and rain and lightning continued throughout the night. Despite the day's turmoil, I had hiked 16 miles. It took a little while to warm up after I got into my bedroll, but neither my bedroll nor my sleeping clothes had gotten wet, so I got a good night's rest.

It had been two days, and I knew someone had to be looking down on me and carrying me safely over the mountains. So many things happened in those two days that could have caused me great bodily harm, but somehow I came through it all without a scratch. Looking back, I know I was not capable of overcoming that many adversities and still being able to hike the next day. All the falls from the vertigo; the disorientation at times; the rain, hail, and lightning; and falling so hard at that bridge: All I can say is it's a miracle! And thank God for His love and His care! I can say without doubt: There was just one set of "footprints on the mountains," and they were not mine those days!

The following morning dawned fresh and cool, especially when I had to retrieve my soaked clothes from my makeshift clothesline, wring them out as best I could, and put them on. The only way to get warm on a morning like that is to start hiking as soon as possible, but it took at least about 30 minutes to take down my tent and pack up, during which time my teeth were chattering. Added to the wetness and cold, my vertigo had returned, but I decided not to take my medicine because it makes me lethargic. Fortunately, my head cleared by about ten that morning, but it took until noon for my clothes to dry.

The Trail up Stratton Mountain is a steep climb up 1,500 feet over five miles, with a considerable number of switchbacks and then drops of about the same elevation on the north side. We always think of the climb going up, and how difficult that can be, but hiking down is harder on your body. The knees and thighs take a beating on each step going down, and every step also shoves your feet farther into your boots, cramming your toes down into the toe of the boot. My second and third toes are longer than the others, so they get bruised and I lose toenails. If properly fitted, boots can be laced up tightly so the shoelaces hold your foot back in the boot, but even then, a sock crumpled in the toe of the boot can cause blisters and bruises. Foot care is a constant problem on the Trail, and wet feet exacerbate the other issues. That morning, my boots and socks were wet, and then I went down a steep, long mountain, resulting in some bruising. I had lost toenails so many times that I was used to having sore toes, so it wasn't a new problem.

The Long Trail joins the AT at the Vermont-Massachusetts state line, and the two trails run concurrently for 105 miles before the Long Trail goes its separate way up to the Canadian border. This puts additional people on the Trail, with hikers going north and south from both trails. More people are competing for camping space and room in the shelters, and the additional traffic also takes a toll on the Trail itself. That summer was the wettest summer since 1908, so the entire area was much wetter, muddier, and more difficult to hike. Mud was a constant problem and was as deep as 16 inches in many places. One place had mud as deep as mid-thigh, and a number of hikers blundered into it, nearly getting stuck. A southbounder had warned me about the deep mud, but I still almost stepped into it before I realized what it was and found my way through the thick woods and vines for about 100 yards to get around it.

Even with the steep climbs and mud, I hiked 19 miles that day. My legs and stamina improved, and I no longer gasped for air or felt my leg muscles burning for a rest stop on most climbs. In fact, I had to remind myself to take breaks during the day. I was getting my Trail legs again.

I spent that night near the Spruce Peak Shelter and found a small area just big enough for my tent. The shelter is rated for 14 people, but after the heavy rains, nearly 20 people crowded into it, trying to find space for hastily hung clotheslines to dry their clothes and gear. A couple of groups had built fires for warmth and to dry out boots and clothing. There is something about a campfire that draws people together and facilitates conversation. Most people went to bed by eight o'clock, but a few stayed up until around ten, their voices and laughter occasionally keeping those nearby awake. Most long-distance hikers fell asleep early, while section hikers were more prone to stay up late and sleep in the next morning. With that many people nearby, I kept my pack with all my food in my tent, trusting that a hungry bear wouldn't venture into the camping area looking for an easy meal.

Bad weather: It isn't a case of 'if' but 'when' bad weather will be experienced. There is a saying, 'No rain, no pain, no Maine.' All hikers will be forced to hike in some inclement weather, so good planning and good sense is always required. It can be a life-or-death decision on when to hike and what rain or cold-weather clothes to wear. If in doubt, find shelter.

The next morning, I was up early and glad to be on my way despite my wet, cold socks and boots, because I was only 2.8 miles from the road leading into Manchester Center, Vermont, where I would zero. I never stopped looking forward to those zero days of hot showers, rest, good food, and clean, dry clothes. Manchester Center has several places to stay. Mado and Low Priority had decided to stay at Green Mountain House Hostel, which cost $20 a night but didn't have private rooms and baths. Freebyrd, Coffeeman, and I wanted a few more conveniences, so we elected to stay at Sutton's Place, which cost $55 for a single or $68 for two in a double room. Sutton's Place was in town, where a shuttle was not needed to get to restaurants, laundromats, drugstores, or grocers.

I arrived at the roadside about seven in the morning to find a couple other hikers already trying to hitch a ride into town. Just as I walked up, a lady in a nice car stopped to pick up two hikers who had their thumbs out for a ride. When the lady opened the trunk for their packs, it was obvious she was dressed for work in a suit, jewelry, and high-heeled shoes. As I walked near, she called, "I've got room for one more," so I piled in with all my gear and sat in the front seat.

All three of us hikers had obviously been on the Trail a few days; we were dirty and still a bit wet. Looking around in the car and at the lady driving, I was self-conscious about how we looked and our aroma of sweat and dirt. I explained we weren't normally this dirty and smelly, and would soon find a motel with a hot shower and then a laundromat. The lady good-naturedly replied, "I come through here every morning on my way to work and pick up as many hikers as I can. My husband always tells me, though: If they don't smell, don't pick them up." Obviously, she knew a good deal about hikers!

I wish I had gotten the lady's name, as she truly was a Trail Angel looking after as many of us hikers as she could. One hiker said he needed to pick up a package at the post office, so she took us there and we waited while he got his package; then she dropped the other two hikers at their motel and took me to Sutton's Place. Freebyrd and I had already decided to share a room, so I waited about an hour until he got there. Coffeeman also showed up and got his own room, so the three of us enjoyed one another's company for the next two days. After showering, we headed to a local restaurant for a late breakfast.

Sutton's Place, owned and operated by Mr. and Mrs. Sutton, is an older, well-kept home in a residential neighborhood about four blocks from the commercial part of town. The front part of the house and upstairs are for guests, and there's a common room with a TV and magazines. The Suttons live in the back part and took good care of us but kept to themselves, which was fine with me. Each morning, I got up to fresh coffee brewing in the coffeepot next to the TV.

My time off the Trail in Manchester Center was relaxing. I had planned to zero the rest of Wednesday and Thursday, leaving early Friday morning, but I was delayed because there was a problem getting my care package from Judy. She had sent it via UPS to General Delivery at the post office. The UPS center that she shipped it from at home didn't realize it was General Delivery, and since UPS doesn't deliver to the post office, my package fell into the non-deliverable bin at the UPS center near Manchester Center. Judy traced the package and changed the delivery address to Sutton's Place, which should have worked but still would have made the package arrive a day late. But for some reason, the package didn't arrive until noon Saturday. All said, I spent the better part of three days zeroing instead of two.

The delay wasn't bad because Freebyrd and Coffeeman were also staying until Saturday morning. Freebyrd had a friend, Rob Ricciutti, who was coming up to hike with him for a week, and Coffeeman was ending his month-long section hike to return to Austria. We filled our time with long meals at local restaurants, going to the laundromat, and relaxing on the porch at Sutton's Place. We had two days to dry out our boots and equipment. I also visited the local drugstore for a Dr. Scholl's insert for my bruised heel and some non-drowsy Dramamine to help treat my vertigo without causing drowsiness.

Friday, August 7, dawned with a beautifully clear sky, the warm sun rising over the mountains, and with me waiting to see if my care package would arrive. UPS had told me the driver would deliver my package "first thing," but he didn't arrive until noon. The driver said no one had told him to deliver to Sutton's Place first, but the important thing was I got my supplies. Coffeeman was still sitting on the porch, waiting for his ride to the airport, so we talked as I consolidated my new supplies into my pack. Freebyrd and his friend had left several hours earlier, so Coffeeman and I exchanged a few last words of goodbye. It's amazing how close people who may have little in common can become while on the Trail, and Coffeeman was always quietly looking out for others. His English wasn't perfect, and neither was my German, but we could always communicate. Sometimes words aren't needed to communicate goodwill. Coffeeman was leaving that afternoon to fly back to Austria, where he lived and worked, and it was a sad moment when I had to turn and walk down the street knowing we would never see each other again, at least in this lifetime.

An inspirational moment captured early in the morning at Griffin Lake campsite.

CHAPTER SEVENTEEN

Climbing through New Hampshire

    I had planned to stay in Manchester Center two nights and one day, but my supply package went to the wrong address. Then the UPS truck didn't deliver it the second day for some reason, so it was noon of the third day before my package caught up with me. Freebyrd and his friend left early the third day and planned to hike about 10 miles a day for five days, and I planned to leave as soon as the UPS truck arrived and would pass them and keep going, as I was going to hike my usual 18 to 22 miles a day. Judy was coming up in another nine days and would stay for four days, so I hoped Freebyrd and I would get back together sometime after that, although it looked a little doubtful. It would take lots of planning, hard hiking, luck, and willpower on both of our parts to make it happen.

    Leaving Manchester Center, I walked about a mile before someone picked me up and took me to the trailhead. I was carrying a full pack and three liters of water. Word was out that the next water was eight miles away so, out of an abundance of caution, I was carrying an extra liter. The Trail started up immediately for almost four miles, climbing 1,500 feet, dropping 800 feet, and then climbing another 1,000 feet to just over 3,400 feet in elevation. On top of the mountain is a ski resort that is closed in the summer, but a refreshment stand was unlocked, so I stopped inside to eat a late lunch out of the wind. The ski lift platform stood a good 20 feet above the ground, which indicated how thick the snow is during the winter and gave me an eerie feeling about what it must be like up there in the wintertime.

After 9.4 miles, the drop into the Griffin Lake tenting area was a relaxing hike compared to the steepness of the earlier trail, and it was scenic with all the surrounding mountains, but nothing prepared me for the beauty of the tranquil lake reflecting the colors of the trees and sky on the water. The Green Mountain Club maintains the area. Like many clubs along the AT, the Green Mountain Club maintains 150 miles of the Trail and several shelters and camping sites, using volunteers who do a great service to their communities and to us hikers. To help cover some costs, a camping fee of $5 per night is charged at the site, and I was glad to pay since I was benefiting from their hard work.

Several hikers were swimming in the lake, but I decided it was too cool for that, so I took the first path off the Trail to find a tenting spot. I had only gone about 50 feet when I recognized the voices of Freebyrd and Rob Ricciutti coming around a turn in the path. They were camping on a wooden pad made for tenting and had left room for me in case I showed up there. The unexpected company was enjoyable.

I awoke the following morning, Monday, August 10, to one of the most scenic views of the entire AT. The lake stretched about 400 yards on three sides with its clear, light blue water, and reflecting off the water was the multi-hued orange of the rising sun. Also reflecting perfectly, like two identical landscapes with one right side up and the other upside down, were the green trees on the other side, with the lake reaching up into the mountains to the blue sky and an occasional wisp of a white cloud that floated by. Mixed with all of that was the rising fog from the warm lake, lifting and slowly evaporating thanks to the sun's rays.

I said my goodbyes to Freebyrd and Rob, and started hiking solo again. Freebyrd and I had decided we would get back together somewhere up the Trail, but neither of us knew when or how we could do that. I was going to take five days off the Trail at North Woodstock, New Hampshire, and that would put me about 80 miles behind. However, Freebyrd planned on only hiking 10 miles a day for the next three days, which would allow me to make up about 30 of those miles. That still left me 50 miles to catch up with him. We would be entering the White

Mountains soon, and neither of us knew how fast we could hike there. I assumed that I wouldn't be able to catch him, and thus this was our final farewell. For that reason, the day was a bit of a downer for me, as I had enjoyed Freebyrd's company and liked the idea that we each could watch out for the other. Two minds are always better than one when making decisions about hiking a dangerous Trail. We both wanted to keep the other from having to wait for several days while one of us caught up on the Trail.

The day was a mixture of the good and bad, as most days on the Trail are. I woke with a bit of vertigo, but it was manageable; the weather was perfect with temperatures in the mid-60s; and the Trail had its ups and downs, but the net was a drop of about 1,000 feet in altitude. Best of all was the Trail Magic from a local hiking club providing a lunch of hot dogs, chips, apples, bananas, watermelon, and soft drinks for all hikers who came by. Sugary soft drinks are always a big bonus because a typical drink will have 100 to 200 calories, which gives an immediate "kick" to your energy level. I often found that if I was dragging with exhaustion, I could drink two soft drinks and feel an immediate recovery due to the high sugar content.

The hike of 19.1 miles into Minerva Hinchey Shelter was good but had limited views of the surrounding mountains. I had a restful night tenting near the shelter despite being nagged by vertigo, but I magically awoke Sunday morning with my head and ears clear.

After Minerva Hinchey, there is a sharp drop of over 1,000 feet to the Mill River suspension bridge over the Clarendon Gorge, and then what begins as a steep climb becomes a steady 3,000-foot ascent up Killington Peak. High winds during the last few days had caused extensive damage to many trees and, combined with the rocky landscape, they had created a web of limbs and rocks that I had to maneuver around and over on the Trail. It appeared that straight-line winds had done the damage, but every tree was knocked down with its limbs broken and twisted, and its roots torn out of the ground, leaving roots and dirt piled high. I had to walk on, or crawl over and through, a tangled mat on the ground formed by the torn-up root systems, tree trunks, limbs, leaves, and huge rocks. It was a mess!

The Trail was nonexistent in many areas, requiring me to simply crawl, climb, and hike in the general direction of the peak and hope I'd find the regular Trail at some point. It was tough going and required me to take off my pack and push it ahead of me to get over some of the toughest places. After about three hours, I finally worked my way through the "jungle" and

Freebyrd fords a river in New Hampshire.

found the Trail again, but it cost me a lot of time and energy. It was perhaps the most energy-sapping three hours of the Trail!

However, as often is the case on the Trail, the worst can turn into the best and vice versa. At one point when I was hot, tired, and needed some rest and energy, I came upon a tree with a small sign that read, "Drinks are in the stream. Help yourself. Please put empty cans in box below." And in the cold stream was one remaining can of soda. Now, diet raspberry is normally one of my least favorite drinks, but that day it was the greatest gift I could have received! I don't know how someone got canned drinks up that mountain, but they must have a great heart and love for others to carry them up those steep, ragged slopes, along with a sign and a wooden box for empties, and they obviously planned on coming back for the empty cans. Those who provided Trail Magic for us hikers must have a great reward waiting for them!

According to Matthew 25:33-35, Jesus himself said, as he was teaching about our final judgment in a life to come: ". . . and He (Jesus) will put the sheep at His right hand and the goats at the left. Then the King will say to those on His right hand, 'Come, you that are blessed by my Father, inherit the kingdom prepared for you from the foundation of the world; for I was hungry and you gave me food, I was thirsty and you gave me something to drink, I was a stranger and you welcomed me . . .'"

I arrived at Copper Lodge around six o'clock after a long day and 16 grueling miles. Built by the Vermont Forest Service in 1939, the lodge is one of the older ones on the Trail. It has several bunk beds built of old timber, and although the charts say it will sleep 16, I saw comfortable space for only about 8 people. The lodge is built of stone and has an uneven stone floor with two old picnic tables in front of two large, open windows that face the valley below. Nearby are several wooden platforms for tenting and a small spring for fresh water. I usually chose to tent, but that night I slept on one of the upper bunk beds for several reasons. First, I was too tired to put up my tent; second, the shelter was truly a four-sided building and was relatively clean; and third, it had an indoor table to cook on and a place to sit down and eat. Three other men who came in later to spend the night gave good company and small talk for the evening. We all left early the next morning; they headed south and I went north.

My first step out of the shelter the next morning caused considerable pain in my right heel, and it took most of the day to work it out by stretching and rubbing my foot and heel, and then walking through the pain. It's tough to hike even on flat ground while trying not to put your heel down, but over the rough terrain of the AT, it's nearly impossible. Fortunately, most of the pain was gone by noon, but my heel was sore for several days. I never knew what the issue was.

Hiking down from the peak, I saw bits of bark and some leaves falling from the top of a tall tree that I passed under, and I suspected it was a bear hiding. After a few general looks up into the tree, I was afraid to spend too much time there for fear, if there was a bear, he might decide to come down and check me out, so I moved on. I can only imagine how many wild animals I walked by without seeing, and what dangers could have occurred.

I entered Gifford Woods State Park about noon. Gifford Woods is a pretty park and is nicely laid out with roads that wind through the wooded camping area, and campsites on both sides made for RVs or tenting. The Trail follows some gravel roads through the middle of the campground and passes near the bathhouse. After several days in the mountains, I badly needed a shower and was excited to discover that not only was there a shower, but it had hot water. After I sat down and took my shirt and my boots off, I looked up at the wall beside the shower and discovered a little black box that I couldn't identify, so I got up for a closer look. It was a coin box with a little sign saying I needed 50 cents for five minutes to take a shower.

I all but emptied my pack, but I could only find one quarter, and there were no campers anywhere to be found whom I could ask to make change for a dollar. Disappointed, I put my clothes and boots back on and continued on my way. I found a ranger station about a mile away that not only could give me change but also had a soft drink machine. I settled on two cans of Coke and decided I'd forgo the shower, as it would have been two miles to walk back and return. Cokes are good, though—with or without a shower!

Since leaving Freebyrd, I had been hiking alone for several days with few opportunities for conversation. At midday I stopped where a southbound section hiker was eating lunch and, during the course of our conversation, after he found out I am a preacher, he shared some things he had done that destroyed his marriage, alienated his children, and cost him his job. We talked for a good while before we left, going in opposite directions. As he walked away, he wished me "happy trails," which is a common way of saying goodbye on the Trail.

I wish I had thought of a way to remind him that life is more than happy. That's aiming too low. I always attempted to tell people I passed on the Trail, "Have a blessed day," as a way to remind them that God is present. Life is much richer, deeper, and fuller than just being happy. Jesus said, in John 10:10, "I came that they might have life, and have it abundantly." This means that life is to be lived with passion and purpose. It also means that, no matter where you have been or what you have done, redemption and new life are available to everyone, including this young man, who was convinced he had ruined his life and everyone's life around him. Yes, there most often are consequences for our past actions, but Christ is about us starting life over with a clean slate and a new purpose. It's not just a promise, but a new life based on the assurance of the blood of Jesus Christ upon a cross.

In the New Testament, Timothy reminds us that our past does not define the person who we become. We are not controlled by our past unless we choose to be. We may focus on the past, but Christ is focused on the future.

2 Corinthians 5:17 says it this way: "So then, if anyone is in Christ, that person is part of the new creation. The old things have gone away, and look, new things have arrived!" And it's not just for a life to be had after we die. It is also life to be lived now!

The Trail that afternoon was filled with roots and rocks, and always going up or down, never just flat. Life is like that. I wish I'd had the words to help that young man, and I pray he has found the help he needs.

> **1 Timothy 1:12-16:** I am grateful to Christ Jesus our Lord, who has strengthened me, because He judged me faithful and appointed me to His service, even though I was formerly a blasphemer, a persecutor, and a man of violence. But I received mercy because I had acted ignorantly in unbelief, and the grace of our Lord overflowed for me with the faith and love that are in Christ Jesus. The saying is sure and worthy of full acceptance, that Christ Jesus came into the world to save sinners—of whom I am the foremost. But for that very reason I received mercy, so that in me, as the foremost, Jesus Christ might display the utmost patience, making me an example to those who would come to believe in Him for eternal life.

I stayed in bed for an extra hour the next morning, Tuesday, August 11, hoping the light rain would stop so I could cook breakfast and take down my tent without getting wet, but the rain only seemed to get stronger, so I ate a Pop-Tart while sitting in my bedroll and then braved the rain. I was soaked by noon, so I ate a candy bar for convenience rather than pulling out my stove.

Mount Moosilauke was the first of the 4,000-foot-plus elevations in the White Mountains of New Hampshire.

I had missed two meals, was thoroughly wet, and was losing my enthusiasm for hiking, so by three in the afternoon, I was glad when I came across the road to a nearby town where I could dry out and find a good restaurant. It was a two-lane, narrow, paved highway called Vermont Route 12, but it appeared to promise everything I wanted that evening: dry clothes, a hot shower, good food, and a real bed. I caught a ride into Woodstock, Vermont, with almost the first car that came by. The young man who gave me a ride dropped me about four blocks from a hotel he recommended. As I walked to the hotel, I noted a restaurant nearby and a grocery across the street, but no laundromat was in sight to dry my clothes.

The Shire Woodstock was a nice hotel with excellent customer service. The lady who checked me in told me where to eat in a nearby restaurant, not the one I had seen. When I asked if they had a washer and dryer I could use, the manager said, "Just bring all your clothes down and I'll wash them in our commercial washer and dryer. There's no sense in you walking all the way across town when we can do it for you here." Two hours later, I went down and retrieved my clothes that he had washed and carefully folded. He accepted my thanks but would not accept any pay or gratuity for his service. Again, Trail Magic is found when you may least expect it!

After walking 8–10 blocks to a nice restaurant in my clean, dry clothes, I ate a steak dinner and dessert that will rival any meal, anywhere, with the best of service. On the way back, I stopped at the grocery and bought snacks and soft drinks for the evening. I spent the rest of the evening drying out my boots with a hair dryer in the room and catching up on the news on TV. The following morning, I ate a breakfast of eggs, bacon, pancakes, and coffee at another restaurant. I couldn't have picked a better place to stop. Unfortunately for hikers and the town, it isn't mentioned strongly in any of the hiking books as a good place to zero.

Hitchhiking back to the Trail was more difficult than usual. I walked six blocks to the highway and thumbed a ride almost immediately, but the driver dropped me in the middle of nowhere with little traffic coming by. I was still three miles from the trailhead and, after 45 minutes, I had decided I'd have to hike it when a man picked me up and took me exactly where I needed to go. He also had done some hiking and knew about hitchhiking and the difficulty in that area. His name has escaped me, but I will never forget his wonderful Trail Magic.

It had rained the day before, and I was fortunate that I was near a town to dry out. Now it was sunny and only a little warmer, and I felt good to be dry and hiking again. But I learned of a new danger. Several different southbound hikers told me about a virus circulating among hikers that was causing severe stomach issues and dehydration. No one knew where it was coming from, and the health department workers were trying to isolate it. They assumed that hikers were spreading it, but they weren't sure if it was from a water source or perhaps bacteria in a shelter. I decided my previous habits of not sleeping or eating in shelters and being careful about my water sources were still the best course of action, and I would be particularly careful to stay away from people as much as I could until I'd gotten through the infected area. That evening, I slept in my tent near Happy Hill Shelter but stayed away from the shelter and used my hand sanitizer regularly. The water source was a brook near the shelter, so I was careful to go upstream past where other hikers might have gotten water, and I made sure I was in an area of fast-moving water. Better safe than sorry! The dangers of the Trail come in many varieties and require constant care and vigilance.

Early the next morning, I came out of the woods onto a small, paved road lined with homes and stayed on it until it turned into a larger road. After about two miles, I was walking beside a four-lane road heavily traveled by cars, and then, a half mile farther, I crossed the Connecticut River Bridge into my 13th state, New Hampshire. The Trail follows the sidewalks through the city of Hanover, and I hoped to find breakfast at a local restaurant and then a motel room for the night, as I planned to spend the day resting and get an early start the next morning. However, all I could find was an upscale coffee shop that advertised the names of various doughnuts and breads I didn't recognize and was occupied by students from Dartmouth College. It wasn't my "eggs over easy with toast and hash browns" kind of place, but I got coffee and a blueberry muffin anyway. The same was true of the hotels. They were upscale and not geared to the finances and needs of hikers. After asking in several businesses where I might go and getting the same answers, I stopped at a Subway for a full meal before hiking through town, across the back of the college's football practice field, and then up into the hills behind the town. I had been on city streets and sidewalks for about four miles going through the heart of Hanover and beside Dartmouth College, which was not what the Trail is normally like. It was another example of how different and diverse the wanderings of the Trail are.

Climbing out of Hanover, I met a group of about 15 Boy Scouts and 4 adult leaders going southbound. They were spread out over about half a mile, and the leaders brought up the rear.

Or so I thought, because nearly a mile behind them, I met another Scout who came off a side trail and turned northbound. He was lost. I helped him find the Trail, pointed out the white blazes for him to follow, and put him on his way. At first, he argued with me as to which way he should go, but after I assured him I had just come from Hanover, he reluctantly headed that way. I was debating with myself whether I should have followed the Scout to make sure he got to the right place when I met two other southbound hikers who assured me they would watch out for him and make sure he got to the football field where all the Scouts were supposed to meet. It goes to show how easy it is to mix up directions or get lost, even when the Trail is well marked. As a former Scoutmaster, I understand how difficult it is to keep up with a dozen young men, but it also points to the importance of a buddy system for those who are not experienced hikers.

I came upon two places where Trail Angels had left ice chests with soft drinks, which brightened the afternoon. The sight of Trail Magic lifts the spirits of a hiker who is hot, sweaty, and lonely. I appreciate every one of those who helped me on the Trail.

My right heel was sore again, so I was trying to walk carefully, and I had begun to take Aleve regularly for it and for my knees. The leather in my boots was showing signs of wear, so I had called Judy and asked her to get me another pair of boots and bring them when she came to meet me in four days in Lebanon, New Hampshire. The Trail was taking a toll on my body, my equipment, and my enthusiasm for hiking the Trail.

I camped that evening near Moose Mountain by a small stream that crossed the Trail. I didn't want to go all the way to the shelter because I didn't want to risk exposure to the virus, but I was isolated where I was. It was a beautiful place to camp, although it was only a small, somewhat flat place near the stream with the forest and the mountain rising on either side. The water was clear and cold, and the sound of the water bubbling in the stream was quiet and calming, but it also drowned out any noises that might have indicated a wild animal was near. From inside the tent, this was a bit unnerving. However, it was nice to have water right beside my cooking area, and the night was comfortable with lows in the mid-50s to low 60s.

Friday, August 14, dawned bright and hopeful, and I enjoyed sitting by the stream watching the dark of night turn to the dawn of a new day. I was up at four thirty and hiking by six. I had three climbs of over 1,000 feet each, including Smarts Mountain, at 3,200 feet; Mount Cube, at 2,911 feet; and Mount Mist, at 3,200 feet. Climbing down the mountains, I could feel the additional weight and stress on my feet and legs. All told, it was a weary day. Coming off Mount Cube is especially challenging due to its 45-degree decline. Metal rebar had been installed in some places to help the climbers, but often I would sit on my rear end and slide down the incline, hoping I wouldn't build up too much speed and start flipping end over end. Each step was a step of faith that the rock would hold and my boots wouldn't slip, but fortunately I got down safely. This was my introduction to the White Mountains, although I wasn't officially at the Whites.

A bright spot of the day came when I was greeted by a sign inviting all hikers to the home of the Ice Cream Man for ice cream and an opportunity to refill water bottles from the tap outside his home. An 80-year-old gentleman lives 50 yards off the Trail and said that, for more than 50 years, he had been giving free ice cream to hikers who came by to sit on his back porch, pitch horseshoes, or play croquet in the yard. His Trail Magic is known up and down the Trail because of his welcoming personality and giving, caring spirit.

That night, I tented near a creek a few feet off the Trail in a makeshift camping area. The gurgle of the creek was peaceful but also made me a bit nervous as the soft background noise muffled any sounds of hostile animals. Despite that, I slept solidly all night.

My boots had deep cuts in the leather and signs of wear on the toes and sides, showing the destructive effects the Trail can have on the best leather and sewing threads available. The soles were also deteriorating, reminding me of how an automobile tire wears evenly all around the tire. Like those tires, the thread was worn and causing me to slip more often as I hiked. Judy would bring my fifth pair of boots with her when she came to meet me in Lebanon, New Hampshire, in a few days, and it would be none too soon!

Cathey Leach—also known as Mama Bear and the wife of a fellow pastor, Rev. Ted Leach—thru-hiked the AT in 2014 and gave me several tips on where to stay. One place she suggested was the Hikers Welcome Hostel in Glencliff, New Hampshire. The hostel was formerly someone's home and has a gathering room with a large collection of tables for hikers to lounge around. This room serves many purposes, including registration, reading, video and TV, Internet, and dining. Outside are several picnic tables, an outdoor shower room surrounded by canvas curtains, and a large tent that has about 10 beds arranged close together. All facilities are available on a first-come, first-served basis with men and women occupying each one equally. I slept in the tent on a bed with no sheets or blankets except my bedroll, and spread the contents of my pack either at the foot of the bed or on the floor beside me. It was close quarters, to say the least, but not bad for $20 a night. About six that evening, an order was placed with a local pizza restaurant, and I got a large pepperoni pizza delivered to my picnic table out back. It was nothing exotic or overly done, but I was out of the rain and cold, and away from most wildlife. Six skunks wandered throughout the backyard all evening, and we gave them free rein, including the time they decided to check out the inside of our sleeping area.

Mount Moosilauke is the first of many mountains called the Whites. Rising to 4,802 feet, it is steep and dangerous on the north side and is the first alpine mountain, extending above the tree line, that northbounders encounter. The Trail on the north side rises from North Woodstock and follows a stream that cascades down the mountain for several thousand feet. The spray from the stream and any rain can make the north side slick; if not for the use of rebar, wooden blocks, and rock steps cut into the mountain, the Trail would be impassable for most hikers. A slip or fall could cost a hiker his or her life. For these reasons, many hikers, including myself, chose to back-slack from North Woodstock to the hostel at Glencliff so we could climb up the steep slope rather than risk trying to find toeholds going down, where one slip could mean catastrophic injury.

I rose early Sunday and was driven an hour away to North Woodstock for the recommended back-slack. I left most of my gear at the hostel in order to lighten my load, which turned out to be a good decision. The climb up Mount Moosilauke was every bit as difficult as I had been told it would be, and several times I realized that not only was I in danger of badly hurting myself, but I was endangering my life with every step on the slick rock. Occasionally, when I came to a place where I could safely stop and look, I admired God's handiwork in the mountains and cliffs immediately around me, as well as the stream and what seemed like a continuous waterfall cascading down the mountain only a few feet away.

After several hours of hard climbing, I reached the mountaintop, where I found a celebration going on for those who had climbed up from the north side. Forming the nucleus of the party were perhaps 20 section hikers who had climbed the mountain from other directions, which were easier. They provided companionship and all kinds of food and treats, including brownies, chips, cookies, Cokes, and beer. I discovered some had climbed there simply to provide Trail Magic for us on the AT, which was greatly appreciated, although I couldn't fathom drinking anything alcoholic that would impair my abilities on the mountain.

Ice Cream Man enjoys hosting hikers.

The mountaintop was above the tree line and covered by large rocks that had to be navigated by stepping from one to another. I sat on some of those rocks while I rested and ate my share of the goodies others had brought, and then I started down the mountain toward Glencliff. I was on a mission, one I was glad to be on finally! I was headed down the mountain about 5.5 miles to the hostel, where I had arranged for someone to drive me into Lebanon, and Judy would arrive the next day for our vacation time together.

The climb down wasn't bad, and it would have been a relatively easy climb up for those who didn't back-slack; it was long and high but not particularly steep, although the climb down the other side was difficult and dangerous. I was counting the miles to Glencliff, looking forward to being off the Trail for six days, and hoping all our plans would come together.

I was now 390 miles from Mount Katahdin in Maine, having hiked 1,794 miles from Springer Mountain. Eighty-two percent of the Trail was done! But I had no idea how tough the Whites would be. Right then, I was focused on meeting Judy the following day and spending the next four days together. I would try my best to push the difficulties of the Trail out of my mind and simply enjoy the moment.

The following is a note I left Judy about the Trail to give more insights to those on her email list while I was hiking: "Wearing layers of clothing is recommended, so I will wear a short-sleeved and a long-sleeved shirt, a light pullover sweater, and then a jacket that doubles for cold weather and/or rain, adding or taking off however much is comfortable. I wear pants with zip-off legs that make into shorts, and I add long johns when it's really cold. Good waterproof boots and two pair of socks are my staple; others prefer running shoes. I routinely change socks every five miles and hang the wet ones on the back of my pack to dry. Heavy perspiration is a constant regardless of the temperature from the extreme exercise of hiking carrying my 38-pound pack, so all of my clothes are continually wet. I carry one extra pair of tights and another long-sleeved shirt to sleep in so I can be dry at night. They also serve as extra clothing in case I tear or damage any of the ones I regularly wear. My wet clothes are hung out to dry during the night, but they rarely dry due to fog and heavy dew. Cold, wet clothes are not the thing anyone relishes putting on in the morning when temperatures can be near freezing, but they quickly warm up after hiking for a few minutes."

Copper Lodge is one of the oldest shelters.

INTERMISSION FOUR

Timeout before the Big Push

 After checking in at my hotel in Lebanon, showering, and making myself somewhat presentable, I went down to the lobby and ate dinner at the bar. A man whose name I cannot recall was sitting at a table next to me, and we began a conversation that primarily consisted of his asking me questions about the Trail. After about 30 minutes, just before he left, the gentleman shared that he was in town to receive a kidney transplant the following morning. I was struck by his interest in me and in hiking when I would have expected him to be locked in on his own health, the surgery he would have the next day, and all the possible consequences and dangers such as rejection of the kidney. After he left, I finished my meal and prepared to go to my room by asking for my bill. The waitress said the man had paid my bill and said to tell me it was simply Trail Magic. This gentleman who was getting a transplant was still thinking of others by paying for my meal! I didn't know who he was, nor did I know how to thank him, but I will never forget him even though I'll never know his name.

 The scripture that fits this stranger has to be Romans 12:13: "Share with God's people who are in need. Practice hospitality."

I spent the next day getting ready for Judy's arrival. I got up late compared to what I had been used to—seven thirty! Then I took care of all the little things such as washing my clothes, drying my equipment, checking each item to see if it needed to be discarded and replaced, and then relaxing and anticipating my lovely bride's arrival that afternoon. The motel room was a mess, as I had all my equipment strung across every conceivable chair and lamp to dry, but I was clean, dry, warm, and had every type of snack available to eat. I was impatient for Judy to arrive, but right then all the world was good! In the afternoon, I got a ride in the hotel van to a car rental place and picked up a car to use for the next four days.

Judy had flown out of Memphis and arrived late that Sunday, August 16. She flew in on a small, twin-engine Cessna owned by Cape Air, and the young, female pilot not only flew the plane, but she helped each passenger out of the plane and opened the cargo door and retrieved their luggage. Judy picked up her luggage planeside and met me inside the terminal. It was great to see her. We had talked or texted every day, sometimes more than once, but holding her in my arms was a dream come true. We were finally back together, even if it was only for a few days.

The following four days are a blur to me. We spent each day touring the area, particularly places where I had crossed a road or visited while hiking. One day, we went to the north side of Mount Moosilauke and walked up the Trail as far as Judy could go, which wasn't very far, unfortunately, since she was still nursing her broken ankle.

Judy shared in an email with friends about part of her trip: "We ventured out Wednesday and drove about 75 miles to Marshfield Station in New Hampshire to ride the 'Cog Train' up Mount Washington, which took one hour to get to the top at 5 mph. Due to the heights, weather, and terrain, there are no trees or vegetation starting about two-thirds of the way to the top, only rocks and boulders. It was great scenery on the way up, but then the fog and clouds obscured any scenery as we neared the top, along with 50 mph winds at an elevation of 6,288 feet. This mountain is in the heart of the White Mountain National Forest and is the highest summit in the northeastern US."

As we rode up the mountain and I saw where I would be hiking in a few days, with the bare rocks and boulders, and the sheer expanse of the Whites, the expression I kept muttering over and over was, "Oh my gosh. Oh my gosh!" At the time, I couldn't imagine having to climb over those mountains. A few days later, I wished I could quickly get over them!

Judy emailed about her trip home: "Saturday was my return to Tennessee and Dennis returning to the AT. The first (planned) leg of my flight home was (to be) from Lebanon to Boston on a small, eight-seat plane. I just happened to check my phone at 4:45 a.m. when we got up and had a message from Cape Air that due to the fog, my flight was canceled out of Lebanon and to find alternate transportation, mentioning the Dartmouth charter bus left at 5:20 a.m. Panic set in as I quickly finished packing, called the front desk, got information on the charter bus, took the hotel van, Dennis at my side, and arrived to buy my ticket with five minutes to spare before the bus left. Made it to Boston with time to spare, but on the last leg in Charlotte had a two-hour delay due to mechanical problems, made it to Memphis finally, and then home sweet home!!"

Judy made it home safely, but we did not have the long goodbye I had wanted. Five weeks would pass before I would see her again.

I was 390 miles from Mount Katahdin, and it was time again to focus my mind and body on reaching that goal before the Trail closed in Baxter State Park on October 15.

From left: Freebyrd, Drop Bear, and Preacher summited Saddleback Junior in Maine at 3,655 feet.

CHAPTER EIGHTEEN

Challenging Mount Washington

    Midmorning on Saturday, August 22, after dropping Judy at the bus station and checking out of the motel, I caught a ride to the North Woodstock, New Hampshire, trailhead, at an elevation of 1,870 feet. Five days had gone by quickly, but I needed that time off the Trail to regain my strength and stamina. Now I needed to concentrate on hiking and all that it entailed, and somehow put behind me, at least for a while, my constant desire to be with Judy and our family and friends. I had to focus and not allow my mind to wander or my willpower to waver before my final ascent on Mount Katahdin in a few weeks.

    The climb out of the valley is steep for the first mile but then flattens out a little on the way up Mount Wolf, which has an elevation of 3,478 feet. Starting late and carrying a restocked, heavy pack slowed me down considerably, so I was only able to hike 7.5 miles to the Eliza Brook Shelter that afternoon, and I camped near the shelter. I had not yet discovered that I would have trouble hiking over 10 miles a day due to the difficulty of walking on boulders rather than a path, the extreme weather conditions of cold and high winds, the scarcity of camping spots, and the sheer steepness of the mountains.

The White Mountain National Forest is strict about protecting the fragile vegetation in the area, and camping is rigidly restricted to designated sites, none of which are in the alpine areas. This made my decisions about how far to hike each day more difficult, and my average daily mileage suffered immensely over the next few weeks. The following day, despite getting up early and pushing myself, I was able to hike only 11 miles and tented at the Liberty Springs Tent Site. The terrain was so steep and hazardous that I often went down inclines by sitting down and scooting on the slick rocks.

Hiking the Whites was definitely more difficult than any of the other mountains I had climbed. I made the following note to myself that illustrates the elevation changes on most days: "Today started out early with a climb up South Kinsman Mountain, 4,358 feet, dropped to 1,450 feet and climbed the North Kinsman Mountain, 4,293 feet."

Another day, I noted: "Very little flat terrain; you are either going straight up or straight down. Climbed the following with valleys in between each one: Haystack Mountain, 4,800 feet; Mount Lincoln, 5,089 feet; Mount Lafayette, 5,260 feet; and Mount Garfield, 4,500 feet."

I was experiencing the White Mountains in all their glory but needed to adjust to being above the tree line in an alpine climate, continually dealing with strong winds, and hiking where the Trail seemed more like a rock pile, and I found it difficult to even distinguish where it was. It was like God had created all these rocks ranging in size from a basketball to a large car and threw them up in the air, and they landed in a pile we now call the White Mountains. I had to learn to step from boulder to boulder and adjust my stride to account for the fact that the wind was gusting up to 50 miles per hour and trying to blow me in any direction except the one I was going. With one misstep, my foot and leg could go down between the boulders and break something. Much of the Trail is like that for some 150 miles in the Whites, or until I was well into Maine. New Hampshire is not fun!

Temperatures dropped both during the day and especially at night, so Judy had brought my winter clothes along with a new pair of boots. I also had swapped out my summer bedroll for my winter bedroll, which is rated down to 10 degrees. The wind chill was always below freezing, even during the day.

Another email Judy sent to friends after talking with me said: "Dennis got up at four thirty. Hiked to Franconia Ridge, foggy, but when the sun hits, you can look down and see the valleys below. It is windy, and when the clouds lift, you can see the ridges above. During the climbs, Dennis saw one of the 'huts' in this area for hikers and stopped for water and a break. Weather cleared off and was a great day where you could see for miles. Hiked 10.3 miles today and stayed in the Galehead Hut on the floor, 3,800 feet in elevation. Dennis decided to work for his stay, which made for a short sleep night. The gathering room on the floor was the room where Dennis and the others doing the work exchange slept after washing dishes and cleaning up. Quiet time was to start at nine, but not everyone went by the rules and they talked until after eleven, and the path to the bathroom came through their room, with people up and down all night. Not a restful night."

Huts are large, enclosed sleep lodges that are sized for 36 to 90 people and are open with full service from June to early September with a crew staff. Rates range from $98 to $118, depending on the day, Appalachian Mountain Club (AMC) membership, and the hut. An overnight stay includes bunk space, pillow, blanket, bathroom privileges, and potable water. Thru-hikers can also do "work exchange" at the huts, working two hours for their food and space on the floor to sleep. With the extreme conditions, this is a welcome respite for hikers with no areas to tent above the tree line in these mountains.

Another email from Judy on Tuesday, August 25, said: "Dennis was up at five and climbed the South Twin Mountain in the first hour, elevation of 4,902 feet. Four and a half hours later, he came to the Zealand Falls Hut. Stopped and ate a hot meal of lentil soup (two bowls and bread for $3), and topped off water supply. Rained off and on all day. More and more difficult to find a place to tent with the rough terrain and protected areas. Finished the day with 14.7 miles and made it to an AMC lodge at Crawford Notch State Park, elevation of 1,277 feet. This was the location for his supply drop from home. Dennis was able to secure an individual room with a 'queen-sized bed, ahhhhhhh!!!' After the night before, this was heaven! They didn't have a washing machine, so he had to wash out all his clothes by hand and hang them in his room to dry overnight."

On Wednesday, August 26, I began my day-and-a-half ascent on Mount Washington, which is the tallest mountain in the Northeast at 6,288 feet. The weather there is perhaps the most undependable and dangerous of any place on the AT, as severe changes can occur without notice within minutes. Normal weather reports are useless because the mountains make their own weather patterns. Winds are always high, and the highest recorded wind speed of 231 miles per hour was recorded in 1934. All hikers are warned to turn back at the first sign of bad weather, as there are no places to seek shelter and no quick ways to get off the mountain. Many hikers have died on the mountain!

The climb out of Pinkham Notch is steep, at 2,700 feet in four miles, and often follows along a ledge where the views are almost straight down to the magnificent valleys below. Judy made the following notes after talking with me: "Terrain was steep and straight up, starting with the Webster Cliffs at 3,250 feet; then on to Mount Webster; 3,910 feet; Mount Jackson, 4,052 feet; Mount Pierce, 4,312 feet; and Mount Franklin, 5,004 feet. All of these mountains are leading up to the tallest, Mount Washington. As he climbs, the temperatures are getting cooler and 60 percent chance of rain. His feet are doing much better with the new boots, but with all the rocks and boulders, it makes your steps uneven and hiking difficult. Finished the day with 11.5 rough miles and sore legs. Camped 1.9 miles from the top of Mount Washington at Lakes of the Clouds Hut. Dennis said there were no less than 110 hikers packed into a roughly 3,000-square-foot building, counting all the spaces in the hut. Fog out tonight and cool. Sleeping on the floor."

Psalm 139:7-8: Where can I flee from your presence? If I ascend to heaven, you are there.

I got up before daylight, by about four, and was met with a fantastic view of the mountains, sky, and stars of the dawning morning. It appeared I would have a beautiful, clear but cool morning for my final ascent on Mount Washington and for the rest of the day—wrong! I decided to eat breakfast on the top of the mountain, so with only 1.9 miles to climb, I began my hike. Stepping from rock to rock with a headlamp to see by isn't ideal but, as the sun came up, the skyline turned various shades of orange and then red. The sun rose directly behind Mount Washington from where I was hiking. It was a glorious and magnificent sight promising a wonderful day on the top of the world!

I had momentarily forgotten that the weather can and will change drastically within minutes on the mountain. Just as I topped the mountain, the fog rolled in like a curtain, shutting down all visibility more than 40 feet away. The winds were steady at 30 miles per hour with gusts nearing 50 miles per hour, and the temperature was about 40 degrees and dropping rapidly. I had reached a milestone in my hike, and an emotional one, too, bringing tears of joy and accomplishment, but it came with the price of bone-chilling winds and poor visibility. I was already wearing double clothes, an all-weather jacket, heavy gloves, and a ski mask covering my entire head and face, but the cold and wind cut through everything I was wearing.

Fortunately, there is a large building on top of the mountain that provides shelter, food, souvenirs, and, most important for me right then, an opportunity to get out of the weather. I stopped in the main building for an hour to warm up and wait for the little food store to open so I could eat breakfast. The coffee wasn't ready, but the hot chocolate was wonderful, along with a couple of prepackaged cinnamon rolls. It wasn't a great breakfast, but I was out of the wind and warm while eating, and I had warm water in the men's room, where I tried to wash a little sweat off my head and brushed my teeth standing at a real sink.

After a bit of rest, I stepped back into the cold wonderland and began my trek down Mount Washington. The fog was heavy, the wind was hollering, and the terrain was treacherous and steep. (As I was discovering, so what else is new in the Whites?) At times I found the Trail difficult to see, as it isn't well defined but rather has cairns, or rocks stacked in a pyramid, every 20 to 100 yards to mark the way. Occasionally, the fog rolled out long enough that I could glimpse God's majesty of one mountain range cascading behind another that seemed to reach forever.

Six miles later, I stopped for lunch of more soup and bread at Madison Spring Hut, at 4,800 feet. I sat at a picnic table inside the hut to eat and change out of my wet boot socks. Not a very appetizing sight, as I ate and changed socks at the same time, but when you're hungry and cold, you do both simultaneously—it's just normal on the Trail! By midafternoon, light rain had begun to fall, changing into sleet and then snow and a bit of hail while I was above the tree line and in the wind. And visibility was diminishing! The conditions got so bad that, for the first time while on the Trail, I began to look for any place to hunker down and wait out the storm, but I was exposed to the elements. Despite the additional danger of snow and ice, I was forced to continue down the mountain. The elevation that day had changed from nearly 6,300 feet on Mount Washington to 4,800 feet at Madison Spring Hut, then down to 3,900 feet and back up again to 5,366 feet on Mount Madison, before dropping to 2,540 feet at the Osgood Tentsite. All of that was over 10.1 miles! It was a memorable day for me and, fortunately, I was not injured in any way despite the winds, weather, and elevation changes. God is good!

On the way down toward the Osgood Tentsite, I passed a young couple who also had come from Mount Washington that day. They had hitched a ride up the mountain on the road that leads to the top and then hiked down with minimal provisions BUT ALSO WERE CARRYING A 10-MONTH-OLD CHILD! The father called himself an experienced hiker and held the infant in a baby carrier attached to his chest. They had gone through the same weather and Trail conditions I had, and they saw nothing wrong with what they had done. I tried to point out that if the man had fallen while coming down the mountain, he would have landed on the baby. Neither parent seemed the least bit aware that they had endangered their infant. As diplomatically as I could, I suggested this was not the place to bring a baby, but evidently they neither understood nor seemed offended. So many people go out on the AT thinking they understand the difficulty and dangers of the Trail and then place themselves and others in harm's way. I don't think anyone can attempt the AT and be completely ready and knowledgeable, but I hope no one else tries taking a baby on one of the most dangerous sections of the Trail.

The Osgood Tentsite is a no-fee, designated camping area with three 10-by-10-foot wooden tenting platforms and a privy provided by the US Forest Service. Its water source is a small stream nearby, where I used a one-quart plastic milk carton that I had cut the top out of, leaving the small finger-hold to dip water from streams or water holes that were too shallow for my water filter. I would dip water using the milk jug and pour a bit of water into my filter, and then repeat the process until I had filled the water bottle, always a long, tedious task.

I arrived at the camping area exhausted but forced myself to cook and eat dinner rather than going straight to bed. I was finally below the tree line again and out of the wind, which was a great relief. The rain and sleet had stopped, and I was beginning to think I might make it over the Whites after all. I slept soundly despite the cold and felt grateful to be out of the mud and up on a tenting platform, which was dry and flat. Morning came early, and my dehydrated eggs and ham, as usual, had no discernible taste and were difficult to swallow, but I made myself eat most of the bag of food.

I had been so intent on just getting through the day before that I had not paid close attention to what came next on the Trail. I was pleasantly surprised the next morning to walk into the Pinkham Notch Visitor Center and find a full restaurant and supply store. I had eaten breakfast only two hours and 4.8 miles earlier, but I "forced down" (don't believe that!) a wonderful hoagie and fries and drank three Cokes. In the supply shop, I found a mouthpiece for my water bladder to replace the one I had lost several days before. I was fortunate that I was able to keep my equipment replenished and in relatively good condition for most of the hike. I saw many others who were not so fortunate.

Later, as was always the case, I had to force myself to leave the warmth of the lodge and venture out into the wilderness, climbing 2,000 feet up Wildcat Mountain and then Mount Hight, where I tented for the night. Judy wrote in her journal for me: "Temperatures are really dropping. Dennis finally found a tent site beside the Trail, was in his tent, and bedded in his winter sleeping bag with several layers of clothes on and said the arm holding the phone as he was talking to me was freezing so would talk with me the next day. He also is wearing his ski mask to bed at night. A total of 13 miles today."

The following are journal entries that Judy made each day after talking with me. I have copied them as she wrote them. Some people may recognize them, as Judy also sent them to a number of friends who were keeping up with my hike via her emails.

Saturday, August 29: "Dennis woke today with more mountains to go up . . . and down . . . and back up and down each time . . . throughout the day. The mountains today were steeper than normal. With each step, Dennis had to find toeholds and fingerholds on the way down the slabs of rocks and boulders on the mountains. Today's mountains included Carter Dome—4,832 feet, Zeta Pass—3,890 feet, South Carter Mountain—4,458 feet, Middle Carter Mountain—4,610 feet, North Carter Mountain—4,539 feet, and Mount Moriah—4,049 feet. As Dennis got off the Trail and neared the White Mountain Lodge & Hostel around Gorham, New Hampshire (780 feet), the Maine Appalachian Trail Club that maintains 267.2 miles from Grafton Notch, New Hampshire, to Katahdin, Maine, provided Trail Magic of grilled hamburgers and Cokes to hikers. A staff member at the hostel also took hikers into town to Walmart that night to replenish their backpack supplies. Time to bed down for the night . . . room was 10 by 10 feet with about 18 inches between beds where hikers slept. It helps that you are so tired that you are asleep by the time your head hits the bed! Thirteen miles today."

Sunday, August 30: Dennis "had a good breakfast at the hostel and then back on the trail. Mountains today have been a little easier. Mount Hayes—2,555 feet, Cascade Mountain—2,631 feet, Mount Success—3,565 feet, and lakes and ponds in the valleys. About 2:30 p.m., Dennis stopped by the trail for a pita bread/Nutella plus peanut butter for extra calories for lunch.

Weather is starting to get a little cooler and the days shorter. Spending the night at Carlo Col Shelter—2,945 feet. Dennis is two-tenths of a mile into his 14th and last state of Maine. A total of 17 miles hiked today."

Equipment

Perhaps a hiker's greatest decisions are about what type of equipment to carry. Every hiker has to make compromises between what might be useful and the factor we all try to minimize . . . weight. An idea of what I would carry includes the following: Backpack, tent, bedroll, sleeping pad, propane stove, first aid kit, personal hygiene items, water, water filter, two hiking poles, broad-brimmed hat, two-inch pocketknife, NO weapons, DEET, a small plastic bag to carry out garbage ("no trace left behind"), headlamp and a small spare flashlight, clothes, food, Bible, etc. Total weight is 30 pounds plus about 8 pounds of food.

Food

It is estimated that the average hiker burns between 4,000 and 8,000 calories a day. High-energy food, and lots of it, is a necessity each day, so preparations and care are required. During my last hike of 900 miles over two months, I lost 25 pounds, and I was determined to eat better this time. It is nearly impossible to eat enough to avoid losing weight . . . but I try. Typically, breakfast is dehydrated eggs and ham or oatmeal; lunch and dinner are chosen from about 20 varieties of dehydrated meals purchased from specialty stores such as REI; added to these are two hot chocolate packets mixed with hot water (for breakfast), two large candy bars, two Justin's peanut butter pouches, and two Probars during the day. These total about 3,400 calories per day. I also take advantage of every little store, restaurant, and grocery store I happen to pass while crossing roads and highways. Also, I generally eat four meals each day while zeroing.

ABOVE: The weather on Mount Washington was all that it promised on the sign. Dennis experienced rain, sunshine, fog, sleet, snow, and high winds.

LEFT: Freebyrd (left) and Preacher (right) thank Fat Man Walking (center) for Trail Magic.

The first sighting of Mount Katahdin was impressive in the distance.

CHAPTER NINETEEN
The Final Steps

Monday, August 31:

    I had hiked into Maine the night before but backtracked about 100 yards to a place I'd seen that was flat enough to pitch my tent. I wanted to go to sleep that night telling myself I had officially reached my 14th and last state. There wasn't any water, but it was already well after dark and my map didn't show any better prospects for the night, so I trampled some weeds and brush and pitched my tent. I had just settled down in my bedroll when someone called out from the nearby Trail announcing he was a hiker and not a wild animal, which is always nice to hear from within your tent when you can't see outside but can hear something thrashing about nearby.

    I asked his name, and he replied, "Alabama."

    "My name is Preacher," I called back.

    "Are you really a real preacher?" he asked.

    I replied, "Yes, from Tennessee. Are you really from Alabama?"

    "Yes," he said, and after a short pause he added, "and pray for me, please." And he was gone.

I immediately knew something wasn't right. I wished that I had offered to pray right then, and I did so silently, but we weren't finished with our conversation yet, because the next morning, I found Alabama asleep in his bedroll in the middle of the Trail about a mile from where I'd camped. The Trail was only about 20 inches wide, so I had to step around him to get by. I tried not to wake him up, but about 20 minutes later, a voice laughingly called out from behind me, "I smell something awful. It must be Tennessee!"

Alabama had grown up in the church, but during a hitch in the Army, he had "strayed," as he put it, and he had been out of formalized church for about 10 years. We had an almost continuous conversation that day where I heard his confession and a desire to follow Christ again. One of the most powerful ways that I saw Christ on the Trail was in the way that God was working His grace and love in that man. I pray that he continues to grow in Christ.

I had gotten up at five thirty and headed out by six thirty. The temperature was warm, around 60 degrees, and the day was breezy, as always. My hike on the Trail that day included Mount Carlo, which was 3,565 feet at the highest point; Goose Eye Mountain East Peak, at 3,765 feet; Goose Eye Mountain North Peak, at 3,790 feet; Fulling Mill Mountain South Peak, at 3,395 feet; Mahoosuc Notch Trail West End, at 2,400 feet; Mahoosuc Notch East End, at 2,150 feet; and Old Speck Trail/Grafton Loop Trail from 3,985 feet to Grafton Notch at 1,495 feet.

Mahoosuc Notch is famous for having ice in the deep crevices, keeping the temperatures below freezing throughout the year, and I often could look down between large boulders and see ice 20 to 50 feet below me. Many call these boulders—which hikers must scramble under, around, over, and between—the most difficult mile on the Trail. It wasn't the most difficult in my estimation, but it was among the slowest due to the narrow crevices, low "tunnels" under huge rocks that required me to take off my pack and push it ahead of me, and the fact that the Trail generally follows the valley rather than white blazes, making it difficult to know where to go. The entire mile is a step valley where landslides have left rocks and boulders of every size piled randomly at the bottom, as if someone had knocked over a bunch of building blocks that tumbled every which way. The Trail snakes its way through the huge boulders rather than going over or around them. Alabama and I hiked most of the day together, and it was really helpful to have two of us pulling and pushing our packs through some of the smaller holes in the rocks that we had to literally pass through on the Trail.

I had been texting with Freebyrd for several days and had been hiking feverishly to catch up with him. I hadn't seen him for several weeks, but about noon, he texted that he was approximately 10 miles ahead of me. I had cut some 50 or 60 miles down between us, so it was good to know he'd be waiting along with Fat Man Walking at Grafton Notch in Fat Man's van. Freebyrd owned a cabin near Andover, so we would zero there and then continue together to Mount Katahdin, some 267 miles away. Alabama decided he needed to press on, so he declined the invitation to join us. I did not meet Alabama again but often wonder what the Lord had in mind for him. I had hiked a difficult 14 miles that day.

Note: Fat Man Walking gave himself that Trail name because he initially, in his words, "was so fat." By the time I met him, he had lost a good bit of weight and no longer fit that description, and he could outwalk most hikers, but he kept the nickname because so many hikers now knew him by that name.

Freebyrd's cabin is on the slope of a mountain overlooking a huge valley and other mountains in the distance. It has two bedrooms, bunks off the great room that sleep four, a full kitchen and breakfast room, indoor plumbing, and a nice fireplace. Wrapping around half the cabin is a wide porch where we loved to sit and look at the sunset and the mountains. Electricity was supplied by a 12-volt system that ran only minimal lighting and got its power from solar panels and a battery system. Freebyrd's hospitality provided a great place to rest and replenish our tired bodies. During the four nights we stayed there, seven other hikers stayed at least one night. Freebyrd had met these hikers on the Trail and invited them to stay with him. This was his way of providing Trail Magic for me and the others, even as he himself was hiking.

Even when we do a good job of informing our loved ones at home, we can't control the circumstances in which they hear our news. After Freebyrd invited me to zero at his cabin, I texted Judy to tell her what I'd be doing and that Freebyrd had said there would not be cell phone service at the cabin. I had gotten to know Freebyrd and fully trusted him, so I assumed Judy would feel comfortable with my plans and be glad I was getting good rest and plenty of food. However, no one can anticipate how the subconscious mind will work, because that night Judy had a nightmare about me that resembled the movie *Deliverance*. You may remember the 1972 film starring Burt Reynolds in which four businessmen from Atlanta canoe down the Cahulawassee River in rural Georgia and encounter crazed men who are out to kill them. It's a horrifying nightmare of twists and turns in which several characters die. In Judy's dream, Freebyrd took me unsuspectingly out to "his cabin in the woods," and I became a victim of foul play. Fortunately, I had cell service the next morning when we went to town, and I was safe, much to Judy's relief. I've never known Judy to react that way, but she said the dream was so real that she couldn't shake the feeling that something had happened to me. She was really upset! It's good to reaffirm one is loved but not at the expense of scaring one's best friend. I'm also glad that my experience at Freebyrd's did not resemble her dream.

Fat Man drove us in his van several times to buy supplies from the small Andover General Store in town; to eat at the only restaurant nearby, the Little Red Hen Diner; and to and from the Trail. After a day of rest, we decided to slack-pack the next day. This means we took only food and water for the day, greatly lightening the load from our normal 40-pound backpacks, and hiked for the day but returned to the cabin for the night. Fat Man drove us to Surplus Pond on the Trail, and we hiked 12 miles back to Grafton Notch, where he met us later that afternoon. Soon after starting to hike, we spotted our first moose wading in a pond several hundred yards away, which was fun to see. We climbed Baldpate Mountain West Peak, with an elevation of 3,662 feet, and Baldpate Mountain East Peak, at 3,810 feet. It was good to get 12 miles "the easier way." We also met Drop Bear from Australia again and invited her back to the cabin.

The next day, we again met Mado, who joined us at Freebyrd's cabin, and it felt like a reunion of hikers we had met previously on the Trail. We slack-packed again but this time went north from Surplus Pond Road to South Arm Road near Andover. We took a shorter hike because rain was coming in, and we enjoyed the cabin and friends gathered there. We only hiked eight miles, but it was a good break and a long-needed breather.

The new hiking boots Judy had brought me in Hanover had threads breaking near the toes after only 170 miles, and Judy was put on the alert for another pair. She called REI, which shipped replacement boots to my next supply point at no charge. I also had worn out a good pair of hiking pants, so I replaced them with a new pair. Most of my equipment was starting to wear badly, and I hoped my pants would last until I reached Mount Katahdin.

Friday, September 4, came early. Five of us were still together at the cabin, so after eating pancakes for breakfast, we all helped shut down the cabin before Drop Bear, Mado, Freebyrd, and I crowded into Fat Man's van and set off for South Arm Road. The mountains we climbed that day included Old Blue Mountain, at an elevation of 3,600 feet, which was a 2,200-foot climb starting out; Bemis Stream Trail, at 3,350 feet; and Bemis Range West Peak, at 3,580 feet. The weather was cooler, and we sensed that winter wasn't far away. I added a layer of clothes when we all bedded down for the night in our tents at the Bemis Stream ford, at an elevation of 1,495 feet. We had hiked 12 miles that day. The hardness of the ground, the coolness, and the closeness of the tent quickly reminded me I was no longer in Freebyrd's comfortable cabin!

Sometime during the night, I woke up to the sound of something walking by my tent. I couldn't tell what it was, but it sounded close. It could be anything from a skunk or raccoon to a deer or even a bear. I called out, hoping to scare the animal away, and the noise stopped for perhaps 30 seconds. When it continued, I scrambled to find my flashlight, unzip my bedroll, unzip the inner mosquito netting on my tent, and finally unzip the outer flap and crawl out of my tent, a routine that usually takes about one to two minutes. When I got out, I shone my flashlight around and could find nothing. Everyone else in tents within 50 yards appeared to be asleep so, seeing and hearing nothing, I got back into my tent. About the time I got comfortable, I heard an animal walking near my tent again. By now, I was alarmed and conscious that the animal wasn't going away easily, so out of my tent I went again. Nothing! This time, I turned off my light and stood there silently. Sure enough, in about a minute, the animal came back. To my great surprise and the source of many laughs since, it was a small, green tree toad jumping erratically in every direction as if it were on steroids! It was jumping on the dead leaves and sounded exactly like an animal walking. I chased it away and, tired as I was, I went back to sleep quickly, with the mystery solved and no bears that night.

All of us woke up by five thirty and followed our normal routines of eating, filtering water, rolling up bedrolls, taking down tents, putting on boots, etc. Then we each hiked out alone, knowing we might not see each other that day or tent near each other that evening. Each of us was doing our own hike and if it coordinated with someone else, so be it. Freebyrd and I, however, were keeping up with each other by text because we hoped to summit together in a few weeks.

The terrain had changed somewhat—not so much in altitude, but with lots of exposed roots due to the hikers traveling along the narrow path. The roots made hiking more difficult and required us to look at our feet to keep from falling, rather than checking out the beautiful

Welcome to Baxter State Park, the location of Mount Katahdin.

landscapes we were walking past, such as Moxie Pond, at an elevation of 2,400 feet; Long Pond, at 2,330 feet; Little Swift River Pond, at 2,460 feet; and South Pond, at 2,174 feet. I noticed a regional difference in terminology. In the South, we have lakes and ponds. In Maine, there are no lakes; everything is called a pond even though some of those "ponds" may be miles across.

That evening, for a cost of $20 each, Freebyrd and I stayed at the Hiker Hut, a hostel near Rangeley, Maine, at an elevation of 1,700 feet. The Hiker Hut is owned by Steve Lynch and his wife, who offered excellent hospitality. Steve also provided transportation into town for meals and supplies, so we accepted a ride and ate a good meal at one of the local restaurants. After dinner, we crowded into a small cabin that had one light and no heat, but it was comfortable, out of the wind, and there were no lumps (rocks) under our bedrolls. Drop Bear came into camp an hour later and elected to stay in her tent to save money even though there was a cabin just for women. We had hiked 14 miles that day.

The following morning, Steve drove us up the mountain and dropped us a mile and a half from the Trail on Barham Stream Logging Road. We slack-packed 15 miles over Sandy River, at an elevation of 1,595 feet; Eddy Pond, at 2,616 feet; Saddleback Mountain, at 4,120 feet; and Saddleback Junior, at 3,655 feet. Temperatures were in the high 60s, and the views were amazing. Since we were in the alpines most of the time, we could see forever with lakes scattered around the mountains and tree lines. Back at the Hiker Hut that night, we were surprised to find that a nearby hostel provided Trail Magic for all hikers in the area, with cooked ribs and all the trimmings. Steve drove us over and stayed for the meal. Among the 20 to 30 hikers eating dinner, I spotted several familiar faces whom I had seen along the trail. It is amazing the camaraderie and community built around the Trail and those who hike it.

I started the next day by suffering a yellow jacket sting on my ring finger, which bothered me for most of the day. The swelling below my ring particularly worried me, and I wondered what would happen if it should cut off my circulation. Fortunately, that didn't happen, but the sting reminded me that a small problem can turn into something big or even life-threatening on the Trail. The weather cooperated, with slightly windy conditions and the temperatures in the 60s to 80s depending on the elevation of each mountain: Orbeton Stream ford, at 1,500 feet; Lone Mountain, at 3,260 feet; Mount Abraham Trail, at 3,140 feet; Spaulding Mountain, at 4,000 feet; Sugarloaf Mountain Trail, at 3,540 feet; Caribou Valley Road, at 2,220 feet; Crocker

Cirque, at 2,710 feet; South Crocker Mountain, at 4,040 feet; and North Crocker Mountain, at 4,228 feet.

Freebyrd and I spent the night in the "luxury" Stratton Motel & Hostel, complete with real beds and hot showers! Fat Man Walking joined us for dinner next door and again for breakfast down the road. He had become a vital part of our hike and acted as our own personal chauffeur. He met us in as many places as he could, and often we'd find him at a road crossing handing out drinks to all who came by. I even had a small box tucked away in his van with a few spare items I didn't want to carry but thought I might need sometime, such as spare socks, an extra shirt, some food items, and an extra hiking pole. In turn, we tried to buy a few meals for Fat Man and help with his fuel costs when we could. It was a long day with 17 miles hiked.

My left knee bothered me somewhat with all the ups and downs of the mountain ranges. I took Aleve for it and later discovered I was covering up issues in both knees that I would have to deal with when I got home in a month.

Tuesday, September 8, was a big day. I covered 17.5 miles in the Bigelow Range with lots of ponds, brooks, and streams along the trail. The Bigelow Range varies from 2,400 to 4,090 feet, with numerous changes in elevation. Judy and I had poor cell service, so I was unable to communicate with her.

Bigelow Mountain, known as Maine's "Second Mountain," might look vastly different now if not for the efforts of many conservation groups, including the Maine Appalachian Trail Club. During the 1960s and '70s, developers planned to turn the Bigelow Range into the "Aspen of the East," but opponents forced a state referendum and stopped the development. Later, in 1976, the citizens of Maine decided to have the state purchase the land and create a 33,000-acre wilderness preserve. Almost every state experiences the constant push and pull between industry and conservation, and many forces influence this balance. I suspect this is a conversation that will go on for many years.

The Trail was a bit easier the following day, as it had fewer elevation changes, with the highest point being just 800 feet. Temperatures hovered in the mid-70s. We hiked around a number of lakes, and other hikers told us we had missed seeing a moose by only a few minutes. Cell phone service was unreliable because there were no mountaintops or cell towers nearby. We camped by a lake at the Pierce Pond Lean-to, where we heard about a fellow hiker who got Lyme disease from a tick bite and had to leave the Trail for three weeks. This confirmed for me the importance of using my insect repellent every day. It also reminded me that the moisture from crossing streams and the sweat streaming off us every minute could wash off the bug repellent, too. We had hiked 16.3 miles, and the distance to Mount Katahdin was only 155 miles. (Or about 10 days, but who was counting?)

We had to get an early start the following morning because we had a canoe trip planned and didn't want to miss the boat. Crossing the Kennebec River can be dangerous. A dam upstream regulates the depth and speed of the current at the crossing depending on whether it is releasing water, especially when generating electricity. Several hikers have died when the dam opened its gates and caused the river to rise rapidly while they were attempting to wade across the formidable waters. For the last 25 years, a canoe funded by two AT clubs has ferried in excess of 22,000 hikers across the river at no cost to the hikers. The ferry runs on a specific schedule, 9:00–11:00 a.m. and 2:00–4:00 p.m. each day.

Up early, we followed the lake down into the valley for four miles, with lots of roots along the path, to the river, where we had to wait over an hour for our turn. To ride in the canoe, we had to sign a release form and wear a life jacket. When we reached the other side, we walked to a nearby road and hitched a ride into Caratunk, Maine, to zero at the Sterling Inn. Waiting for me at the inn were a package from Judy to replenish my supplies and a new pair of boots from REI to replace my two-week-old boots that were breaking stitches.

I spent the day doing the usual zero-day tasks such as washing clothes, taking a hot shower, restocking my pack, and lots of eating! The inn is an old house with a number of bedrooms and private bathrooms and a dining area downstairs for breakfast.

This zero day was different than most. Because we reached Caratunk after only a four-mile hike and a canoe ride, we stayed only one night. We had planned to get an early start the next day, but hard rain kept us at the inn until noon. We hiked only 12 miles over mountains that were not as tough as those we had already hiked, and we camped for the night at Moxie Pond.

The terrain was starting to change, with lots of roots and rocks to navigate, but the rocks in no way compared to the White Mountains. We camped that night at an elevation of 970 feet and climbed up Moxie Bald Mountain, at 2,629 feet, the next morning. By then, climbs of nearly 2,000 feet in elevation had become commonplace and my legs and lungs were in top shape, so we seldom made rest stops. Two river crossings slowed us down because we had to ford the west and east branches of the Piscataquis River; each branch was about 50 feet across. We were fortunate to have had little rain, so the river was only knee-deep, but it can be dangerous during periods of heavy rainfall. Fording means we took off our shoes and socks and walked across the river, stepping carefully from rock beds to who knows what. After we forded the river, it took 5 to 10 minutes to dry our feet before putting on our socks and boots. All told, a ford usually takes a good 20 to 30 minutes.

After 22 miles, we stopped for the night around seven at Shaw's Lodging in Monson, where a semiprivate room cost $28, laundry cost $5, and breakfast cost $8. The local hiking club was having a free dinner in town, and I gladly accepted an invitation. The dinner was outdoors on card tables with lawn chairs. I can't begin to describe all the wonderful food they had prepared and the delightful fellowship. I was a total stranger, but everyone made me feel welcome. I weighed myself later that evening and, even after a huge dinner, I found I had lost 22 pounds. Late that night, a strong thunderstorm came in, making me glad I was in a house and not outside in my tent.

The next morning, Freebyrd and I met up with a friend of his named David Murtough. David was moving to Monson and was building a new home. It was only partially completed, but David had a small building out front where he stayed when he was in town. He invited Freebyrd and me to throw our bedrolls down on the floor in it, and David slept on the floor in the house. David drove us around the community to see all the sights, and we visited several beautiful lakes, all of which I enjoyed immensely. We spent the evening at a nearby restaurant, where I attempted to put on a few pounds before our final push for Katahdin. Freebyrd sent the following email, which I echo, to several people: "I want to send out a special thanks to my longtime friend David Murtough for lodging the Preacher and myself in Monson prior to entering the Hundred-Mile Wilderness."

On Monday, September 14, David drove us in a misting rain to the Trail, where we entered the Hundred-Mile Wilderness. It is often called one of the wildest, most challenging areas to navigate and traverse, but we found it to be one of the easiest. Granted, some southbounders described it as one huge mud pond with mud up to six inches deep, but we found it dry and easy to hike. Most Trail guides recommend planning for 10 days of hiking and carrying at least that many days' supply of food, but we carried only 6 days' supply and completed the hike in 5 days. I was motivated for two reasons, though. First, I wanted to summit on Sunday morning as a symbol of God's presence on my journey and His sustaining power in getting me there. Second, I was simply ready to finish and go home!

Freebyrd, otherwise known as Scott Garner, wrote the following email to his friends as we entered the Hundred-Mile Wilderness:

"I left Monson this morning in rain under cover of darkness with the preacher and we have limped into the Hundred-Mile Wilderness. We are targeting to summit Katahdin next Sunday, but this is only an estimate, as the Trail is very muddy, rocky, and rooty with many challenges ahead. We have already had to do two full river fords requiring footwear removal today and there are more ahead. We also need to average 18 or 19 miles per day over six days in order to summit Katahdin by Sunday, a very lofty goal requiring long hiking days and short breaks during those days.

Thank you all for your prayers and support.

Best wishes to all, Scott "Freebyrd" Garner

On our first day in the Hundred-Mile Wilderness, it misted or rained enough to keep us wet all day but not enough to affect the Trail, as we hiked 19.4 miles. The second day started out slowly but got better throughout the day. That part of the Trail had gotten wet from the rain, and the rocks and mud slowed us down to about a mile per hour compared to about 2 to 2.5 miles per hour normally. By day's end, we had traveled 18.4 miles before stopping at the Carl A. Newhall Lean-to, where six or eight other hikers were gathered. This was an encouraging day because it was the next-to-last day of tall mountains before we reached Mount Katahdin. We had gone over Fourth Mountain, which was 2,380 feet at the highest point; Third Mountain, at 1,920 feet; Columbus Mountain, at 2,325 feet; and Chairback Mountain, at 2,180 feet. We also forded the west branch of the Pleasant River, at an elevation of 680 feet.

On the third day in the Hundred-Mile Wilderness, we covered 18.6 miles and four mountains, the last of which was White Cap Mountain at elevation of 3,650 feet. White Cap Mountain was the last tall mountain and the one I'd been looking forward to for a long time. It crept up on me suddenly, as somehow I had lost track of exactly where I was and thought I still had a mountain

Rock cairns mark the route on the climb to Mount Katahdin.

to go. When I finally arrived on top, I found a beautiful view of the surrounding mountains, and I saw Mount Katahdin in the distance and realized for the first time that I really would finish the Appalachian Trail! To top it off, the weather had been perfect, and I'd seen three moose, one of which was a bit too close. I hadn't seen them until a young moose bolted out of the brush nearby, causing me to stop and look around. Just to my right, with her rear end sticking toward me, was a momma moose standing dangerously close. She seemed unconcerned that I was standing a mere 15 feet from her, so I did the unsafe thing: I pulled out my camera and took several pictures, spending perhaps 10 minutes watching her. Her two calves were grazing nearby, which made the whole experience one of the more hazardous things I did on the Trail.

In the afternoon, we hiked through the forest, where my footing was a little easier and my pace a little quicker. We only had to ford the east branch of the Pleasant River and climb Little Boardman Mountain, at an elevation of 2,017 feet, before camping near Jo-Mary Road, at 620 feet, for the night. We ended the day at 18.6 miles hiked.

On Thursday, we had only small elevation changes of 500 to 600 feet, although we encountered a few rocks and lots of tree roots. The lack of water when we tented that evening caused me to settle for a power bar and peanut butter for supper, but we were 22.3 miles closer to finishing than we'd been that morning.

We were getting close! Friday was a relatively easy day of 23 miles with only minor elevation changes, dry trails, and the usual rocks and roots. It was a most memorable day, as Freebyrd and I arrived at the Abol Stream and the Baxter State Park boundary. We had survived five days in the Hundred-Mile Wilderness. Now we were just 14.4 miles from the summit!

As previously planned, Fat Man Walking picked us up late in the afternoon and took us into Millinocket to the Appalachian Trail Lodge for food and rest. Millinocket is a small town that has experienced more than its share of economic losses and relies on the Trail hikers for much of its economy. We tried to help by eating often and a lot! We ate dinner and breakfast at the Appalachian Trail Cafe and enjoyed both excellent food and excellent service.

The Appalachian Trail Lodge is a three-story building catering almost entirely to AT hikers. Most thru-hikers come through in about a two-month period, so it is either feast or famine for the lodge. It was full when we called for reservations, but the owner agreed to let us stay in a suite that wasn't normally open to hikers. It had two bedrooms, a breakfast room, and a large bathroom. We made reservations for two nights. The first was only for Freebyrd and me, and the second night also included Freebyrd's wife, Phyllis, and another friend of Freebyrd's who came up to wish us well as we reached the summit of the final mountain of the Trail. But we still had nine miles from the park entrance to the base of Mount Katahdin, weather permitting.

Mount Katahdin, Maine's highest mountain at 5,268 feet, is the northern terminus of the Appalachian Trail. It is located in Baxter State Park, 5.2 miles from the Katahdin Stream Campground. The mountain, along with the surrounding landscape, is part of a 209,644-acre wilderness sanctuary and forest preserve. It is exposed to extreme weather including high winds and has gotten snow during every month of the year, so the park registers all hikers and limits the number of people climbing each day. Hikers can never take anything for granted until they are off the mountain because of many factors including unexpectedly high winds, rain, sleet, or snow. All hikers are advised to plan their summit of Mount Katahdin by October 1 if possible and definitely before October 15, as the mountain is usually closed due to bad weather after that date and sometimes before.

We woke up well rested and met Fat Man Walking at the Appalachian Trail Cafe before driving back to the park entrance at Abol Stream. The Trail was almost completely flat along the well-marked, wide path. Signs along the way advised hikers of the strict rules and regulations imposed by the park. Among those rules: Camping in the campsites was allowed only by reservation; campfires were prohibited; no dogs or other pets were allowed; we must stay on marked paths; and we were not to disturb the wildlife and plants. After many miles of seemingly few rules and regulations except those we imposed on ourselves, these rules seemed a bit intimidating and reminded us that we would soon be back in civilization with all its rules, regulations, timetables, and routines. I felt a little like all my freedom was about to be taken away from me.

We hiked nine miles in about three hours and arrived at the park services office, where we got instructions for the next day's ascent up the mountain. We learned we could not enter the park before seven the next morning; there was limited parking, so each car must have a permit to enter the park; we must sign in before going up the mountain and report when we were back down; no alcoholic beverages or glass containers were allowed; we could have no more than six people in each climbing party; we must be down before sundown; if bad weather threatened, we must turn around and come down the mountain, no matter how close we might be to the summit; and we must be prepared for every contingency, such as snow and ice, winds as high as 75 miles per hour, temperature drops well below freezing, etc. After 2,171 miles of few rules and regulations, we were shocked back into reality.

We were not sure if Freebyrd's wife, Phyllis, would be able to get a car permit to enter the park and pick us up, nor did we know exactly when she would arrive, so without cell phone service, we hitched a ride to the main park gate. As luck would serve us, we met Phyllis coming into the park at the entrance. After reunions and introductions by all, we drove back into Millinocket to the Appalachian Trail Lodge, where we had spent the previous night.

Dinner that evening was one of the best of the entire journey. We ate at the Scootic In Restaurant, where Freebyrd insisted on buying not only my dinner but a Maine lobster. I had never had one and didn't know how to break the shells properly, so not only was it good, but I had lots of help, and good-natured kidding, from around the table on how to eat it. We retired early, knowing we had to get up around four thirty, clean up the room, pack our belongings, eat a big breakfast, and drive back to the park by seven in the morning.

Early the next morning, Judy's last journal entry, which she sent to friends who had been following me as I hiked the Trail, said: "Continue to pray for a successful and safe summit of Mount Katahdin and Dennis as he journeys back home. I know that your prayers joined with family prayers have kept him safe, healthy, and with energy to accomplish this amazing goal of completing the entire Appalachian Trail from Georgia to Maine. Thank you so much for sharing this journey with us! We love you all. If all goes well, Dennis and Freebyrd will summit today. I know it will be an emotional end to a long journey. Freebyrd's wife will be meeting them at Millinocket and they are giving Dennis a ride to Bangor, Maine, to the airport to fly home!" Later, plans changed and they dropped me in Boston.

Weather is always an issue on the "Great Mountain," as the Native American word "Katahdin" is translated, because the conditions change rapidly. The Weather Channel showed a good possibility for rain, but it was expected to diminish later in the morning. We went to bed hoping for the best but knowing that any rain during the night could mean snow on the mountain and, at best, the rocks would be wet and slippery, making the ascent more dangerous. When we got to the base of Mount Katahdin at about seven thirty and the rain continued to drizzle, we began to lose hope that we would summit that day. We stood under the cover for a picnic table and waited

At last, Dennis broke through the clouds as he climbed Mount Katahdin.

about an hour for the rain to stop. Finally, the rain stopped and the sky began to clear, allowing us to go for it, although we knew that the mountain was wet and we would have to be even more vigilant with every step and every handhold.

Four of us—Freebyrd, two of his friends named Dan "Tinker" Kutcher and Eric "Greenie" Greene, and I—started up the Trail knowing that Dan would only go about a mile due to health issues. He would stay behind with Phyllis near the parking lot until we returned. Eric was an experienced hiker and a good addition to help keep all of us safe on the wet, windy day. All hikers must sign in and out so the rangers will know who is on the mountain and can be sure everyone gets down safely. We signed the register as we left the parking lot and received the standard polite but stern lecture from the ranger: "Do NOT forget to sign back in on your return or else."

The first mile is a slight grade in elevation and is relatively smooth. Then, after crossing a large stream on a wooden bridge, the Trail turns a bit steeper and more difficult. I felt adrenaline pour through my veins from knowing this was the day I had looked forward to for months. Right then, it was easy going, though. My legs were as strong as they had ever been, and I knew physical strength and endurance would not be a problem that day. I was confident and began to think maybe the mountain was overrated. But when the Trail broke out above the tree line, it was like I was stepping into a new world. The winds increased significantly to a steady 25 to 30 miles per hour, with estimated gusts to near 50 miles per hour. The temperature dropped in the higher elevation, and the wind chill became much worse. I was wearing gloves, four layers of clothes, and a hat with a hood, and I was still cold. I had left much of my gear at the parking lot to lighten my pack for easier climbing. I left behind everything I didn't think I needed, such as my bedroll and sleeping pad, cookstove, all my extra food, and, unfortunately, some of my extra clothing. I wished I had kept a few more clothes to put on, but I would just have to tough it out.

Soon the Trail turned to more climbing than hiking and required the assistance of steel rebar sunk into the rock for handholds and toeholds. Even with the rebar to assist me, I often found myself reaching up and outside my comfort zone of what was safe. In the midst of the steepest, most dangerous section of the climb, I was climbing almost straight up using toeholds and rebar stuck into the rock for handholds. In that section, I could lean back and see at least a thousand feet below, which is where I would have fallen if I had lost my grip. I held my two hiking poles in my left hand and was attempting to grasp the rebar and rock using my fingers when a strong gust of wind, which I would estimate approached 50 miles per hour, hit me suddenly. The wind struck so hard that it shocked my entire body and blew my hat and prescription glasses off my head. In a desperate attempt to grab my hat and especially my glasses, I reached for them with my left hand, which still held the two poles, and knocked one of the poles out of my hand. Now I had my glasses, my hat, and one of my poles floating around on the rock in front of me as I tried to hold on against the wind. Somehow I switched hands to hang onto the fingerhold and, with one swing of my arm, managed to grab all three items out of the wind. I quickly put the glasses back on my head, my hat into my pocket, and the pole back into the hand holding the other pole. There was no time to think or to pause right then. Later, when I got to an area where I felt safe to adjust my equipment, I got my hat out of my pocket, pulled the chinstrap into my mouth, and kept my hat on using my teeth for the rest of the climb. Things happen quickly on the Trail, and reflexes often are called upon more than rational thinking. God is good! All the time!

At some point, the Trail changed from almost vertical rock to a path that reminded me of the White Mountains. The rocks were of every size and shape, and the Trail was not marked like a path but went from cairn to cairn in the general direction of what looked like it must be the summit . . . only to find out there was another crest farther up the mountain that surely was the summit . . . but it never was. The wind was extremely cold and strong, and pushed me around on the rocks; fortunately, I remained on top of them and not down between them.

Near the top, the Trail flattens out to almost level and becomes something of a defined path, although it is still just as rocky and rough. And then in the distance, through windblown eyes and nearly frozen eyelids, I saw the wooden sign that denotes the summit. It's there that (it must be a park rule) everyone must stand on the sign and have their picture taken. Freebyrd paused and waited for me near the top, and then we looped arms and together stepped to the top of Maine. We had come up the mountain, stopping only to add more clothes or decide where the Trail went, in 3.5 hours, hiking 5.9 miles and 3,089 feet in elevation before reaching the summit. Now, we had made it . . . and I'm not ashamed to say tears of relief and thanksgiving flowed for several minutes.

I truly had the sense that I was at the top of the world, looking down through the clouds at the mountains and valleys below. It was an awesome experience to stand there with Freebyrd knowing we had dreamed of this moment for months and wondered if we had the stamina and physical and mental strength, and if we would be lucky enough to avoid any injuries that would have stopped us from continuing. We both knew we would not have made it to the top without the help and encouragement of countless other people, some of whose names and faces we knew, but many we will never know. It's not something I would want to do again, but I am thankful that I completed the Trail from end to end.

I stood and enjoyed the moment, taking the mandatory pictures for perhaps 10 minutes, but then reality drifted back. I was extremely cold but, more than that, I couldn't stop there. I had to get down the mountain the same way I had climbed up—past those vertical rocks where only my fingertips clasping the steel rebar would hold me on the mountain and keep me from freefalling thousands of feet down to the valley below, and going down is always more hazardous than going up!

I had hoped that I would summit on a Sabbath morning and, of course, that was on my mind as I climbed that day, but it wasn't until I returned home and saw a picture of me standing on the summit that I realized, unbeknownst to me, the date and time stamp had been activated on the camera and it showed "9-20-2015, 10:39 a.m." Not only did I summit on the Sabbath, but I did it at 10:39 eastern time, or 9:39 central time, when Judy and others were worshipping at my home church, Northside United Methodist. I texted Judy: "Just summited Mount Katahdin. God is good."

We descended the same way we went up: carefully! Phyllis and Dan waited patiently for us in the parking lot below. After pictures, some snacks Phyllis had brought, and a bit of celebrating, we drove back into Millinocket and had drinks and dinner at the Blue Ox, where Freebyrd, Phyllis, Dan, Eric, and I were joined by two of Freebyrd's other friends, Steve Perrone and Rob Ricciutti. While we ate dinner, Judy and I texted and she found me a flight out of Boston, leaving at six the next morning and arriving in Memphis four hours later. Freebyrd and Phyllis offered to drop me in Boston on their way home, even though it was about two hours out of their way, they had originally planned to spend the night in Maine, and they would have to drive until about three in the morning! Thanks to their generosity, I was able to eat breakfast with Judy in Memphis just hours after summiting the "Great Mountain." It was great to be back home with Judy, sleeping in my own bed, playing with our grandkids next door, and not sleeping in a tent, eating dehydrated foods, or wondering which mountains I had to climb that day.

I had damaged both of my knees and both of my shoulders, requiring three months of physical therapy to reach the point where it was comfortable to walk again. The damage is probably permanent, but I can live with it. My doctor says it will prevent me from doing any more long-distance hiking. As he put it: "At your age, you need to be listening to your body more carefully."

Today, I am more convinced than ever that I would not have made it the entire 2,186 miles unless it was:

God's
"Footprints on the Mountains"
that carried me from Georgia to Maine.

Dennis summited Mount Katahdin after 2,186 miles on Sunday, September 20, 2015.

Dennis remembers the journey—the challenges and accomplishments!

CHAPTER TWENTY
Epilogue

In the summer of 2016, Judy and I spent two weeks following the Trail as best we could from Fontana Dam in North Carolina to Kent, Connecticut. This time, we went in our 40-foot, fifth-wheel camper, which has everything imaginable: four slide-outs, including two king-size beds; a full kitchen, including a refrigerator, stove, oven, and microwave; a toilet and shower with hot and cold water; heat and air conditioning; an electric fireplace; and an awning to sit under in the evenings and mornings. I pulled the camper with a Ram diesel truck that we used to follow some of the less-traveled roads near the Trail after dropping the camper at a campsite nearby. Along the way, it was great to reminisce and again experience the great scenery and animals. We gave rides to numerous hikers and shared a little Trail Magic with those who were crossing the road as we passed by. Judy took numerous pictures of the towns and trailheads as we drove. It also helped me remember many of the towns I had been in with their restaurants, hostels, and hotels.

A word of thanks:
I owe a great deal of gratitude to hundreds of people who made my hike possible. Judy's

constant encouragement, prayers, supply packages, and love kept me going when I otherwise would have quit. Our children helped me in so many ways and supported Judy in all the extra things she had to do.

Freebyrd (Scott Garner) became a great friend and companion whose encouragement and knowledge of Maine were of immeasurable help, as was the ride by car from Mount Katahdin to the Boston airport in the middle of the night so I could get home to my wife and family.

Our son, Denny, flew into Asheville, North Carolina, and spent three days with Judy and me in the Smoky Mountains taking pictures for this book, and then he helped with editing the pictures for the book.

Then there are those who came in and out of my hike such as Coffeeman, Drop Bear, Fat Man Walking, Mado, and Alabama, who were great companions and gave meaning to my hike. And how can I thank those who so generously gave Trail Magic along the way, and the thousands of volunteers who blazed the Trail and now maintain it by trimming trees and branches, cutting grass, keeping the Trail in shape so it doesn't erode away, building and maintaining shelters and privies (toilets), and so many more necessary tasks?

My thanks and gratitude go out to each one . . . a few whom I know by name and many anonymous Trail Angels who made it all possible. But most important, I give God the thanks and the glory for creating such great, generous people and for keeping me safe along the way!

Coffeeman:
Recall: He is from Austria and hiked with me for about two weeks. We zeroed together in Manchester Center, Vermont, where we stayed at Sutton's Place for two days. We had fun communicating—he in German mixed with English, and I in "Southern" English!

He emailed the following shortly after I summited: "Hi, Preacher: What a great moment! You guys have done a really great job! And the most important thing you finished well and healthy! It was great for me to meet you guys and to hike some miles together. I have got important experience because for me it lasts two years more to stand where you guys now! But you inspired me to continue my section hike next year! Freebyrd got also a Fotograf (German for "photograph") from Mount Katahdin! So again congrats, I hope we stay connected! Best regards, Coffeeman"

Fat Man Walking and Drop Bear:
  Two months after I got home, Fat Man Walking and Drop Bear called from Memphis. They were touring the South and had gone to Elvis Presley's home in Memphis, and they asked if they could take me up on my invitation from months before to visit Judy and me in Jackson. They spent the night with us, and we reminisced about the Trail until late into the evening. Having Fat Man's big van parked in the driveway was great to see, too.

Freebyrd:
  I correspond with Freebyrd occasionally via email. He has gone back to working in his family's business on a limited basis. He has done some hiking and fishing on or near the Trail and has enjoyed leaving Trail Magic when he can. During one of our conversations, he shared: "I was compelled to make the journey. I met amazing people along the way who blessed me in wonderful ways. I am thankful for that time away as it has changed my life in wonderful ways. . . . God let me think only of myself on the Trail; and now I can think only of others and of God."

Mado:
  An email from Mado says: "Hello, 'Preacher': Hope you're well and recovering from the prior months. I am OK and still feel it, but getting better every day. I am researching what it's going to take for me to climb Mt. Rainier . . . a whole different animal and it won't take months. It is the 5th tallest in North America and glaciated. Just an idea at the moment. Just wanted to say congratulations on your successful thru-hike."

More hiking:
  My knees still give me a lot of trouble, and the doctor has suggested that I not hike anymore. The mountains still draw me back, and I have taken two short hikes since finishing the Trail.
  In the fall of 2016, I planned to hike from Springer Mountain to Dicks Creek Gap but had difficulty obtaining water along the Trail. The entire area was experiencing a drought, but I didn't expect to find it that difficult to get water. In two days of hiking, I missed two meals because I couldn't find water to hydrate my food. The second morning, after missing supper the night before, I started hiking and hoped to come across some water but could not find any

Isaiah 40:28: Don't you know? Haven't you heard? The Lord is the everlasting God, the creator of the ends of the earth. He doesn't grow tired or weary.

natural sources. I was fortunate to see a military water supply truck that was parked beside the Trail for Army maneuvers in the area. I ate breakfast and lunch, brushed my teeth, and refilled my water bladders there. After talking with some other hikers coming south, I realized it was too dangerous to continue hiking due to the water shortage, so I stopped at Neel Gap.

In August 2017, Camille, our oldest daughter, and I took five days to hike from Springer Mountain to Dicks Creek Gap, a distance of 72 miles. It was much easier than before; the "long, steep" climbs were not quite as long or steep as I had remembered. It was fun to be back on the Trail and even better to spend time with Camille. We had two notable wildlife sightings. First, we saw a bear that wasn't the least bit afraid of us and stayed around for about 15 minutes until we got tired of watching him, and then we moved on. And a large buck with a big rack came out of nowhere, chasing a doe, and almost ran over Camille. He came within about four feet of her as we were walking along the Trail.

DEVOTIONAL
Do You Want to Get Well?

I met many people on the Trail, and each person had a different reason for being there. For some, they were fulfilling a longtime dream of being in nature and experiencing the terrain, vegetation, and animals. For some, it was a challenge and an accomplishment that drove them to go as far as they could each day. For some, it was a time to get away and think or rethink what they wanted to do with their lives. For some, it was just fun.

For a few, though, it was a way to escape a past hurt, a personal loss, or a broken dream. Some were suffering from personal tragedies, such as the death of a loved one or a lost job, which changed everything they had ever dreamed of doing or being. Some had graduated from high school, college, or a trade school and then, for whatever reason, could not get or sustain a job, leaving them with a bleak future and loss of direction for their lives. A few had never had direction in their lives. Perhaps the family they were born into had never given them direction or, perhaps, the family and community had been there for them, but they were rebelling against everyone and everything. Some had grown up in a church or synagogue but found their religious affiliation had let them down or had not given them the training and hope in God that would sustain them when their world turned upside down. And for some, the church had been more about telling them how bad they were instead of how much God loves all of us—even when we do some very unlovable things.

Someone of great importance in the Bible initially was like that. The Apostle Paul, in his earlier years, was adamantly opposed to Christianity and to the church. He spent a number of years persecuting the church and arresting the followers of Jesus Christ. But one day, on the way to Damascus to arrest more Christians, he experienced Jesus Christ in a vision and was converted to Christianity, and he spent the rest of his life spreading the Christian faith.

In Paul's letter to his friend Timothy (1 Timothy 1:12-16), he explains how grateful he is that God forgave his past and then used him in a mighty way to spread the Gospel (a word derived from Greek meaning "good news") so that "Jesus Christ might display the utmost patience, making me an example to those who would come to believe in Him for eternal life."

One of the major teachings of Christianity is that our past does not define us. Paul wrote in another letter, in 2 Corinthians 5:17: "So if anyone is in Christ, there is a new creation: Everything old has passed away; see, everything has become new!"

Although past experiences, hurts, pains, deaths, or words can make us feel broken, they do not control us unless we choose to let them. Christ offers us forgiveness, a new start, a new way of relating to others and to God, and a new way of thinking about ourselves. Paul had lived his life up until he met Jesus on the road to Damascus thinking he knew all about God and what God wanted for his life and the world. But that day, he discovered God still loved him and wanted to forgive him and make a new life for him. That same offer is available to us all.

We have a choice to make, though. We can continue to be defined by our past, or we can decide to accept Jesus's offer of acceptance, forgiveness, and a new direction for our lives. Jesus often asked those who sought healing and forgiveness a question. Perhaps He asks you the same question today: "Do you want to get well?"

About the Author

Dr. Dennis Renshaw was born in Brownsville, Tennessee, but grew up in Iran, India, and Indonesia as his father was with the United States State Department.

At age 15, Dr. Renshaw climbed Mount Damavand, Iran, elevation 18,406 feet, the highest mountain in Iran and the highest volcano in Asia. It's snow-covered year-round.

"You have to climb the last 3,000 feet in the dark and summit at sunrise so you can quickly descend due to toxic sulfur emissions caused by the heating of the sun," Dr. Renshaw said.

He attended high school at the Tehran American High School and received his B.S. in math and chemistry at Lambuth College in Jackson, Tennessee. He ran track and cross-country in high school and on scholarship in college.

He studied engineering at the University of Tennessee–Knoxville and graduated cum laude in 1992 from Union University with a degree in marketing and management. At Memphis Theological Seminary, he received his master of divinity in 1999 and doctor of ministries in 2006. He has worked as an industrial engineer, manager of engineering, in industrial sales, and as an industrial sales manager.

He has been an ordained elder in the United Methodist Church since 2002 and has served churches for 14 years as a pastor.

Dr. Renshaw hiked the Appalachian Trail over the summers of 2013 and 2015. Hiking 2,186 miles over hazardous mountains into steep valleys through every kind of terrain and weather imaginable turned into a 5.5-month adventure, especially at age 66. Dr. Renshaw started this trek as a challenge to himself because his research of the Appalachian Trail said only a small percentage of those starting the hike actually finished.

Newly retired as a United Methodist pastor, he felt God's presence in unique ways as he trekked across the 14 states to Mount Katahdin in Maine. Read about his adventures, challenges, danger, and resolve in being God's hands and feet as he felt God's *Footprints on the Mountains*.

Dr. Renshaw is an avid golfer, a certified scuba diver, and has a commercial pilot's license. He built half of his home and can do most maintenance on the home, including electrical, plumbing, framing, woodwork, and yard work.

He's married to Judy Renshaw and they have four children and seven grandchildren. They love to travel in their fifth-wheel camper. They've traveled to Canada and Alaska twice and 26 states in total.

www.ingramcontent.com/pod-product-compliance
Lightning Source LLC
Chambersburg PA
CBHW061152010526
44118CB00027B/2951